Audacious Aging

edited by

STEPHANIE MAROHN

www.AudaciousAging.com

Elite Books
Santa Rosa, CA 95404
www.EliteBooksOnline.com

Library of Congress Cataloging-in-Publication Data

Audacious aging / edited by Stephanie Marohn.
    p. cm.
ISBN: 978-1-60070-061-3
1. Aging. 2. Gerontology. 1. Marohn, Stephanie.
    612.6'7—dc22
                        2009006056

Cover design by Victoria Valentine
Edited by Stephanie Marohn
Typeset by Karin A. Kinsey
Typeset in Mona Lisa and Palatino
Printed in USA by Bang Printing
First Edition

10 9 8 7 6 5 4 3 2 1

CONTENTS

FOREWORD:
What If We Took More Risks?

Joe Laur and Isabelle St-Jean

W e want to lay out a bit of our individual journeys and the collaborative thinking that led to this book. So here we share with you how the volume in your hands and the concepts it contains came to be.

Joe's Path

On my fifty-fifth birthday, I took a little time for reflection. I had always had a lighthearted notion that I could live to the ripe age of 110, the same age Joseph, my namesake in Genesis, achieved. After all, three of my four grandparents lived into their nineties, and the youngster of the four died at eighty-five. I figured with a little luck and healthy living, I could make 110 in reasonably good shape. In any case, at fifty-five, at least as much of my life span lay behind me as before me. That got me thinking: Regardless of longevity, how did I want to spend the rest of my days? What could I do in the years remaining to me? What would the second half of my life mean, and how did I want to live it?

I began to frame in my mind and heart some of the key questions that would later be addressed by the contributors to this anthology. Instead of playing it safe, as is often the tendency as we age, what if we took more risks, spoke out on what was most important to us, moved boldly (at least in spirit, if not always physically), and lived each day more fully than the next?

Around this time I met Isabelle St-Jean at a conference on business and sustainability that I had conceived and facilitated. As we talked, we discovered our common interest in inspiring our peers to partici-pate even more fully in the grand endeavor of passing on a more lov-ing, just, and healthy planet to future generations. We had a wonder-ful and deep conversation about the need and opportunity for those in the "second act" of life to take action boldly and to live ever more audaciously as the years pass. We also both felt a strong desire to do something to counter our culture's fear of aging.

In true collaborative fashion, we decided to help launch an anthology of writings by people both well known and little known who were living and aging audaciously. The stories told by these people would model audacious aging and inspire the rest of us to take our own audacious acts at every stage in life. As Muriel Rukeyser stated, "The universe is made of stories, not atoms."

It is our hope that this book will contribute to the radical redefinition of aging under way in our society. Many baby boomers thought the revolution would take place in the Sixties. Now they are awakening to the reality that it may take place in their sixties!

Isabelle's Story

When I attended the Society for Organizational Learning's conference on sustainability in 2006, I heard Joe Laur deliver a powerful call to action to those of us at the gateway of our life's second half. At that time I was in the midst of writing my own book, *Living Forward, Giving Back: A Practical Guide to Fulfillment in Midlife and Beyond.* Joe and I quickly got fired up in an exchange of ideas and talked from our respective coasts for several months after that, intent on helping to ignite a collective spirit among elders and baby boomers regarding the future—our own and that of the planet.

I told Joe about one of my models for audacious aging: my friend Jan Furst, who is ninety-five as of this writing. Jan has kept up his practice of fencing, just published his third book, and recently started a nonprofit organization to sponsor education in Ghana. Being with Jan stimulates in me questions about how I will keep making a significant contribution as the decades stack up and bring me closer to my last year, my last month, or my last week.

Perhaps you too are reflecting on these kinds of questions. We hope this trailblazing anthology, filled with provocative and empowering ideas, will inspire you to live more boldly and audaciously. We urge this, not for the mere sake of boldness or audacity, but with the knowledge that time is of the essence for the human race.

No matter our age, each of us has the opportunity to be continuously reborn. We are reborn when we take a stand on behalf of the future and bring it forth with both our deep yearning and the power of our actions and words. We are reborn when we unleash our creativity and our fire to re-enchant the world with a love for nature and for everything alive. And we are reborn when we shed the remnants of our guarded, timid ways to reveal our true, divinely imperfect beauty, core identity, and authentic strength. These are the rebirths needed to carry the human race and the planet into the future.

We invite you to ride with us on the wings of courage, from the heightened perspective afforded by years of journeying. This book provides tools, information, and inspiration for the ride. May we all rise to the challenge of transforming our society from a youth/appearance-worshiping culture into one that fosters the values of the heart, supports the evolution of consciousness, and leaves to future generations a legacy of which we can be wildly proud.

Joe Laur
Isabelle St-Jean

October 2008

INTRODUCTION

Stephanie Marohn

What does it mean to age audaciously? Patch Adams says the term is redundant, that aging by its very nature is audacious. Asha Clinton says that audacious aging comes from audacious living. Zalman Schachter-Shalomi says the key is in turning age-ing into sage-ing. Christiane Northrup says that audacious aging is the new order of aging. Deepak Chopra says that aging in the new way means stepping out of "the hypnosis of social conditioning." Nikki Giovanni says, "Audaciousness comes in refusing to be silenced."

These and the other contributors to this thought-provoking anthology share their personal stories of aging and audaciousness, their views of aging, and how their work contributes to the ability to be audacious in life. You will likely be surprised by what they have to say.

The view of aging is undergoing a radical transformation in the Western world. With rising consciousness and extended life spans, after sixty is no longer the "go gently into the night" stage of life. With decades of quality life left to live, continued engagement is the order of the day. When the tsunami of the aging baby boomer population hits, the redefinition of aging that is already under way in our society will be carried forward by that giant wave.

The contributors to *Audacious Aging* give us a glimpse of the new view of aging that will emerge. They give us the new science of aging, dispel the myths that have until now ruled how we age, and offer us the new paradigm of body, mind, and spirit health throughout life. Alternately personal and global, practical and transportive, the chapters in this anthology are on the forward edge of this amazing revolution: the transformation of elderhood.

As with all revolutions, the aging revolution involves changing the language. The very way we speak of aging is in the process of shifting. Here are some of the new terms that reflect the change in how we view aging: creative aging, sage-ing, spiritual eldering, aging as a path to spiritual awakening, lifelong learning, elder adventure, conscious aging, the third age, the second journey, mitigated aging, new elderhood, and positive elderhood.

As editor of this anthology, I want to share with you that the book changed my view of aging before it even went to press. Simply editing the work of the visionary contributors shifted my thinking and perspective. And it brought to light the subtle age-ism I was carrying within me. Opposed to all isms as I am and have long been, I was, however, unaware that I was harboring this one. Through working on the book, I discovered that I was carrying a highly negative view of aging, even though I have great respect for elders and elder wisdom.

Two years ago, when I turned fifty, I began to get mail from AARP. With a feeling of aversion, I would toss the unopened membership invitations into the recycling as quickly as they arrived. There are so many things wrong with that simple ritual of denial and the beliefs it reflects (*Audacious Aging* explores such issues), but suffice it to say here that it was not an act of self-love and it undermined who I am, all that I know and have accomplished, and my very future. It revealed a belief in a future of limitation rather than expansion. I saw aging as a shrinking of options and a gradual loss of everything. What a dismal view! I was not alone in this view. It is the societal view of aging under which we currently operate.

How wonderful to discover that it is a delusional view! The contributors to *Audacious Aging* produced a sea change in me, as I'm sure they will for many who read this book. The blinders created by our youth culture have been removed, and I am excited about the future— for me and for all of us. I am excited to be part of the revolution that is bringing elders back to the vital, rightful place of elders in our society, and I look forward to seeing what this transformation will bring about in our world.

The above photo shows Patch Adams and Susan Parenti on a peace mission to Serbia and Croatia in 2001. Patch Adams, MD, is a political activist for ending capitalism and creatinga value system based on compassion and generosity. Two areas of focus in this are medicine and clowning. In 1971, he created the Gesundheit Institute, a hospital model posing solutions to problems in health care delivery, which includes free services and no malpractice insurance. In 1984, Patch began leading clown trips all over the globe as intensive seminars in compassion and to bring love, fun, and aid to the horrors in the world. Patch Adams was born on May 28, 1945, in Washington, DC.

PATCH ADAMS

Another Aging Option

"They say that age kills the fire inside of a man, and when he hears death coming, he opens the door and says, 'Come in, give me rest.' That is a bunch of lies. I've got enough life in me to devour the world, so I fight."

—Zorba in Nikos Kazantzakis' *Zorba the Greek*

There is an implication in the title "Audacious Aging" that aging means getting old. Aging audaciously may be first cousin to aging gracefully. Everything is aging. The greatest aging of mind, body, and spirit in one's life—the most dramatic aging—occurs in the nine months inside mother. So relax! We're aging…from day one. So aging…is living.

In a beauty and youth culture, aging is often spoken as a whine, curse, loss, something to be fixed, burden, even something to lie about. Regrettably, this shallow culture supplanted the cultures where old people were the elders, the carriers of wisdom. The two major themes of twentieth-century literature—alienation and meaninglessness—show that aging in this system deepens loneliness. These contexts give aging a bad name. Every age in a human's life is an epoch of one's aging.

I had such a loving mother, a schoolteacher, who gave me self-esteem and made me fully loving, full of wonder, curiosity, and fun, so aging was more and more of these. She did the same for my older brother (we're sixty-two and sixty-four) and we work together, part of a commune, serving humanity full-time all over the world. My aging in her presence influenced me to lean away from manly things: competition, winning, greed, and a lust for power over. I got interested, instead, in an engagement in nature and the arts, friendship, and the thrills that come from caring. All along I was aging into ways of being and seeing.

Then my father died from war when I was sixteen (he was a career soldier and we grew up overseas on army bases) and we had to move back to the United States in the south in 1961. I was instantly devastated by segregation. It shattered my illusions of our society, fake democracy, fake religion, fake government. After three hospitalizations in one year (at eighteen), trying to kill myself, I realized you don't despair over violence and injustice, you make revolutions for peace and justice. I became a wild nerd studying economic, political, social, and environmental systems, beginning a lifetime of study and altruism. So aging was the vital participation in the movements to change the global value system from one based on greed and power over to one based on compassion and generosity. To age in this context gets geometrically sweeter because I'm able to do much more over time. So aging is being ecstatic for one's life.

I never had a religious thought in my life. When I hear those rare sincerely faithful people speak so sweetly about their god, I hear them use a language I use for friend. So friend is God to me. Aging's most precious gift is all the friends I have met over time and the richness that glows with the hundreds I've kept long-term contact with. Friends over time is the closest thing I have as a measurement of wealth. There is a spectre in our society of aging meaning being alone in a nursing home for the end of life. The problem is not aging; it's the design of our society. I started a commune thirty-eight years ago with a massive outreach attracting thousands of people to our work. Aging (time) in persistence with our ideals and learning from mistakes has made the project much more stable, intelligent, and fun.

So aging is audacious...that is the resting state of aging! You are fully alive, engaged in living, oozing appreciation for millions of things—literally. For example, my favorite thing to do in life is kissing. And it has definitely improved with aging. At sixty-two, I'm doing my best kissing ever, with Susan. The capitalist system thrives on the dissatisfactions of aging, and cosmetic surgery and Botox have made that discontent a multibillion-dollar industry.

Aging is not a disease. In summary, the adjective "audacious" *is* redundant. Aging is audacious. If one chooses to engage one's intellect throughout one's life—in school, in nature, in community, in the arts—and apply it in all endeavors, then aging is the enchantment of life. Aging expands thinking in the moment by standing on its entire past. In aging I've found how to be maximally useful to our society.

Jean Shinoda Bolen, MD, is a psychiatrist, Jungian analyst, clinical professor of psychiatry at the University of California–San Francisco, and internationally known speaker who draws from spiritual, feminist, Jungian, medical, and personal wellsprings of experience. Among the many books she has authored are *Goddesses in Everywoman, Gods in Everyman, Crones Don't Whine,* and *Urgent Message from Mother.* She is a Distinguished Life Fellow of the American Psychiatric Association and the recipient of numerous other professional honors and awards. Dr. Bolen was born on June 29, 1936, in Los Angeles, California.

Jean Shinoda Bolen, MD, is a psychiatrist, Jungian analyst, clinical professor of psychiatry at the University of California–San Francisco, and internationally known speaker who draws from spiritual, feminist, Jungian, medical, and personal wellsprings of experience. Among the many books she has authored are *Goddesses in Everywoman, Gods in Everyman, Crones Don't Whine,* and *Urgent Message from Mother.* She is a Distinguished Life Fellow of the American Psychiatric Association and the recipient of numerous other professional honors and awards. Dr. Bolen was born on June 29, 1936, in Los Angeles, California.

Jean Shinoda Bolen

How to be a Green and Juicy Crone

On becoming fifty, most of the women I know are celebrating instead of denying their age. Turning fifty may have been an over-the-hill marker for their mothers, but it's a day to break out the champagne for them. Becoming fifty is inspiring reunions of girlfriends who have reached this passage year together. It's party time for some, and a time for rituals or retreats for others. Most women at fifty are celebrating how young they still feel and look. Even so, there is a certain unease at growing older. Women reaching fifty do not have many clues about who they might become, or know of the potential energies that menopause can bring, or understand that they are on the threshold of a phase of their lives in which they may become more themselves than at any other time before.

At some point after fifty, or postmenopausally, every women crosses a threshold into the third phase of her life, thereby entering uncharted territory. In a youth-oriented patriarchy, especially, to become an older woman is to become invisible, a nonentity. From the archetypal perspective that I elucidate, however, it is possible for this third trimester to be a time of personal wholeness and integration; when what you do is an expression of who you deeply are. In the active years after fifty, you may become more visible in the world than ever before, or you may develop your inner life and pursue creative interests, or you may be the centering influence in a family constellation. Far from being a nonentity, it is in the third trimester that it is possible to be more defined and substantial a person than ever. In the Native American tradition, a woman becomes fully grown at the age of fifty-two.

Women who came of age during the feminist movement in the late sixties and seventies have been rejecting stereotypes, exploring new possibilities, challenging old limitations, and insisting on defining themselves anew each decade. As the baby-boomer generation of women pass into this third crone phase, I anticipate that the connotation of the word "crone" itself will shift. It is my intention to help to redeem the crone word, the third stage of life, and, most of all, to help women recognize the archetypes that become accessible as sources of energy and direction at this time. It is in this third phase of a woman's life that the crone goddess archetypes most naturally make themselves known.

There is something delightfully outrageous about the phrase "green and juicy crone." The descriptive adjectives "green" and "juicy," used together with "crone," boggle the mind before they grab hold. Several years ago, I gave a talk on the wisewoman archetype, and out came this phrase, which was immediately embraced by the almost all-women audience. I think this aptly describes a woman in her crone years, who has integrated the archetypes and tasks of maiden and mother as aspects of her personality. Her attitude and spirit are like the fresh green of spring; she welcomes new growth and possibilities in herself and in others. There is something solid about her being an adult whose life has borne fruit through cultivation and pruning, as well as tempering and work; she knows from experience that it takes commitment and love for budding possibilities in herself or in others to grow into reality. There is also something about her passion for life that is like the juiciness of summer's ripe fruit. Now, at menopause, she enters a new phase and is alive to new possibilities.

To be a green and juicy crone comes from having lived long enough to be deeply rooted in wholehearted involvements, of living a personally meaningful life, however unique, feminist, or traditional it may appear to others. It has to do with knowing who we are inside and believing that what we are doing is a true reflection or expression of our genuine self. It is having what Margaret Mead called PMZ, or *postmenopausal zest* for the life you have.

My inspiration for "green and juicy" was the *viriditas* ("greening power") theology of Hildegard of Bingen, a remarkable woman who lived eight hundred years ago. Hildegard was a Renaissance woman before there was Renaissance and a feminist before there was feminism. In *Illuminations of Hildegard of Bingen*, theologian Matthew Fox introduced Hildegard to a reading audience. Hildegard (1098–1179 CE) was a woman of considerable influence, a Benedictine abbess, a mystic, a physician, a theologian, a musician, a botanist, and a painter. At a time when few women could write and most were denied a formal education, she corresponded with emperors, popes, archbishops, nobility, and nuns. She traveled, preached widely, established monasteries, and was politically astute and outspoken. At key junctures in her life, she defied the authority of her church superiors and prevailed.

Hildegard's authority and creativity grew as she grew older. She had an exceptionally long life for her time (eighty-one years), which will not be at all unusual for women entering their crone years now. To achieve what she did and be the person she was, Hildegard had to develop her intellect and talents. This was possible then only because she lived in a religious community of women, which allowed her to pursue her interests. She was able to take herself seriously, to draw spiritual support from meditation and prayer, and over and over again, to react to external events. Hildegard, as an exemplar of a green and juicy crone, was what I call a choicemaker.

To be a choicemaker in the third phase means that what you choose to do or be must correspond with what is true for you at a soul level. What you do with your life is then meaningful; it is something you know in your bones, at your core, in your soul. It is impossible for anyone else to know your truth or judge it, particularly since the same role and set of circumstances can fulfill one woman and constrict another. Why this is so can be understood through the archetypes of the collective unconscious, which C. G. Jung, the Swiss psychologist, saw as inherent potentials in the psyche. When an active archetype rather than an external expectation is the basis for a role we take, there is depth to the choice. When we find meaning as well, then the archetype that Jung called the Self is also engaged. I think of the Self as a generic term for whatever we experience as sacred, divine, or spiritual. It has to do with personal values and integrity, and what is deeply right for each of us in particular. There are significant choice points in everyone's life, when what we choose and who we become are linked. At these moments of truth, we find ourselves at a fork in the road and have to choose which path to take. There is always a cost to such choices. The price we pay is the path not taken, that which we give up.

A green and juicy crone has a life that is soul-satisfying. Maybe you can fall into such a life with the help of serendipity and grace. But for a contemporary crone-aged woman, a soul-satisfying life usually involves making choices, as well as taking risks. For so many of us, the obligations and demands made on our time and energy have a way of expanding to take up our whole life. There are conflicting loyalties to sort out and unchosen circumstances and limitations, including the reactions of others who may be angry at us for not fulfilling their expectations.

Think of yourself as the main character in a novel or motion picture that is being written by the choices you make or the roles you play, and by whether you are committed to your own story. Your parents' positive aspirations for you, or their negative expectations, or the examples they set, may have provided you with a ready-made script to follow. That prescribed path may have helped you to develop in ways that were positive, or may have done you great harm if there was a major discrepancy between who you were supposed to be and your own potential and needs. Others in your life, especially any that you gave authority to, or loved, further defined you. As a result, you may see yourself in a perennial supporting role, or as a victim, instead of as the protagonist in your own story. There are, as fiction writers often note, only so many basic plots, and only so many typical or archetypical characters—which is true in life, as well.

When you see yourself as a choicemaker, you take on the role of protagonist in your life story. You know that what you choose to do, or not do, has an effect. You learn that when circumstances are unavoidable or even terrible, then how you respond inwardly is a choice that may make all the difference.

The choices that shape your life and give it meaning may also depend on the possibility of imagining what you could do or having a name or image for what is stirring in your psyche. This is where stories and role models may make the difference. This is also when you need spiritual resources, especially if others do not support the changes that you are making.

There will soon be over forty-five million women on the far side of fifty, whose lives and attitude have been shaped by the women's movement. Never before in recorded history have there been so many such women with so much competence, experience, independence, and resources. At fifty, most women can look forward to several decades of prime time. For them, seventy is what fifty used to be. And as each woman turns fifty, she joins a growing tide of crone-aged women now in their sixties and many in their seventies and older who have learned to trust themselves and each other.

Joan Borysenko, PhD, is a pioneer in the health-care revolution that regards a sense of meaning and the spiritual dimensions of life as integral to health and healing. She is author/coauthor of thirteen books, including *Minding the Body, Mending the Mind,* which has sold over 400,000 copies since its 1987 release, *Your Soul's Compass,* and *Seven Paths to God.* She directs the Interspiritual Mentor Training Program at the Claritas Institute for Interspiritual Inquiry, of which she is co-founder. Joan Borysenko was born on October 25, 1945, in Boston.

JOAN BORYSENKO

Looking Beneath the Surface of Life

I like to say to people that it looks like I'm a scientist who then became interested in psychology and spirituality, but in fact it was the opposite. When I was ten, I had a very serious mental illness from which I recovered in what we would call, scientifically, a spontaneous remission. But the remission came after a very particular experience of realizing I could not live any longer in the health state I was in. I was psychotic and I had obsessive-compulsive disorder. I won't go into all of the elements of that, other than to say that when you're ten and you hear your parents cry themselves to sleep every night, you can't tell anymore the difference between the dream state and the waking state, and you don't know what's real, it's a difficult place to be.

One day I was in complete despair and said, "If there is any force out there that can help me, please help me." I then had an experience that I certainly had no understanding of at that point. I would say it was an experience of cosmic consciousness or divine union, during which I underwent a shift from terror to unimaginable peace. At that moment, I recognized that it was possible to recover from this mental illness and I actually knew precisely how to go about it. I like to say at this point in the story that this doesn't mean that other people who are mentally ill could follow what I did and recover. I think it was very specific to my situation.

Within three or four days of that experience, and doing what it was that I felt was going to alleviate the mental illness, I recovered entirely, went back to school, and that was that. At ten, with the limited experience one has at that age, I looked for a way to make sense of this. I saw three things. One was that I wanted to help other people who had similar problems. A lot of children who get sick do that; helping others with what they learned becomes their life's calling. The second was that in my illness and recovery something in my brain had undergone a major shift. Knowing this led me to feel that I really needed to study the brain and study behavior. So I wanted to become a scientist. The third and most compelling part of the experience was that I realized there was a state of consciousness in which peace, wisdom, and absolute love were the only possible description, and that is not the consciousness that I, or most people, lived in during daily life. I wanted to understand that state so that I could get back to it again. I recognized that it was the state I wanted to live from. Those three strands of psychology and practically helping people, understanding the science, and getting back to that spiritual state became, truly, the road map for my life and the driving force behind it.

How Far We've Come

So there I was years later, a scientist and a psychologist, trying to help people with life-threatening illnesses such as AIDS, cancer, and stress-related disorders. I led two lives at that time because back then medicine and spirituality were strange bedfellows. I had become a student of the world's great spiritual tradition and that was where my life was anchored, but that came into my work only at the most subtle levels. The role of the mind in health and healing wasn't even acknowledged then, so spirit didn't have a chance in conventional medicine.

When I started doing this work in the early 1970s and said things like "What you think can affect your health," my colleagues looked at me like I was crazy, even though, as a Harvard-trained medical scientist, I had credibility. I devised a simple way to illustrate the body-mind connection. I said to my male colleagues, "Have you ever looked at the pictures in *Playboy* magazine? There's the mind-body connection." It is so simple, yet people were remarkably resistant to the very notion of a connection, until this last generation. With the scientific interest in the brain, neuro hormones, and how thoughts might affect the limbic system, the existence of the mind-body connection has been established. We now know that the connection goes through the emotional centers of the brain.

Today, what we have in the field of medicine is more of an emphasis on what's called "evidence-based medicine," which looks at treatment results instead of relying solely on the conclusions of double-blind, placebo-controlled studies. The role of the mind and spirit in healing is difficult to study with the conventional research design. Evidence-based medicine allows us to look at energy medicine and other modalities that incorporate mind, body, and even spirit in healing.

Spiritual Mentoring

Though the role of spirit has been important to me all along, at this phase in my life I've shifted toward considering more specifically the spiritual aspects of life. My husband, Gordon Dveirin, and I founded a school called the Claritas Institute. *Claritas* is the Latin word for "clarity." The basis for the work we do there is that within every person is what Quakers call an "inner light," Buddhists call "true nature," and mystical Christians might call "the Christ within." The work of being human is to remove the obscurations to that inner clarity, like parting the clouds over the sun. Our interest has been in the mystic heart of all religious and spiritual traditions because mystics, whether they're Islamic, Jewish, Christian, or Native American, will tell you the same thing about the experience of touching into that greater field.

At Claritas, we train people in that kind of interspiritual tradition and in the ancient art of spiritual mentoring. In Buddhism, this ancient art is called *kalyana mita*. The word *mita* comes from the same root as *metta*, loving kindness. So *kalyana mita* is a soul friend, a beautiful friend who loves you, who loves not your false self, not your stories, but your true nature. In the Christian tradition, there were the desert mothers and fathers; people would come to them for help on their spiritual journey. So that's what our school does: it trains mentors who accompany you on the journey.

A very important part of the spiritual life is what the Buddhists call *sangha*, the group of people who make inquiry into the same questions you ponder on the spiritual journey: What is it that makes me happy? What is it to generate compassion? So that not only am I happy, but the people around me begin to look at their lives in a way that they then become free from suffering, that they can drop some of those old beliefs, opinions, and habits that keep them stuck in a box and that prevent their own true nature from shining forth. On our spiritual journey, the company we keep is very important, as is our intention, and the two can be synergistic.

The Age of Sagehood

We baby boomers haven't been a group to go lightly into the good night. We have wanted to carve our own path. Ours is a generation that's been very interested in personal growth, in bringing compassion out in the world, in social justice, and in making a difference in this world. Generations before us might characterize themselves similarly. What's changed in this generation is our ability to know what's happening. The media, the Internet, and global communications have given us so much access to wisdom, in a way that is different from any previous generation.

Baby boomers are bringing all of this to how we approach aging. Here I must mention Reb Zalman Schachter-Shalomi (see chapter 32), who came before us (he is in his eighties) and has given us a model of the wisdom approach to aging. His book *From Age-ing to Sage-ing* looks at what aging is about—not our physical health, how we look externally, or how we're going to manage our retirement, but what that fourth phase of life is. There are lots of ways to break down the human lifecycle. I use four quadrants: birth to twenty-one, twenty-one to forty-two, forty-two to sixty-three, and the fourth quadrant, sixty-three and beyond. The last quadrant of life is a time when we're harvesting our wisdom, looking beneath the surface of our life, and seeing the deeper meaning and the way our soul has matured. We are then in a position to mentor young people and others across the life span, to take what we have learned and allow it to come out to the world in whatever form of expression that might be. This is healthy aging.

We know that people who retire go downhill fast. Retirement is not good for us. We might shift and change what we're doing, but when that shift is toward greater meaning and sharing in a way that increases the amount of potential in the world, then that makes for healthier aging, and that's what makes us happy in the end. There are lots of approaches to this, but I think it's important to stay in society and make use of what's continuing to evolve in us.

There is some wisdom in the idea of retirement. It is the phase of life referred to in the East as "time to go into the forest," to let go of some of the outer busy-ness and draw closer to the divine, draw closer to ultimate reality. I do think that in the last phase of life it's natural to require more time in stillness. This allows us to delve more deeply within and to bring forward that meaning for our family, for our children. The stillness also allows doing to come organically from this state of being. If we look more carefully as we go along the path, we'll see that's true. When we take the time to center ourselves, what comes out in action is so much more elegant.

Assistance for the Journey

At any stage of life, we have to punctuate the busy-ness with time out, otherwise it is as Wayne Muller said, that everything you're doing in your life can be terrific, but without time out, it's like music without rests. Without the rests, it's just noise. So it's important to take respites in nature and spend time with soul friends, those who are interested in the inner life.

To monitor your stillness needs, you can measure your state of being: how calm you are, how stressed you are. I use a scale of one to ten, with one indicating feeling peaceful and ten being incredibly stressed. If you ask yourself several times a day, "Where am I on the scale?" you get a sense not only of your immediate state, but also of where you usually are. If you realize you're usually stressed, that's good feedback and you need to help yourself because it's not a happy state of mind or even a productive way to be.

The biggest issue in our whole life span is resisting what is. What we resist may be different at different ages. An example that may have application for later years is getting up in the morning and feeling your arthritis. You're already doing everything you can for it and there's nothing further that you can do about it. If you start in on yourself with "I can only be happy if the pain goes away" or "This is a terrible thing; I'm falling apart," that's what will make you miserable. We do this all the time. We resist what is.

When my husband and I wrote *Your Soul's Compass,* we interviewed sages from a variety of spiritual traditions, including Ajan Sona, the abbot of a Buddhist monastery in British Columbia. He had this to say about being present in the moment: "There's no point resisting reality, no point resisting what is, because the forces that have led up to this moment, the karma that has led up to this moment, has ripened." So it's false hope to think you're going to change this moment. If you have arthritis in this moment, or if you're fearful in this moment, or if your kids are acting up in this moment, you can't change it because it is what is. But what you can do is, after accepting this moment, see within it whatever seeds can be planted toward a more skillful future.

Retrospection is another practice I recommend. At the end of every day, you look back through your day and say what things you were grateful for. It helps you change your mindset; you get up the next day ready to start looking for things to be grateful for. That brings you into presence and into mindfulness of the beauty of life. Also, when you retrospect, you might say, "Gee, I wasn't very kind to that person" or "I dropped the ball over here," not to make yourself guilty but to say, "Here's what I'll do tomorrow to bring those things back into harmony." If we don't do a retrospection, time passes and it all runs together. So, last thing before bed, retrospect your day. Go from the point of gratitude to recreating harmony where it's been missing.

The quandary we're in as a culture right now is that we know more about how to stay healthy, every molecule of what to eat, how to reduce stress, and how to exercise than we ever have before, and yet, as a society, we have more obesity and more chronic illnesses and are more sedentary than ever before. We have to look at the slip between the cup and the lip. I think it's this: when we feel disenfranchised, when we feel depressed, when life rushes by so fast we can't find meaning, we don't care about the future and we don't care about our health. We do what is most intrinsically human—we try to find comfort in this moment. Zone out in front of the TV and eat something full of fat and calories. I believe that as more people approach their lives with a focus on meaning and begin to age audaciously, that slip between the cup and the lip will get smaller and the unhealthy patterns in our society will change. To the extent that we find meaning in our lives, that we keep good friends, that we make a little time for ourselves, that we place love as primary, that we give and receive in this lifetime, then we'll have the motivation to stay well.

Helen Gurley Brown's first book, the somewhat autobiographical *Sex and the Single Girl* published in 1962, became an immediate bestseller and liberated and redefined a generation of women. In 1965, hired as editor-in-chief of the flagging *Cosmopolitan,* she transformed the magazine into a testament to the pleasures of womanhood and a gold mine for the Hearst organization. The recipient of many journalism awards, she has also been designated a "living landmark" by the New York Landmarks Conservancy. Helen Gurley Brown was born on February 18, 1922, in Green Forest, Arkansas.

Helen Gurley Brown

Flower Smelling— Not for Me

Everybody, he or she, is lucky is get to be eighty or ninety and it always astonishes me that people make such a big whoop-de-doo about your being that age. I'm also astonished that people don't do everything they can to have a good time, to make those years palatable, sometimes pleasant—not unpleasant. So, my point about the eighties—you are just lucky to be there and you want to make the most of it, and those people who have done so I think are pretty admirable.

Back in 1965, I took the helm at *Cosmopolitan* magazine. I transformed it to show the joys of women excelling at work, enjoying life's better things, and beguiling men. The Hearst ownership wouldn't have had me there if they didn't decide to go ahead with it. After all, it was their magazine. They owned it. But it was hemorrhaging and I think they would have closed it down if I hadn't come along.

There were people, I'm sure, who were horrified that I had been allowed in there. A man named Richard Deems, who was president of Hearst Magazines, was the one who made the decision. They looked at my proposal, they looked at the magazine—they knew about the book I had written, *Sex and the Single Girl*. Then they looked at my comprehensive outline for a new magazine. They made the decision to go ahead.

My first issue sold more than 90 percent of its print order. That's a tremendous sell-through. Magazines nowadays sell 35 percent or 45 percent of their print order and figure they get along with that. To sell 90 percent of your print order is really sensational. I knew at once, they knew at once, that the buyers of magazines liked it immensely and it wasn't very long before the advertisers came in. Advertisers want to be where the readers are.

I don't think I would be capable of editing such a magazine anymore. Any editing job is not a barrel of fun. The biggest deal is to make it good so people will buy it. That's an hourly proposition, a minute-by-minute proposition. You have to work with writers; you have to work with your editors. You have to work terribly hard all the time.

I work for a wonderful company that has always rewarded me for making money for them. On my twenty-fifth anniversary, they gave me a silver-gray Mercedes Benz 550 and a driver just as a little present. I didn't expect anything. I didn't even know what my anniversary was, but they kept track and they did that for me.

I was not privy to any of Hearst's financial statements. But they knew that *Cosmopolitan* was making money and that it immediately brought advertisers in. I came from that world. I had been an advertising copywriter. I knew how to respect and appreciate advertisers. Every Thursday, as long as I was the *Cosmo* editor, we had a luncheon at Twenty-One and we'd ask a big advertiser and his agency to have lunch with us. There'd be about twenty people and we would all visit. I would sit at the table and I'd put the head guy next to me. I would say, "You know that your secretary, your wife, your girlfriend, your daughter—they all love the magazine. But I want to explain to you why they like it so much. Would you hold the pages for me?"

At the end, when it was time to have a younger editor, they knew I would throw myself under a train if I didn't have a job. I worked all my life, ever since I was eighteen years old. They found a job for me to be the editor of *Cosmo*'s international editions. There were about twenty of them when I took the job. Now we have fifty-six. We open them up in new countries every year.

I'm too old to be the editor of *Cosmopolitan*, that's for sure. Could I edit a magazine for a somewhat older woman? I might be able to do that, although it's a lot of hard work. I can do what I'm doing, and I don't miss the other, because I did it for thirty years.

I'm not smelling the flowers today. I tried a little flower smelling when I stopped being the editor-in-chief. I went to the Metropolitan Museum a couple of times. I took piano lessons because we have a baby grand that never gets played. I took a couple of French lessons because I do not speak a foreign language. I did all that. I don't know if you can call it "smelling the flowers." I did try doing something different from what I've been doing. Just to sit on the veranda with iced tea and listen to a CD. No, that's not for me. Everything good that's happened to me has come from my work. I can have lots of flowers if I want them.

I'm the luckiest person because I still have a husband (producer David Brown), and he and I embrace life together. We're going to a fancy resort in the Caribbean. We'll be soaking up the sun, eating wonderful food, and enjoying ourselves.

David's *Dirty Rotten Scoundrels* was a hit play on Broadway and that's the most life-embracing thing imaginable. We went to see it nearly every week. Some said that was because David was the producer, but I did it because I was just nuts about it, and he liked it, too. We had to pay for our ticket each and every time. Producers don't get free tickets. They get good locations. David is a Tony member so we go to all the new shows. We'll be going to some that we haven't seen.

We went to City Hall to watch Mayor Bloomberg be inaugurated. That isn't something you have to do, but we're glad we did it. It was icy cold out. David came home and got a cold, but it was a very special experience to watch the ceremony. The emcee of the show was John Lithgow, who was David's star in *Dirty Rotten Scoundrels*. Mike Bloomberg is a good friend. It wasn't convenient to go clear down there to Twentieth Street on a frosty afternoon and spend two hours outdoors, freezing to death. But we did it. That's embracing life.

We have been all over the world at this point. I can't think of any place I haven't been. We don't have to go to other countries to embrace life, but we go there. I'm involved with my work and we do go to Paris and London every year and usually to Tokyo.

There's a slight difference between the way I handle stress today and as a young woman. In those days, stress had a lot to do with making enough money to support my invalid sister and my mother. I had to start working when I was eighteen. A lot of my stress through the years came from taking care of my sister in a wheelchair. That was a specific kind of stress, which I met by being good at my work. Stress today has to do with not feeling as good as you did when you were fifteen years old. There is some stress in that.

I've done everything I'm capable of doing. I want to keep this job at *Cosmo*. There are two countries we haven't gone into yet that I feel we must. One of them is Singapore and the other is Denmark. We are in Norway, Finland, Sweden, but we're not yet in Denmark. We did just get a commitment.

My two favorite words today would be: "Hanging on." Quite a lot of my last book was a memoir. It's called *I'm Wild Again*. That has considerable biographical material in it. I don't think I'll write another one. I don't think I have anything else to say. All I try to remember is to be grateful for how well off I am. My wonderful husband has been mine for forty-nine years. He had two previous wives. He finally got it right.

I can't think of any advantages to being older. David uses a cane sometimes and he gets on the airplane first. All I can do is to try to remember to be profoundly grateful for the things I have to be grateful about. I try not to be a dumbbell. I do regret that I can't do some of the things I used to do. I just try to appreciate what I've still got.

I do have some advice for the generations that are following me. I don't want to sound pontifical and I don't know whether I'd call it advice. All I can call it is what I've learned. And what I've learned is that if you do the best you can, no matter how bad the situation, you probably are going to come out okay. That's something to remember.

The important thing is you're lucky if you get to be eighty-six, so why don't you come to your senses and be thankful for that? You've got to get through it as you have the rest of your life. Do the best you can.

Robert Byrd became U.S. senator (Democrat) from West Virginia in 1959 and has held the office ever since. He is the longest-serving senator in the history of the United States and is currently the oldest member of Congress. Some call him a "walking encyclopedia" of information on both the American and the Roman Senates. As of April 2006, he had cast a total of 17,591 votes, far and away the most of any U.S. senator. Robert Byrd was born on November 20, 1917, in North Wilkesboro, North Carolina.

Robert Byrd

Age Is Just a Number

I may no longer be able to run a hundred-yard dash, but my mind is as sharp as the day I took office, and my passion to serve my state and my country has never been stronger. Gray hair—or white hair, in my case—and wrinkles are signs of maturity and that life experiences and hardships are important sources of wisdom.

Some people fear and dread growing old. I don't. I think there are some good examples to follow, if only we take the time to learn.

Individuals of exceptional accomplishment have been known at every age and in every quadrant of the globe. Neither geography nor chronology of life is a barrier to continued achievement. Confucius was still teaching at his desk at age seventy-three in 479 BC. Michelangelo was still painting, sculpting, and writing poetry when he died at the age of eighty-nine on February 18, 1564. Rosa Parks served as a role model in social activism until she passed away at the age of ninety-two. Indeed, it seems that very little can hold some people back.

It may seem cliché, but with age comes experience. That has been the case for hundreds of years. From the Book of Job in Chapter 12 we read, "With the ancient is wisdom; and in length of days understanding." I frequently find that I have an advantage in my dealings in the Senate because there are not many matters that come before me that I have not previously dealt with and learned from in one form or another.

For me, age is just a number. The passion that I have for the Constitution, the fervor that I feel for the liberties of the American people, and the courage that I draw from the heroism of our founding fathers—that is where I draw my inspiration. That is where I find my own fountain of youth. The greatest thing a person can do for this country is to continue to serve, to engage in public service. What was the challenge that President Kennedy offered? "Ask not what America will do for you, but what together we can do for the freedom of man." It is that ideal that drives me in public service and in defense of our Constitution, the premiere spark of genius in the framers' mind.

I embrace life through the lessons of my faith. I am a Christian. I don't go around making a big deal over that fact. But my faith teaches me a great many things, including the way to live life in service of one's neighbor. "In as much as ye have done it unto one of the least of these my brethren, ye have done it unto me." In large part, my Senate career follows that biblical direction. I have sought to lift this country, to help people overcome adversity and build a better future for themselves and their families.

Recently, I had the chance to give the commencement address at Marshall University in Huntington, West Virginia. It was inspiring to talk to those newly minted graduates, and to see the pride in the faces of their families. I told them, like I tell most young people, the days in their life's journey won't always be blue skies and sunshine. Storms and rough weather will surely come. But, remember this— problems are for solving. Almighty God, in His infinite wisdom, gave man a brain for the purpose of using it to better his lot. Never, never give up. Never become the scourge. As George Bernard Shaw once observed, "I don't believe in circumstances. The people who get on in this world are the people who get up and look for the circumstances they want."

I have spent my life overcoming obstacles and jumping hurdles. I didn't have enough education, so I got more. I wanted to help West Virginia, so I went into politics. I wanted a law degree in order to be a better senator, so I went to school at night. I wanted to understand the Constitution to which I have sworn an oath many times, so I studied it—read the Federalist Papers, read Roman history, learned about the roots of the constitutional language, and the lives of the framers. None of it was easy. I had to work for all of it. Our young people can, too. Great satisfaction comes in being the master of oneself, being able to discipline oneself to beat all the odds and achieve a goal.

That's the real fun in life: Achieving something when everyone says you can't. Pulling it off against all odds. One's feeling of pride is what makes life the exciting adventure that it is.

"To be ignorant of what happened before you were born," admonished Cicero, "is to remain always a child." If Cicero were to look at history lessons for America's schoolchildren today, he might conclude that they will never grow up.

Washington, Adams, Jefferson, and Madison lived in a revolutionary time, a revolution fed by their own eloquence and erudition. These men read widely and deeply. Their interests and their libraries spanned the ages and included works on philosophy, history, economics, agriculture, and the arts—every facet of the human condition. Their knowledge of history, of the mistakes and triumphs of past civilizations and forms of government, permitted them to formulate a simple, flexible political doctrine that worked with our human flaws and allowed individual talent to thrive, regardless of the circumstances of one's birth. They believed that the ultimate security for this new government lay in an informed populace, one that could recognize would-be tyrants and prevent their return to power.

We, too, live in a revolutionary time—a time of great technological change and globalization. We face new and uncertain threats. In our fear, we have sought protection from a more powerful and intrusive central government. But if we are to remain a role model of government, by the people and for the people, we must not simply wear red, white, and blue and proclaim ourselves patriots. We must cherish the heritage of governance bequeathed to us by our founders. And even more important, we must understand its underpinnings and historical roots, lest in our ignorance we allow the return of tyrants.

We cannot let others think for us, no matter their office or their media ubiquity. We must as a people have the wisdom to think, and think well, for ourselves. We have not lived under a tyrant, so we have only history to teach us what one looks like.

Perhaps at no time in our history has the study of history been more important. History is not the recitation of dead facts—it is relevant for the present and for the future. Our schools should give history its proper place and encourage a love of it. For more than half a century, I have repeatedly taken a sacred oath to protect this republic and our constitution against all enemies, foreign and domestic. Today I see programs and policies that threaten the foundations of the Constitution and of this country. I am not willing to sit idly by and allow that to happen. I will continue to stand in defense of the Constitution and the people's liberties. The American people need to wake up to what is happening to their country. A poem by Louisa May Alcott reads:

A little kingdom I possess,
Where thoughts and feelings dwell;
And very hard I find the task
Of governing it well.

Like Alcott, most of us find self-control difficult. We do get mad. At work, while driving, even at home, people get on our nerves and make us very angry. We are tempted, as the saying goes, not just to get mad, but to "get even."

The Bible advises against such a solution. It holds us to a higher, nobler standard. In the Sermon on the Mount, Jesus advised us to turn the other cheek when someone strikes us. Well, that is still too noble for many people. But the place for all of us to begin is with self-control.

In Washington, in Congress, and really throughout the country, we must cultivate the ability to listen to one another. We've got to always keep in mind that the other side can be right and that legislation can often be removed by constructive amendment. No political party has a corner on the market of wisdom, and no proposal or policy is beyond the possibility of improvement.

I always have hope. There's a story from the Constitutional Convention that might best answer this question. Benjamin Franklin was the oldest man at the Constitutional Convention in Philadelphia. He was eighty-one years old. At the end of those meetings, after the documents had been signed by the representatives of the people, Dr. Franklin was asked about the president's chair at that convention. It featured a sun. Was it a rising or a setting sun? Ben Franklin believed that it was a rising sun, the rising sun of America.

I believe in the Senate. I believe in the people of this great nation.

And I still believe that we see a rising sun, not a setting one. Some days may have clouds obscuring the view, but those clouds are not enough to hold back the sun's rays.

Deepak Chopra, MD, a leader in the field of mind–body medicine, has authored more than forty books, including *Quantum Healing* and *The Seven Spiritual Laws of Success.* He taught at Tufts University and Boston University medical schools, was chief of staff at New England Memorial Hospital, and established the American Association of Ayurvedic Medicine. In 1996, he cofounded the Chopra Center for Wellbeing in Carlsbad, California, which integrates Western medicine and natural healing traditions of the East. Deepak Chopra was born October 22, 1946, in New Delhi, India.

Deepak Chopra

The Land Where No One Is Old

I would like you to join me on a journey of discovery. We will explore a place where the rules of everyday existence do not apply. These rules explicitly state that to grow old, become frail, and die is the ultimate destiny of all. And so it has been for century after century. However, I want you to suspend your assumptions about what we call reality so that we can become pioneers in a land where youthful vigor, renewal, creativity, joy, fulfillment, and timelessness are the common experience of everyday life, where old age, senility, infirmity, and death do not exist and are not even entertained as a possibility.

If there is such a place, what is preventing us from going there? It is not some dark continental landmass or dangerous uncharted sea. It is our conditioning, our current collective worldview that we were taught by our parents, teachers, and society. This way of seeing things—the old paradigm—has aptly been called "the hypnosis of social conditioning," an induced fiction in which we have collectively agreed to participate.

Your body is aging beyond your control because it has been programmed to live out the rules of that collective conditioning. If there is anything natural and inevitable about the aging process, it cannot be known until the chains of our old beliefs are broken. In order to create the experience of ageless body and timeless mind, you must discard ten assumptions about who you are and what the true nature of the mind and body is. These assumptions form the bedrock of our shared worldview.

They are:

1. There is an objective world independent of the observer, and our bodies are an aspect of this objective world.

2. The body is composed of clumps of matter separated from one another in time and space.

41

3. Mind and body are separate and independent from each other.

4. Materialism is primary, consciousness is secondary. In other words, we are physical machines that have learned to think.

5. Human awareness can be completely explained as the product of biochemistry.

6. As individuals, we are disconnected, self-contained entities.

7. Our perception of the world is automatic and gives us an accurate picture of how things really are.

8. Our true nature is totally defined by the body, ego, and personality. We are wisps of memories and desires enclosed in packages of flesh and bones.

9. Time exists as an absolute, and we are captives of that absolute. No one escapes the ravages of time.

10. Suffering is necessary—it is part of reality. We are inevitable victims of sickness, aging, and death.

These assumptions reach far beyond aging to define a world of separation, decay, and death. Time is seen as a prison that no one escapes; our bodies are biochemical machines that, like all machines, must run down. This position, the hard line of materialistic science, overlooks much about human nature. We are the only creatures on earth who can change our biology by what we think and feel. We possess the only nervous system that is aware of the phenomenon of aging. Old lions and tigers do not realize what is happening to them—but we do. And because we are aware, our mental state influences what we are aware of.

It would be impossible to isolate a single thought or feeling, a single belief or assumption, that doesn't have some effect on aging, either directly or indirectly. Our cells are constantly eavesdropping on our thoughts and being changed by them. A bout of depression can wreak havoc with the immune system; falling in love can boost it. Despair and hopelessness raise the risk of heart attacks and cancer, thereby shortening life. Joy and fulfillment keep us healthy and extend life. This means that the line between biology and psychology can't really be drawn with any certainty. A remembered stress, which is only a wisp of thought, releases the same flood of destructive hormones as the stress itself.

Because the mind influences every cell in the body, human aging is fluid and changeable; it can speed up, slow down, stop for a time, and even reverse itself. Hundreds of research findings from the last three decades have verified that aging is much more dependent on the individual than was ever dreamed in the past.

However, the most significant breakthrough is not contained in isolated findings but in a completely new worldview. The ten assumptions of the old paradigm do not accurately describe our reality. They are inventions of the human mind that we have turned into rules. To challenge aging at its core, this entire worldview must be challenged first, for nothing hold more power over the body than beliefs of the mind.

Each assumption of the old paradigm can be replaced with a more complete and expanded version of the truth. These new assumptions are also just ideas created by the human mind, but they allow us much more freedom and power. They give us the ability to rewrite the program of aging that now directs our cells.

The ten new assumptions are:

1. The physical world, including our bodies, is a response of the observer. We create our bodies as we create the experience of our world.

2. In their essential state, our bodies are composed of energy and information, not solid matter. This energy and information is an outcropping of infinite fields of energy and information spanning the universe.

3. The mind and body are inseparably one. The unity that is "me" separates into two streams of experience. I experience the subjective stream as thoughts, feelings, and desires. I experienced the objective stream as my body. At a deeper level, however, the two streams meet at a single creative source. It is from this source that we are meant to live.

4. The biochemistry of the body is a product of awareness. Beliefs, thoughts, and emotions create the chemical reactions that uphold life in every cell. An aging cell is the end product of awareness that has forgotten how to remain new.

5. Perception appears to be automatic, but in fact it is a learned phenomenon. The world you live in, including the experience of your body, is completely dictated by how you learned to perceive it. If you change your perception, you change the experience of your body and your world.

6. Impulses of intelligence create your body in new forms every second. What you are is the sum total of these impulses, and by changing their patterns, you will change.

7. Although each person seems separate and independent, all of us are connected to patterns of intelligence that govern the whole cosmos. Our bodies are part of a universal body, our minds an aspect of a universal mind.

8. Time does not exist as an absolute, but only eternity. Time is quantified eternity, timelessness chopped up into bits and pieces (seconds, hours, days, years) by us. What we call linear time is a reflection of how we perceive change. If we could perceive the changeless, time would cease to exist as we know it. We can learn to start metabolizing non-change, eternity, the absolute. By doing that, we will be ready to create the physiology of immortality.

9. Each of us inhabits a reality lying beyond all change. Deep inside us, unknown to the five senses, is an innermost core of being, a field of non-change that creates personality, ego, and body. This being is our essential state—it is who we really are.

10. We are not victims of aging, sickness, and death. These are part of the scenery, not the seer, who is immune to any form of change. This seer is the spirit, the expression of eternal being.

These are vast assumptions, the makings of a new reality, yet all are grounded in the discoveries of quantum physics made almost a hundred years ago. The seeds of this new paradigm were planted by Einstein, Bohr, Heisenberg, and the other pioneers of quantum physics, who realized that the accepted way of viewing the physical world was false. Although things "out there" appear to be real, there is no proof of reality apart from the observer. No two people share exactly the same universe. Every worldview creates its own world.

I want to convince you that you are much more than your limited body, ego, and personality. The rules of cause and effect as you accept them have squeezed you into the volume of a body and the span of a lifetime. In reality, the field of human life is open and unbounded. At its deepest level, your body is ageless, your mind timeless. Once you identify with that reality, which is consistent with the quantum worldview, aging will fundamentally change.

Dawson Church, PhD, founded Soul Medicine Institute to research and teach emerging psychological and medical techniques that can yield fast and radical cures. His book *The Genie in Your Genes* pioneers the field of epigenetics, explaining the remarkable self-healing mechanisms emerging from this science. Through EFT Power Training, he teaches groups how to apply these breakthroughs to health and athletic performance. Publisher of Elite Books and Energy Psychology Press, he has worked with many eading authors during a long career in health publishing. He was born on November 15, 1956, in Cape Town, South Africa.

Dawson Church, PhD, founded Soul Medicine Institute to research and teach emerging psychological and medical techniques that can yield fast and radical cures. His book *The Genie in Your Genes* pioneers the field of epigenetics, explaining the remarkable self-healing mechanisms emerging from this science. Through EFT Power Training, he teaches groups how to apply these breakthroughs to health and athletic performance. Publisher of Elite Books and Energy Psychology Press, he has worked with many eading authors during a long career in health publishing. He was born on November 15, 1956, in Cape Town, South Africa.

Dawson Church

Your DNA
Is Not Your Destiny

"Josephine Tesauro never thought she would live so long. At ninety-two, she is straight backed, firm jawed, and vibrantly healthy, living alone in an immaculate brick ranch house high on a hill near McKeesport, a Pittsburgh suburb. She works part time in a hospital gift shop and drives her 1995 white Oldsmobile Cutlass Ciera to meetings of her four bridge groups, to church and to the grocery store. She has outlived her husband, who died nine years ago, when he was eighty-four. She has outlived her friends, and she has out-lived three of her six brothers.

"Mrs. Tesauro does, however, have a living sister, an identical twin. But she and her twin are not so identical anymore. Her sister is incontinent, she has had a hip replacement, and she has a degenerative disorder that destroyed most of her vision. She also has dementia. 'She just does not comprehend,' Mrs. Tesauro says.

"Even researchers who study aging are fascinated by such stories. How could it be that two people with the same genes, growing up in the same family, living all their lives in the same place, could age so differently?"

Josephine Tesauro and her sister have identical genes. Not similar genes or closely matched genes, but an absolutely identical set of genes. Yet with exactly the same genetic information to work with since birth, they have had radically different health paths. One is healthy and active, living large in her nineties. The other sister is constrained by her many physical ailments, and the loss of her mental faculties, according to the *New York Times*, which published their story recently.

Josephine Tesauro and Her Sister

What creates such different health outcomes as we age? The media is full of stories of the power of genes, identifying a gene for this or that characteristic. Yet examples like those of the Tesauro sisters contradict the popular notion that your genes determine your destiny. People with the same genes can diverge in appearance, life span, and health. James Vaupel, director of the Laboratory of Survival and Longevity at Germany's prestigious Max Planck Institute, says that, on average, identical twins die more than ten years apart. Same genome, divergent life spans. So if your genes don't determine that much about your health or life span, what does?

The new science of epigenetics shows that many factors from the environment outside the cell, even from outside the body, can trigger changes in genes. Genes need to be "turned on" by a stimulus in order for the body to act on the information contained in the genetic code. For instance, when you are healthy and at rest, your body keeps your immune system at a low "standby" level, like a computer in sleep mode. But if you get a cut or a cold, it puts the immune system into high gear, and shunts enormous resources into repelling invading bacteria and viruses. The hard disk is spinning and the processor is churning in high gear. Infection is the epigenetic trigger that signals the body to turn on the genes necessary for a strong immune response. We have a huge and complex set of switches in our bodies. Genes are being switched on or off all the time, based on the signals our bodies are receiving. The body activates the genes it needs to face its current challenges, and turns off the genes it doesn't need at the moment. Just because you have a particular gene (for example, a gene associated with obesity, dyslexia, or cancer), that does not mean it's turned on.

Some epigenetic triggers are beyond our control. But some are completely within our control. What we eat and drink and whether we choose to smoke or take drugs are simple examples. One of the first scientific experiments to demonstrate the epigenetic effects of food intake was done with mice, which are often used in experiments since they are genetically quite similar to human beings.

The researcher, Randy Jirtle, PhD, a professor at Duke University, fed pregnant mice a diet rich in a substance called methyls. These methyl groups eventually made their way from the digestive tract to the brains of the mice, where they attached to a gene called the agouti gene. When a methyl group attaches to a gene, it inhibits the ability of that gene to turn on. By feeding the expectant mice a diet rich in methyls, Dr. Jirtle suppressed the activity of the agouti gene. The result was astounding. The agouti gene is associated with a yellow coat rather than brown fur. Agouti mice have yellow coats and are also much more prone to cancer, diabetes, and obesity than those in whom the gene has been supressed. They die at about half the life span of agouti-suppressed mice. So two mice with identical genes can have completely different disease profiles and life spans when just a single gene is epigenetically modified.

Genetically Identical Mice (Suppressed Agouti Gene on Right)

A study published by Dean Ornish, MD, in 2008 showed the epigenetic effects of lifestyle change in human beings. His subjects were thirty men with low-risk prostate cancer, and he did "gene scans," using advanced DNA microarray technology, of all 23,888 of their genes. This allowed the researchers to see which genes were switched off and which were switched on. Rather than submitting to medical treatment with drugs or surgery, the experimental subjects agreed to change their lifestyle. They ate a healthy diet rich in whole grains, fruits, legumes, soy, and vegetables, exercised moderately (such as walking) for half an hour a day, and spent an hour a day in a stress reduction activity such as meditation.

After three months, they again had all their genes scanned to determine what changes had occurred. The researchers found that 48 genes had been turned on, and 453 had been turned off—an epigenetic effect on 501 genes triggered solely by the positive lifestyle changes the men had made.

Norman Shealy, MD, PhD (see his chapter in this book), coauthored, with me, the book *Soul Medicine,* which explains the world of energy medicine and how to find and work with your ideal practitioner. Norm recently broke new ground in studying the epigenetics of aging. He examined a genetic marker called a telomere. These are the "tails" of genes, and they get about 1 percent shorter each year. Experts can tell how old a cell is by the length of the telomeres, though if you have unhealthy habits, your telomeres shrink faster. After measuring the telomere length of his six subjects, he put them on a healthy diet and exercise routine, and had them use his patented RejuvaMatrix, which bathes the body in an electromagnetic field with the same frequencies as human DNA. After three months on Norm's program, the telomeres of his subjects stopped getting shorter, and actually began to lengthen! After ten months, they were almost 3 percent longer, suggesting that we can reverse many of the signs of cellular aging by a healthy electromagnetic environment and a supportive lifestyle.

Nurture Changes Nature

It's not just what we eat and drink that gives epigenetic signals to our bodies. Our emotional experiences also change the functioning of genes in our brains. Another famous researcher, Moshe Szyf, PhD, of McGill University, found that nurturing is epigenetic. Nurturing creates changes to the genes in our brains that help us deal with stress. Dr. Szyf's experiments used genetically identical rats. Some rat mothers nurtured their offspring, licking and grooming them constantly. Other rat mothers were neglectful. He found that the baby rats who were nurtured showed epigenetic changes in parts of the brain that handle stress. Molecules called acetyls, which help DNA turn on, had attached to the genes that mediate the stress response. When baby rats who had been nurtured by their mothers grew up, they had a much better ability to handle stress.

Dr. Szyf then wondered what would happen if he chemically stripped the acetyl groups out of the brains of the nurtured rats. He tried this and found, sure enough, that these rats then became fearful and easily stressed. He then injected acetyls into the brains of rats that had not been nurtured, and they suddenly showed the ability to handle stress. This was a convincing demonstration that it's not just physical factors such as diet that result in molecular epigenetic changes to the brain, but that emotional factors such as nurturing produce molecular alterations too. I emphasize again that there is no change to the DNA itself; with identical genes, we can see very different results in well-being and other life factors.

The brains of human beings with disorders such as schizophrenia show similar changes in the acetylization of the parts of the brain that mediate the stress response. And, as with the rats, children who are not nurtured lose their ability to handle stress. Love produces the same results in human beings as it does in other animals. Love and nurturing are epigenetic interventions that can make a huge difference in the quality of our lives.

In a large-scale study of 17,400 adults done by the U.S. Centers for Disease Control and Prevention with Kaiser Permanente, a group of researchers looked at the link between emotional trauma and health. They found that children who had experienced traumatic emotional events were more likely to have serious diseases as adults. The more traumatic the childhood, the higher the disease risk. Traumatized children had higher rates of heart disease, cancer, diabetes, hepatitis, obesity, bone fractures, and other conditions. They were three times as likely to smoke, and thirty times as likely to attempt suicide. Badly nurtured children not only have the same inability to handle stress as badly nurtured rats, they also have a higher likelihood of disease than their well-nurtured counterparts.

A 2007 study published in the journal *Biological Psychiatry* looked at the genetic profiles of eighteen medical students. Nine months later, just before their licensing examinations, the researchers did a second gene scan. They found that many genetic switches had been tripped by the stress under which the students were laboring just before the exam. Other studies, looking at people who are lonely and depressed, find more than two hundred gene switches that are tripped in such emotionally traumatized people. Many of these genes regulate the immune system and our response to inflammation, showing another compelling link between our emotional states and our physical health.

By way of contrast, a group of nineteen subjects was taught to de-stress themselves using the relaxation response. Developed by Harvard psychologist Herbert Benson, the relaxation response has people tense and release their muscles sequentially in order to induce a sense of well-being and release tension. Dr. Benson examined the genetic baseline of his subjects before and after they began practicing the relaxation response. He also compared them to another nineteen subjects who were long-term practitioners of relaxation response techniques. He found that many genes were turned on or off after relaxation, especially those relating to cell health, inflammation, and how the body handles free radicals, which unless neutralized can damage tissues.

Love is good for your health, and the ability to nurture yourself and release your emotional upsets is an epigenetic gift, if you are able to accomplish it. And as the Benson experiment demonstrates, even if you did not have a nurturing childhood, you can learn new skills as an adult to help you reverse the epigenetic signals that you were sent early in life.

It Is Never Too Late

So how can we nurture ourselves, and nudge the complex of epigenetic switches in our bodies to make us as healthy and happy as possible? If you are like me, you did not learn much about self-nurturing when you were growing up. By the time I reached thirty-eight years of age, I was running a big publishing company and taking good care of my employees and clients, as well as my wife and children.

There was only one person I was not taking good care of, and that was me. I had frequent respiratory ailments, and my back ached every day. My joints went out of alignment easily, and I suffered from gout. Some days I was in agony, and I could not move in any direction without screaming involuntarily from the severe pain. I battled depression, addiction, and insomnia. I had time for everyone else, but no time for me. When I tried to take some time for myself, there was always someone else's need to attend to.

Now, in my fifties, I take much better care of myself, and I feel vibrantly healthy. As well as diet and exercise, I pay great attention to emotional health. When I have an upset, I resolve it as fast as possible. And I have a daily routine that supports a peaceful and serene state, despite a busy schedule of lectures and consulting. It took a lot of effort to retrain myself in the art of self-nurture.

Here are the concrete steps you can take to create an emotional "love nest" for yourself. These are all practical methods to help you handle stress, create inner peace, and release the emotional charge of traumatic events. Best of all, most of them are free, and easy to learn:

- Meditation
- Prayer
- Optimism
- A positive attitude
- Energy medicine
- Energy psychology
- Positive beliefs
- Positive visualizations
- Acts of kindness
- Love
- Nurturing
- Spirituality

By "energy medicine," I mean methods such as Reiki, Donna Eden's energy medicine, Quantum Touch, Therapeutic Touch, and other methods that alter the body's electromagnetic state. A full list appears in the book *Soul Medicine*.

By "energy psychology," I mean methods such as Emotional Freedom Techniques (EFT), Thought Field Therapy (TFT), Tapas Acupressure Technique (TAT), and other similar therapies that release the emotional charge of traumatic events. In my book *The Genie in Your Genes*, I provide a full explanation of how energy psychology works, and how to use some of the most popular methods.

The key to epigenetic health is releasing as much as possible of the unhealthy programming we received as children, and then releasing stresses that occur in present time right after they occur.

Try this simple experiment from energy psychology to see how easy it is. Think of a recent incident that deeply upset you. Give it a number from 0 to 10, with 0 being complete peace, and 10 being the most extreme upset possible. Write down your number. Now cross your hands over your heart, and take three deep breaths. Tap on the center of your chest with one hand ten to fifteen times. Take another breath. Now think about the incident again, and write down your number. Most people report a big drop in the intensity of their feelings after doing this fast and simple exercise to release emotional charge. Rather than storing all that emotion in your body, you're letting it go. Do this whenever you have a big emotional reaction and you start to create a life in which you aren't being the neglectful rat mother to yourself! Clean up enough of your real-time emotional reactivity and you can then work on your childhood deficits with the aid of a good coach or psychotherapist.

That's the kind of work I do now, much of it with veterans of the wars in Vietnam, Iraq, and Afghanistan. We teach EFT to soldiers suffering from posttraumatic stress disorder (PTSD). After they learn to release the intense emotional energy of their combat experiences, many of them apply these methods to their personal lives. This is part of the Iraq Vets Stress Project (www.StressProject.org), which connects coaches who are teaching EFT with veterans suffering from PTSD. In witnessing the powerful positive changes in the veterans' lives after EFT, I am awed and humbled to see the difference that self-nurturing makes.

I've also tried this with elite athletes. Helping healthy people release emotional memories enhances their performance. I performed a rigorous type of scientific experiment called a randomized controlled trial (RCT) with the men's and women's basketball teams at Oregon State University. We split them into two groups. One received EFT and the other received a placebo treatment, a fake intervention. Before and after treatment, we tested how high they could jump, and how many free throws they could accurately deliver into the basket. Although both groups performed about the same beforehand, their performances afterward were very different. The group that received EFT scored an astonishing 38 percent better at free throws than the group that got the fake intervention!

I teach EFT to groups through an organization called EFT Power Training and we're seeing major changes in the stress levels of executive groups, sports teams, professional organizations, and other collections of people who learn EFT. When you release your stress, you perform better at any task, no matter whether you're hitting a business sales target, putting a golf ball on the green, doing surgery, or coaching a client. As your stress level goes down, all your body's biological resources become available for cell repair, combating the effects of aging, and filling you with lightness and energy.

The bottom line is that you are not living a life script programmed into your DNA at conception and out of your control ever since. You have it in your power to change the on-off switches on many of your genes. In fact, you're doing this every day already, through your emotions and your lifestyle. As you learn the skills of self-nurturing, you consciously select responses that support a long and healthy life. You can increase your physical energy, sharpen your intellectual powers, boost your spiritual practice, and live a life brimming with optimistic promise at any age. So love yourself, and choose the best life possible!

Asha Clinton, MSW, PhD, is the developer of Advanced Integrative Therapy (AIT). Her forty-year background as a cultural anthropologist and analytic psychotherapist has given her a deep understanding of the traumatic causes of personal and societal affliction. AIT is the culmination of her lifelong mission to help reduce suffering and replace it with hope and freedom. She trains therapists on three continents and has headed AIT's humanitarian aid projects on the Navajo Reservation and among the Maya of Guatemala. Asha Clinton was born on August 6, 1943, in New York City.

ASHA CLINTON

Creating the Freedom to Age Audaciously

Imagine waking up on the morning of your eightieth birthday. You get out of bed without stiffness, pain, or illness. You feel content with your existence whether you are planning a day of solitary beauty or a party with those you love. You are comfortable in yourself and in your accumulated knowledge and wisdom. You know that, should something unsettling arise, you have the tools to resolve it harmoniously. You have enthusiasm for living and the capacity for giving and receiving. You feel that your life has value and purpose and know that you make a difference.

How many people do you know who, even at half that age, feel that good? It will be another fifteen years before I become an octogenarian, but my life experience has shown me that authentic, courageous, and audacious aging comes from authentic, courageous, and audacious living.

Few of us experience such quality of life because we carry within us the steadily growing burden of old suffering. Each new wounding event that we experience is laden with the emotional and physical load from every other such past experience, and this backlog is what blocks the flow of free, joyful living and health.

In the following pages, I will share some profound benefits that can emerge from a new therapy that is gentle yet deeply effective in healing our wounded pasts, reconnecting us to our potential, and liberating present and future from the oppression of pain, frustration, and inner limitation. The therapy is called Advanced Integrative Therapy (AIT; formerly Seemorg Matrix Work).

An Answer

I developed this therapy because my life's work has been about removing the obstacles that get in the way of humans' potential to live full and fascinating lives. My journey began in 1998 when the skeleton of what was to be AIT first appeared as I woke up from a Sunday morning nap in the tub.

I was an experienced psychotherapist with a solid background in Jungian psychotherapy, object relations, self psychology, systems therapy, traumatology, and twenty years of private practice. I was also trained in cultural anthropology, healing, and spiritual practice in the Buddhist and Sufi traditions. Always integrative in orientation, I had already helped many people find insight, transformation, and physical healing. But some of my clients felt that what I could do was not enough—and they were right. I shared their frustration as I struggled to make the methods available to me succeed, especially when I was treating a client with a more difficult disorder such as obsessive-compulsive disorder (OCD), a personality disorder, or bipolar disorder. Their suffering was great, and the available modalities took years to help only a little.

My search for a deeper, more thorough, faster way to alleviate suffering brought me to many workshops and seminars. I trained in several techniques in the emerging field of energy psychology, which uses the movement of energy in the body to effect significant change. I felt that these techniques showed real promise. I hoped that, soon, someone could teach me to use energy movement to produce progressively deeper levels of physical and psychological healing and spiritual freedom. In fact, I was waiting for someone to develop a new therapy that used energy toward this end.

I dozed off that Sunday morning a therapist wanting a better way to relieve people's pain, and awoke knowing that I'd been given what I had been looking for: the skeleton of a new therapy that would combine the best of the traditional modalities—psychodynamic, cognitive, behavioral, and transpersonal—with the movement of energy. Such a combination had the potential to make therapy highly effective and to broaden psychotherapy into therapy that treated the whole person. I jumped out of the bathtub and ran down to my computer because what I had seen was something I did not want to forget. I wrote down the first two protocols of what was to become AIT as if I were taking dictation. I've felt grateful for this gift every day since then.

My first tentative AIT experiments on myself left me breathless with excitement. Through research with traditional energy centers such as the chakras and experimentation with others, I found thirteen major energy centers in my body that held my emotional, physical, conceptual, and spiritual reactions to trauma. I held each center in turn, repeatedly named a traumatic incident, and moved my hands from one energy center to the next to direct the wounded energy down and out of my body. In a matter of hours, by repeating this process for a group of related traumas, I was able to treat the harsh self-judgment that had dogged me all my life! By the end of that afternoon, the unforgiving voice inside my head had changed its tune. It became compassionate, and remains so to this day. Twenty-two years of the best talk therapy I could find had failed to do this.

I tried the method with many different issues. Once I saw how well it worked on me, I asked my husband and daughter whether they were willing to try it out, and they were. The results were equally good, and showed me that AIT was suitable for children as well as adults. Then came my colleagues and friends and, finally, my clients. Afraid they would say no, I asked my clients, one by one, if they would like to try something totally experimental that had great potential to heal them. All but one volunteered.

As new clients replaced those who had been healed, this gave me the opportunity to work with many different issues, and to develop new protocols and methods for a growing number of psychological disorders and physical illnesses, as well as spiritual malaise. Many clients told me that our sessions produced a lightness of being, an increase in energy and vitality, greater clarity, more physical strength, new interests and the ability and energy to pursue them, elimination of depression and anxiety, and sometimes altered states of consciousness. I observed the remission of one illness or disorder after another. In all my years as a therapist, I had never seen responses like these, especially with intractable disorders.

While I was busy in my practice, I was also busy at the computer and in the classroom. In the late evenings, I wrote new protocols based on the research I was conducting daily with my clients. On the weekends, I taught each new segment of AIT to my intrepid, forward-looking colleagues. Some of them began to do AIT research as well, and contributed protocols and other methods. Fifteen training seminars grew out of this work, and more are in development. Most important for me, it was the answer to my deepest dream: to be able to help lessen the suffering in the world.

It took a few years to discover what the longer-term therapeutic results of AIT might be, and they were even more exciting to me than the short-term results. I began to observe them first in myself, and then discovered that many of my AIT colleagues and clients were enjoying similar experiences. It was a movement, for all of us, from suffering into joy and contentment that took months for some people and a few years for others, depending on how deeply wounded they had been. AIT transformed us into people who no longer suffer emotions, sensations, and negative ideas from the past and who, as a result, live in a state of peacefulness, clarity, and presence most of the time. When I first realized how gentle and sporadic my more difficult emotions had become, I asked one of my colleagues to work on me to discover whether I had repressed or dissociated them. Imagine my joy when I realized, with her help, that they simply were not there, and that my own spiritual connection had become amazingly strong just because so many of the traumas that had blocked it had been removed!

Trauma, Energy, and Treatment

A growing body of AIT theory and methodology emerged from my experimental work with willing clients in the decade that followed. The more it developed, the more it demonstrated the relationship between energy and the actual incidents and patterns that wound us and distort our way of experiencing the world. AIT does not rely on talking as a cure because, although talking helps people gain insight into their issues, it does too little to remove them. Issues consist of energy. AIT is able to remove issues completely because it removes the energy of which they consist.

Quantum mechanics, with its dictum that everything is energy, informs AIT. Just as material objects, light, and sound consist of energy, so do emotions, beliefs, and physical sensations. In other words, our anger and grief consist of energy, as does a headache or a prayer. The problem, then, is not the hurtful incidents we experience; it is our unresolved and long-lasting reactions to them that are held in our emotional and physical memories. To heal our issues fully, we need to transform or remove the energies in us made up of our particular responses to the incidents and patterns that hurt or upset us. The more of these we remove or transform, the greater our clarity, lightness, vigor, and contentment, and the more audaciously we can grow.

It works like this. Trauma—the things that happen that are painful or negatively life-changing whether they impact you physically, psychologically, conceptually, and/or spiritually—occurs repeatedly throughout your life. For instance, your mother tries to control you from birth until you finally leave home and can stop having to fight her off on a daily basis. Your dad, a poor man who never had a chance for an education, nags you daily to make a success of yourself because he needs you to but doesn't think you can. The kids at school tease you because you study a lot to achieve your dad's dreams. And later there are those who dump you and whom you dump, the divorces, the hurt children—all your failures and humiliations. Later still there are all the deaths of family members and friends, of hopes and dreams, of your health, of your ability to shrug things off and move on. Trauma, then, is the stuff of normal life.

Trauma has an incredibly pervasive effect on us. On the emotional level, it causes us to feel things like fear and anxiety, depression, rage, and grief—or to stop feeling altogether. Whether we feel them consciously or not, these emotions, in turn, cloud our ability to think through our situation and act with clarity. Trauma also causes most psychological disorders, from garden-variety anxiety to narcissism, and many physical illnesses.

As I treated more and more clients with AIT, I began to see that, once a significant trauma occurs in childhood, it tends to repeat. The person who has suffered it is conditioned to what happened during the original trauma, as well as to how she or he reacted to it. It's as if the first trauma becomes a kind of magnet that draws similar circumstances, events, or experiences in the future.

For example, Gina's father left the family for another woman when Gina was three. During high school, two steady boyfriends left her for other girls; her first two husbands left her for other women as well. This kind of patterning in life is not coincidental; it is the original trauma repeating because the person who suffered it is conditioned to its circumstances and effects. AIT can quickly eliminate such traumatic patterns of conditioning by removing their constituent energy.

Trauma and Illness

To age with optimal health and well-being, it is also important to treat our physical illnesses successfully. Before the emergence of AIT, I had specialized in working with cancer patients, so numerous clients came to me with physical illnesses in addition to the psychological issues they wanted to resolve. As we worked with AIT, I discovered some important connections. To begin with, trauma results in physical as well as psychological and cognitive aftereffects. When we do not express our posttraumatic emotions fully enough, these energies can remain captive in our bodies, settling into organs, joints, or other body parts that are symbolically related to the emotions and the traumas that caused them. If the emotions remain in parts of the body long enough and are intense enough, these parts often seem to sicken. Though it is hardly the only cause of illness, such emotional displacement can be at the root of some autoimmune disorders, heart prolems, cancers, and respiratory infections as well as other physical conditions, including chronic pain.

For example, I treated Kate, who had a lifelong heart murmur. Once we discovered and treated the traumatic cause of the murmur, a frequently broken heart caused by her childhood family's frequent moves and her concomitant loss of friend after friend, the murmur completely disappeared. And then there's Bill, whose prostate cancer went into full remission once we treated the sexual indiscretions of his youth and the shame and guilt that accompanied them.

Most important, to the degree that the causes of an illness are psychological in nature, they can be successfully treated with AIT energetic methods. These methods include: finding and treating psychologically caused weaknesses in the immune system in order to cure infection; finding and treating all the psychological, physical, and spiritual causes of an illness, its symptoms, and the relationship between causes and symptoms; and, where relevant, finding and energetically treating the allergies and food intolerances that, because they weaken the immune system, function as a covert underpinning for the development of other illnesses. Since these methods were developed, AIT practitioners have addressed a wide variety of illnesses, successfully enabling their clients to regain health and vitality.

Mike came into therapy with me at the age of seventy-two because his lifelong asthma was getting worse. His energy and enjoyment of life were deteriorating as his asthma attacks became more numerous. He said that life was not worth living when it was threatened so frequently. I asked him when his asthma had started and when, recently, it had begun getting worse. It had started after the death of his father when he was seven; it had worsened after his brother had died two years ago.

We quickly discovered that his asthma had three major causes: multiple food allergies; a smothering, invading mother whom he had internalized; and unresolved grief, especially from the loss of his father and brother. Using AIT, I energetically treated his grief issues, the smothering, and his allergies. During the grief treatments, his asthma began to recede. By the end of his treatment six months later, his asthma was gone. He felt energetic and optimistic, and decided to learn to play tennis, something his asthma had never allowed him to do. More important, he became conscious of his own depths for the first time in his life. He said of his AIT therapy:

> From the very first session, I felt transformed as we peeled off layers of pain I'd carried around for decades, and as we transformed the limiting beliefs and expectations I'd absorbed from my family, ancestry, and culture and carried

into my marriage. I learned I wasn't to blame for them; they had been created by events I would never have imagined were related. Looking back, what I got from AIT was a miracle. It gave me a deeper connection to who I really am and the clarity and strength to take my new, stronger voice into the world with purpose and love. And I get to play tennis too!

Trauma and Spirituality

Aside from traumas that cause psychological pain and physical illness, my clients and I discovered certain types of trauma that blocked the spiritual dimensions of life. I tailored the methods of AIT to address them, offering help to those who were unable to meditate, pray, or engage in meaningful ritual. As a result, some clients found themselves able to connect to God and to develop awareness of their spiritual dimensions as their traumas were healed. For many of my older clients, this work has been pivotal in healing their immense grief as growing numbers of family members and friends die. For others, awakening to a larger identity through treatment offered peace where there had been fear of death.

For instance, Anne, seventy-six years old, had spent her life painting lively, vivid abstract canvases. Though many people found them intensely spiritual, Anne had no conscious spiritual connection. When we looked for the traumatic causes of her spiritual disconnection, we discovered that she had been brought up in a rigidly atheistic household where spirituality, feelings, and personal authenticity were anathema. As Anne and I energetically treated these linked issues, she began to dream of a great cavern in the earth where she went to worship the Goddess. As this series of dreams progressed, Anne contacted her own ecstasy, love, and peace. Most important, she experienced a deep connection with her own spiritual essence and with the feminine side of God. During her last session, she said: "I came here alone and isolated from my deepest ground. Now I leave connected to the earth, to the universe. I'll never be alone again."

Aging in Freedom

What are life and aging like after the energetic removal of trauma that has limited us, which Advanced Integrative Therapy makes possible? Inwardly, we flourish by transforming our interior landscapes and our capacity to experience the fullness of human life in all circumstances and on all levels. We come to terms with the limitations and finiteness of existence in a way that not only acts as a model of hope and courage for younger people, but also brings about experiences of wonder, joy, deep gratitude, and presence. We own our truth not just by surviving, but also by thriving in our own authenticity. By our example, we change the world for the better.

Outwardly, freedom from the energy of past trauma allows us to live spiritedly in full authenticity and integrity, to dare to be fully present in each and every minute, and boldly complete our life's work. It can mean strengthening our bodies and using them creatively for work and play. It can involve contributing compassionate service by lovingly focusing on our families, friends, and those in need; becoming politically outspoken and active; and feeling free to do these things and others in a way that uniquely and authentically expresses us and our unique potentials.

In short, it is aging with a minimum of psychological pain, a minimum of illness, and a maximum of spiritual contentment.

Gene D. Cohen, MD, PhD, is founding director of both the Center on Aging, Health, and Humanities at George Washington University Medical Center and the think tank Washington DC Center on Aging. He cofounded the Creativity Discovery Corps, which is dedicated to identifying and preserving the creative accomplishments and rich histories of under-recognized talented older adults. His book *The Creative Age: Awakening Human Potential in the Second Half of Life* brought the concept of "creative aging" to the public discourse on age redefinition. He was born on September 28, 1944, in Boston, Massachusetts.

GENE D. COHEN

CHAPTER
9

The Myth of the Midlife Crisis

I was taken by surprise several years ago when my colleagues start-ed to worry that I was going through some sort of midlife crisis. I was in my late forties, and after two decades as a gerontologist I was pursuing a new passion: designing games for older adults. My first game, a joint effort with artist Gretchen Raber, was a finalist in an internationally juried show on games as works of art. Though I still had a day job directing George Washington University's Center on Aging, Health, and Humanities, I was now working hard on a second game.

"Are you turning right on us?" one friend, a neuroscientist, kid-ded me. He wasn't talking about politics. He was asking whether I'd scrapped the logical, analytical tendencies of the brain's left hemi-sphere to embrace the more creative, less disciplined tendencies of the right brain. But I wasn't scrapping anything. As a researcher, I had spent years documenting the psychological benefits of intergen-erational play. Now I was using both sides of my brain to create new opportunities for myself. Instead of just measuring and studying the benefits of mental stimulation, I was finding creative ways to put my findings to work. What my friends perceived as a crisis was, in truth, the start of a thrilling new phase of my life.

In thinking about this experience, I realized that our view of human development in the second half of life was badly outmoded. We tend to think of aging in purely negative terms, and even experts often define "successful" aging as the effective management of de-cay and decline. Rubbish. No one can deny that aging brings chal-lenges and losses. But recent discoveries in neuroscience show that the aging brain is more flexible and adaptable than we previously thought. Studies suggest that the brain's left and right hemispheres become better integrated during middle age, making way for greater creativity. Age also seems to dampen some negative emotions. And a great deal of scientific work has confirmed the "use it or lose it" adage, showing that the aging brain grows stronger from use and challenge. In short, midlife is a time of new possibility. Growing old can be filled with positive experiences. The challenge is to recognize our potential—and nurture it.

Until recently, scientists paid little attention to psychological development in the second half of life, and those who did pay attention often drew the wrong conclusions. "About the age of fifty," Sigmund Freud wrote in 1907, "the elasticity of the mental processes on which treatment depends is, as a rule, lacking. Old people are no longer educable." Freud, who wrote those words at fifty-one and produced some of his best work after sixty-five, wasn't the only pioneer to misconstrue the aging process. Jean Piaget, the great developmental psychologist, assumed that cognitive development stopped during young adulthood, with the acquisition of abstract thought. Even Erik Erikson, who delineated eight stages of psychosocial development, devoted only two pages of his classic work *Identity and the Life Cycle* to later life.

My own work picks up where these past giants left off. Through studies involving more than three thousand older adults, I have identified four distinct developmental phases that unfold in overlapping twenty-year periods beginning in a person's early forties: a midlife reevaluation (typically encountered between 40 and 65) during which we set new goals and priorities, a liberation phase (55 to 75) that involves shedding past inhibitions to express ourselves more freely, a summing-up phase (65 to 85) when we begin to review our lives and concentrate on giving back, and an encore phase (75 and beyond) that involves finding affirmation and fellowship in the face of adversity and loss. I refer to "phases" instead of "stages" because people vary widely during later life. We don't all march through these phases in lockstep, but I've seen thousands of older adults pass through them— each person driven by a unique set of inner drives and ideals.

What sparks this series of changes? Why, after finding our places in the world, do so many of us spend our forties and fifties reevaluating our lives? The impulse stems partly from a growing awareness of our own mortality. As decades vanish behind us, and we realize how relatively few we have left, we gain new perspective on who we are and what we really care about. This awakening isn't always easy—it often reveals conflicts between the lives we've built and the ones we want to pursue—but only 10 percent of the people I've studied describe the midlife transition as a crisis. Far more say they're filled with a new sense of quest and personal discovery. "I'm looking forward to pursuing the career I always wanted," one forty-nine-year-old woman told me. "I'm tired of just working on other people's visions, rather than my own, even if I have to start on a smaller scale."

While changing our perspective, age also remodels our brains, leaving us better equipped to fulfill our own dreams. The most important difference between older brains and younger brains is also the easiest to overlook: older brains have learned more than young ones. Throughout life, our brains encode thoughts and memories by forming new connections among neurons. The neurons themselves may lose some processing speed with age, but they become ever more richly intertwined. Magnified tremendously, the brain of a mentally active fifty-year-old looks like a dense forest of interlocking branches, and this density reflects both deeper knowledge and better judgment. That's why age is such an advantage in fields like editing, law, medicine, coaching, and management. There is no substitute for acquired learning.

Knowledge and wisdom aren't the only fruits of age. New research suggests that as our brains become more densely wired, they also become less rigidly bifurcated. As I mentioned earlier, our brains actually consist of two separate structures—a right brain and a left brain—linked by a row of fibers called the corpus callosum. In most people, the left hemisphere specializes in speech, language, and logical reasoning, while the right hemisphere handles more intuitive tasks, such as face recognition and the reading of emotional cues. But as scientists have recently discovered through studies with PET scans and magnetic resonance imaging (MRI), this pattern changes as we age. Unlike young adults, who handle most tasks on one side of the brain or the other, older ones tend to use both hemispheres. Duke University neuroscientist Robert Cabeza has dubbed this phenomenon "hemispheric asymmetry reduction in older adults" (HAROLD) and his research suggests it is no accident.

In a 2002 study, Cabeza assigned a set of memory tasks to three groups of people: one composed of young adults, one of low-performing older adults, and one of high-performing older adults. Like the young people, the low-performing elders drew mainly on one side of the prefrontal cortex to perform the assigned tasks. It was the high-scoring elders who used both hemispheres. No one knows exactly what this all means, but the finding suggests that healthy brains compensate for the depredations of age by expanding their neural networks across the bilateral divide. My own work suggests that, besides keeping us sharp, this neural integration makes it easier to reconcile our thoughts with our feelings. When you hear someone saying, "My head tells me to do this, but my heart says do that," the person is more likely a twenty-year-old than a fifty-year-old. One of my patients, a fifty-one-year-old man, remembers how he agonized over decisions during his twenties, searching in vain for the most logical choice. As he moved through his forties and into his fifties, he found himself trusting his gut. "My decisions are more subjective," he said during one session, "but I'm more comfortable with many of the choices that follow."

As our aging brains grow wiser and more flexible, they also tend toward greater equanimity. Our emotions are all rooted in a set of neural structures known collectively as the limbic system. Some of our strongest negative emotions originate in the amygdalae, a pair of almond-shaped limbic structures that sit near the center of the brain, screening sensory data for signs of trouble. At the first hint of a threat, the amygdalae fire off impulses that can change our behavior before our conscious, thinking brains have a chance to weigh in. That's why our hearts pound when strangers approach us on dark side-walks—and why we often overreact to slights and annoyances. But the amygdalae seem to mellow with age. In brain-imaging studies, older adults show less evidence of fear, anger, and hatred than young adults. Psychological studies confirm that impression, showing that older adults are less impulsive and less likely to dwell on their nega-tive feelings.

An editor I know at a New York publishing company provides a case in point. He was in his sixties, and contemplating retirement, when he realized that he had finally matured into his job. Despite a sharp intellect and a passion for excellence, this man had spent much of his career alienating people with brusque, critical comments and a lack of sensitivity. Now, he told me over lunch, he was finally begin-ning to master interpersonal communication. As his emotional devel-opment caught up to his intellectual development, he morphed from a brilliant but brittle loner into a mentor and a mediator of conflicts. "I feel like a changed man," he said with a bemused smile. His best work was still ahead of him.

Clearly, the aging brain is more resilient, adaptable, and capable than we thought. But that doesn't mean we can sit back and expect good things to happen. Research has identified several types of activ-ity that can, if practiced regularly, help boost the power, clarity, and subtlety of the aging brain.

Exercise physically. Numerous studies have linked physical exercise to increased brainpower. This is particularly true when the exercise is aerobic (continuous, rhythmic exercise that uses large mus-cle groups). The positive effects may stem from increased blood flow to the brain, the production of endorphins, better filtration of waste products from the brain, and increased brain-oxygen levels.

Exercise mentally. The brain is like a muscle. Use it and it grows stronger. Let it idle and it will grow flabby. So choose something appealing and challenging—and don't be surprised if, once you start, you want to do more. One of the programs I cochair, the Creativity Discovery Corps, strives to identify unrecognized, talented older adults in the community. A ninety-three-year-old woman we recently interviewed advised us that she might find scheduling the next interview difficult because she was busy applying for a PhD program.

Pick challenging leisure activities. Getting a graduate degree isn't the only way to keep your brain fit. An important 2003 study identified five leisure activities that were associated with a lower risk of dementia and cognitive decline. In order of impact (from highest to lowest), the winners were dancing, playing board games, playing musical instruments, doing crossword puzzles, and reading. Risk reduction was related to the frequency of participation. For example, older persons who did crossword puzzles four days a week had a risk of dementia 47 percent lower than subjects who did puzzles only once a week.

Achieve mastery. Research on aging has uncovered a key variable in mental health called "sense of control." From middle age onward, people who enjoy a sense of control and mastery stay healthier than those who don't. The possibilities for mastery are unlimited, ranging from playing a musical instrument to learning a new language to taking up painting or embroidery. Besides improving your outlook, the sense of accomplishment may also strengthen the immune system.

Establish strong social networks. Countless studies have linked active social engagement to better mental and physical health and lower death rates. People who maintain social relationships during the second half of life enjoy significantly lower blood pressure, which in turn reduces the risk of stroke and its resulting brain damage. Social relationships also reduce stress and its corrosive effects, including anxiety and depression.

The brain is like the foundation of a building—it provides the physical substrate of our minds, our personalities, and our sense of self. As we've seen, our brain hardware is capable of adapting, growing, and becoming more complex and integrated with age. As our brains mature and evolve, so do our knowledge, our emotions, and our expressive abilities. In turn, what we do with those abilities affects the brain itself, forging the new connections and constellations needed for further psychological growth. This realization should embolden anyone entering the later phases of life. If we can move beyond our stubborn myths about the aging brain, great things are possible. Successful aging is not about managing decline. It's about harnessing the enormous potential that each of us has for growth, love, and happiness.

Raines Cohen, a community organizer active in the aging-in-community movement, helps people connect with their neighbors to take care of each other. He cofounded the Berkeley Macintosh Users Group (BMUG) and adapted the mutual-support model and his technology journalism, business development, and consulting experience to help people create and thrive in real-world communities. He helps people form and grow village networks and intentional neighborhoods such as Berkeley (California) Cohousing, where he lives and runs Planning for Sustainable Communities with his wife, community researcher Betsy Morris. He was born on October 4, 1966, in Beverly, Massachusetts. Photo by Scott Beale/laughingsquid.com.

RAINES COHEN

CHAPTER
10

Aging in Community

A quarter century ago, I was privileged to be involved in the beginning of a grassroots revolution in the computer industry. In high school and college, setting up and operating self-help peer-to-peer computer "user groups" taught me more than I could ever learn in classrooms about how people can build trust and community through voluntarily engaging in relationships for mutual benefit. People shared expertise in an openhearted way. Working together, we brought accountability to the hardware and software makers and found new paths to independence and self-determination through the combination of technology and sociability.

Now, I feel blessed to be part of a parallel evolution in the field of aging, a newly emerging phenomenon we in the movement call "aging in community" (not to be confused with the important but narrower "aging in place" concept from which it grew). New community-based, people-powered institutions and models for cooperation are giving us the opportunity to resist the multibillion-dollar aging-industrial complex trying to put us into prefabricated generic slots in nursing homes and the well-intentioned efforts of our own families to "take care of us" in ways that strip us of autonomy.

We can gain control of our lives, and even add elements of choice in our deaths. We earn independence through interdependence. Empowerment comes from people's discovery that, in sharing information and ideas, access to a greater whole becomes integral to each individual's success, as my wife, Betsy Morris, a longtime community researcher, phrases it. Passionate groups of users—amateurs and professionals interacting freely in structured settings—become a community of stakeholders with the power to reshape the systems itself, first through voluntary exchanges among themselves, and then by translating social connections and trust into economic and political clout.

A Movement of Many Parts

Aging in community is a ragtag movement of ordinary people banding together to fill in gaps in the patchwork of care with overlapping efforts on both regional and national levels. These "multiple centers of initiative" have just in the past decade:

- Built "village model" support structures that can help us stay in our homes, connecting to neighbors rather than isolating ourselves as we age.

- Created new cohousing neighborhoods and ecovillages specifically designed to provide homes in which people can live out the rest of their lives, transforming their collective impact on the earth for the benefit of future generations.

- Formed Elders' Guilds, Second Journey workshops, and study groups for conscious aging/positive aging in which people reimage old age and embody the wisdom to help heal the future.

A few groups are exploring new areas of development in the movement, including:

- ElderFire communities, ElderShire neighborhoods, and "Green House" nursing homes.

- Strategies to remake our cities and towns into aging-friendly communities prepared to meet their populations' needs.

- Senior support networks that keep people connected and engaged across distances through computer communications.

The term "aging in community" appears to have been coined early this century by participants in Second Journey workshops on "Spirit, Service, and Community." (Based in Chapel Hill, North Carolina, the organization Second Journey is dedicated to "awakening human potential in life's second half.") I credit White House Conference on Aging member Janice Blanchard of Colorado as the one who has done the most to popularize the term through presentations at American Society on Aging national conferences and throughout the "industry of aging."

It's going to take a lot of us working together to grow the movement. We're still in the early stages of finding each other, and as a self-help, citizen-organized movement, we're in the de-commodifying business, so you can't (yet) just look up your local aging-in-community center and say "I'd like one of those villages by next week, please." A few national organizations support matchmaking and group development for some types of community efforts, but at the moment, if you want one of these groups to meet your housing or care needs, the odds are you'll have to step up and make it happen, working a bit to find others to share the load. Fortunately, help of all kinds is available along the way.

Curious? Join me, if you will, on a brief journey through some of these innovative efforts and what makes them so essential to our revolution in aging.

Villages: Supporting Each Other Where We Live

As we age and go through all the changes that life brings, it is not uncommon for us to find ourselves living in homes that no longer meet our needs. Kids growing up, partners passing or moving away, shifts in our social networks, losing our automotive mobility, and suddenly we can find ourselves in a house that is too big, too tall, too isolated, or simply too much work to maintain.

Growing up near Boston, I sometimes bicycled through the charming historic Beacon Hill neighborhood northwest of down-town. The same characteristics that caused me to steer clear when bicycling—the steep and narrow cobblestone-paved, traffic-clogged streets—made it a challenge for elder residents to get safely to the store or appointments, with or without driving, and fostered isola-tion. Sure, some elders there could afford to move to a beautiful (and expensive) "community" or "home" in the 'burbs. But faced with the loss of independence and giving up their social networks, the familiarity of friends close at hand in a known place that had served them for decades, many resisted pressure from family and neighbors concerned for their health and well-being.

So elders who didn't want to be displaced from their longtime homes in this urban oasis banded together to organize mutual sup-port networks and membership-based cooperative buying clubs for all the services they needed to continue their active, healthy lives without displacement. Beacon Hill Village pioneered a one-stop shop-ping "concierge" service coordinating transportation, in-home care, maintenance, and health-care referrals, along with regular socials, classes, and monitoring services organized by members. Service pro-viders offered discounts and knew that they better provide prompt, quality results, thanks to leverage that no individual member would have on her or his own. And the members were in charge, setting up a nonprofit in 2001 and hiring a coordinator, rather than being passive consumers of services or captive clients of an institution.

This "village model" is rapidly spreading around the country and being adapted to different needs and conditions, with experienced community organizers playing a key role in helping people unite around their shared interests. The National Cooperative Bank's NCB Capital Impact division recently launched a "Village to Village Network" to make it easier and faster for aspiring village founders to build a critical mass, especially in suburban or rural areas that lack the density of the original Boston example.

Cohousing: Creating Co-Care Connections

The roots of the cohousing model lie in Denmark in the early 1970s. Families looking for deeper connections with neighbors and support for raising kids together pioneered a new form of neighborhood, one combining private homes with a large shared area. A common house included a shared kitchen and dining area that they could use together a few times a week, while retaining the independence of their own kitchens. Cars were pushed to the edge, the design aimed at walkability. Residents could share in childcare but weren't forced to do everything together. This "yes, and..." principle of adding choices turned out to provide a high quality of life without adding much cost to basic homeownership.

More than one hundred cohousing neighborhoods across the United States offer homes with community, developed by the residents. In these "intentional neighborhoods," knowing your twenty to forty neighbors and sharing experiences builds trust. Cities will approve cohousing projects and banks will finance them (even when the economy is stalled everywhere else) because the future residents invest and share an interest in the project's success; they've got "skin in the game."

The cohousing neighborhood design can further offer:

- Shared guest rooms to accommodate visiting family members or long-term care providers whose services are shared by community members; having your care provider live independently rather than in your house is beneficial to all concerned.

- Regular shared meals to keep people talking to one another and aware of significant events in each other's lives.

- Community connections that keep people active because they know they'll hear from their neighbor if they don't get up and get the paper by midday.

Senior cohousing, promoted in the United States by Charles Durrett (decades after he imported the original intergenerational form with his architect/author wife, Kathryn McCamant), is just

getting off the ground here, with a handful of communities established in California, Virginia, and Colorado, and a couple dozen more
in the development process. The Cohousing Association of the United
States (Coho/US) is helping these bold pioneers challenge bureau-
crats, land-use regulations, and their own fears that can keep them
from realizing their visions.

Part of what is driving this elder-rich movement, according to
cohousing's Durrett, is the tendency of baby boomers to reinvent
society's institutions as they engage them. "What is more audacious
than twenty-five seniors deciding that they should build their own
neighborhood?" Durrett asks. "What is more audacious than twenty-
five seniors deciding, 'Hell, they don't know how to do it. We're
gonna figure out how to do it.' All these seniors should be able to stay
in their houses, not just be told to be happy in assisted care. This generation understands that the Stepford country is not where it's at."

The Danish national aging curriculum, which Durrett is adapting for domestic consumption, helps people band together in "study
groups" to talk about all the taboo topics of aging adults that are
important to discuss before crises arise:

- Health
- Death
- Finances
- Co-care agreements
- Spirituality

By working together, cohousers are able to partner efficiently
with professional developers and cocreate neighborhoods that will
better meet their needs. This increases the odds that they can
remain in their homes over time without becoming a burden to
their neighbors.

In my experience in coaching people in creating village models
and cohousing groups, I have found that people who want to stay in
their own homes in their elder years often start with the community-
in-place path, and in the process of creating it gain the self-knowledge
and confidence they need to participate in building something new.
Idealists with a vision look first at cohousing, and after move-in,
often connect with their neighbors, sharing services in a village-style
approach. Each model can act as an on-ramp to the other, getting people to the point where they can more fully cocreate what they need.

Getting Greener as We Age

Cohousing, both intergenerational and age-specific, is the only form of development I know of that doesn't just start green (as part of the New Urbanist movement, well ahead of LEED and Energy Star standards), but gets greener over time. While the "sticks and bricks" of green building make a difference, the biggest long-term savings in energy, water, car trips, and everything else that matters to the planet comes from how people live in sustainable communities: cooperating and supporting each other, and providing tools and models for mutual progress.

Ecovillages, evolving in parallel with cohousing, strive not just to be "carbon neutral" but also to have a net positive impact on the earth. They are designed to be sustainable both economically and environmentally. This involves analyzing where and how residents work, shop, travel, and consume, and creating solutions to minimize environmental insults and maximize positive effects. Ecovillage design seeks synergies to create a win-win situation, in which small changes have enormous benefits. The permaculture movement calls this "stacking functions," that is, looking for how a single element can serve in more than one way; an example is a planted field that both absorbs rainwater runoff and provides a place to relax, and both absorbs carbon dioxide and serves as a bird habitat.

As we retire, slow down, look back at our lives, and take time to consider the legacy we are leaving for the generations to come, we have the opportunity to forge new settlements like these that incorporate the wisdom we've gained, individually and collectively. There's not just one path to ecovillage-hood, or even a single definition. A rural off-the-grid farm community may end up with shared values similar to those of an urban building-rehab project like St. Louis's Culver Way EcoVillage, even as the two look very different and offer a different experience for the people living there.

Elder Inspiration

The greatest potential of the cohousing and intentional communities movement, I believe, is in the people it attracts and how it helps them fully express their passions, through connection, examples, and the confidence to pursue their life visions. I draw daily inspiration from the life and work of fellow Fellowship for Intentional Community (FIC) board member Fred Lanphear, now in his seventies. He helped create Songaia Cohousing near Seattle, where he has lived for decades, and is currently writing a book about it.

When Fred turned seventy, his community organized an eldering ceremony, the men taking him out into the woods for a ritual they had created to formally welcome him to elderhood.

When he learned he had ALS (Lou Gehrig's disease), his neighbors helped him organize life celebrations while he was still able to participate and appreciate them, rather than waiting for a funeral. It's one thing to say you'll carry on the work of someone after he's buried, but I found it so much more meaningful to make the commitment to him in person, in front of his friends and community, when we could still talk about what really matters. In so doing, I am held accountable for my actions (like writing this chapter) that continue his legacy.

Several aging-in-community initiatives draw on the work of the Spiritual Eldering Institute and its founder, Rabbi Zalman Schachter-Shalomi (see his chapter in this book).

I'm involved in growing a pilot Elders' Guild in Berkeley, California, where I live. The principle of the guilds is to foster community discussions around the topic of "Conscious aging for the greater good" and share tools for self-assessment. Guild founder Barry Barkan studied under Reb Zalman and created a definition of an elder that reframes the conversation (see sidebar).

Reb Zalman's disciples also created the Sage-ing Guild, based on his pioneering book, *From Age-ing to Sage-ing*. The guild is devoted to network professionals trained in "growing older with wisdom, maturity, and understanding." I've joined the Sage-ing Guild for its intensive "becoming a sage" training, to learn how it complements the peer-to-peer community educational model of the Elders' Guild.

An Aspiring Elder

Friends in my age group have asked me over the years, as we moved through our thirties and into our forties, why I hang out with all these "old people," involving myself in stuff that my peers would rather not think about until it is forced on them by crisis or gradual deterioration, decades from now (so they hope).

My response is that I am an aspiring elder. I want to be as experienced, as considerate, and as full of wisdom as the folks I'm meeting in the movement. I want to help build places where people of all ages can connect with each other, have quality time together, and share the unique characteristics of our ages. Most important, I want to build a society where everybody is recognized for their own special contributions and age is merely a number.

What makes aging in community so exciting, so motivating, and so powerful that people dedicate great time and effort to creating new support structures and maintaining existing ones? Why does this mutual self-interest get people engaged far more consistently and deeply than even well-intentioned institutions like senior centers? The answer, my friends, is in the relationships that result from these communities and the movement that seeks to form them.

I invite you to join me in creating these rich connections, for yourself as well as for the world. The journey is the reward.

Definition of an Elder

- An elder is a person who is still growing, still a learner, still with potential and whose life continues to have, within it, promise for and connection to the future.

- An elder is still in pursuit of happiness, joy, and pleasure, and her or his birthright to these remains intact.

- Moreover, an elder is a person who deserves respect and honor and whose work it is to synthesize wisdom from long life experience and formulate this into a legacy for future generations.

Reprinted with permission by Barry Barkan, The Elders' Guild, www. eldersguild.org

Rose Cole, CNC, CNHP, a holistic nutrition coach, certified nutrition consultant, and certified natural health professional, is author of the book *Eating for Optimal Energy* and a nationally recognized speaker on the subject of health and nutrition. For more than a decade, she has helped clients use her step-by-step natural methods to overcome their health obstacles, achieve permanent weight loss without dieting, and increase their energy so they can take back control of their life and health. Rose Cole was born on October 29, 1977, in Santa Cruz, California.

Rose Cole

Conscious Eating
for Optimal Aging

I don't know about you, but I'm not content with just "going gently into that good night." I see midlife and beyond as a gateway to accelerating my personal transformation and helping to change the planet. But in order for me to live my life to its fullest potential and give my biggest gifts to the world, I don't just want to live a long time; I want to be active, healthy, independent, and thriving into my nineties.

To some that may be an audacious plan, but I know it is possible. Everyone has a unique message to bring to the world. Mine is about how attuning the physical body with health, wellness, and nutrition increases energy and vibration and ultimately elevates consciousness. It's from this conscious place that anything is possible.

I like to think of myself as a spiritual warrior. When I'm running on the treadmill or fasting, I know I'm not just doing it for myself. I'm in training—in spiritual boot camp, if you will. Unless I'm physically, emotionally, and mentally attuned, I know I'm not giving the world my best.

Contrasts in Aging

When I was growing up, both my mother and my aunt worked in a convalescent hospital. If you've ever been in a convalescent home, you know how depressing they can be. Yes, the residents are often kept alive for a long time nowadays, but with what quality of life? Many would not be alive but for the tubes or machines to which they are attached, or for handfuls of medication and spoon-feeding by nurses. Some move through hallways in wheelchairs as if in a daze and with no real destination.

What saddens me most is that the majority of them didn't have to end up this way. I am always amazed that one person in their seventies stares off into space most of the day, not having the cognitive function to know where they are, or even who they are; while another person in their nineties still drives a car and has their friends over for lunch. A friend of mine recently went with friends to Las Vegas to celebrate her ninetieth birthday.

What causes people to age so differently? Is aging predestined by genetics, or is there something we all can do to age audaciously? I don't believe genetics alone can be blamed for the way we age. Studies have shown, in fact, that the state of your health, and your waistline, have much more to do with your lifestyle, diet, and your way of life than what you inherit genetically.

This truth yelled out to me loud and clear growing up. My great-grandmother lived to be a hundred years old. She was driving until the age of ninety-five. She was able to live on her own until the last four years of her life. When she did have to go to a nursing home, the only reason she went was that her eyesight was bad. She was always slim and fit her whole life. She was totally "there" mentally. In fact, she was the one pushing other people in their wheelchairs to their rooms. Some of the people she helped were thirty years younger. She was even on the nursing home's board, and was elected president at ninety-eight years old. Just lucky? Or did she realize something that most of the other folks at the nursing home didn't? If it's just genetics, then why did my grandmother, her daughter, end up practically confined to a La-Z-Boy recliner while her mother was out and about? And then how did my mother, the next generation, end up carrying around an extra eighty pounds, plus a whole slew of other health conditions?

My great-grandmother owned an organic farm and vegetable garden and ate organic foods. She had a positive state of mind and took classes into her nineties. She lived in an era without an accessible grocery store and with no frozen meals. She had to grow her food and trade with the other folks in the neighborhood. In fact, she had the best little organic farm and vegetable stand in Kentucky. My grandmother, on the other hand, has eaten junk and processed food most of her life, binge eating and developing an eating disorder. She raised her family in the fifties, when packaged and processed food became vogue. She actually took a cooking class for using the microwave! Even today, she relies on Hamburger Helper, Rice-A-Roni, and frozen TV dinners, and on holidays whips up her famous Jell-o mold.

My grandmother is well over a hundred pounds overweight, and my mom, who also eats junk and processed food, is close behind.

Watching the daughter of my super-active great-grandmother not taking care of herself and become practically confined to a chair has been sad for me. She had dreams of traveling the world and having an impact on the lives of young women through the Girl Scouts of the USA, but now she lives vicariously through me. It's because of her that I realized that what you eat and put into your body makes the difference between surviving and thriving. I did not want to be dependent on others to spoon-feed me and make me take my medications. Watching my mother follow in the footsteps of my grandmother made me realize I didn't want to go down that same path. And at twenty years old, I already was.

Waking Up

I was twenty-five pounds overweight, with perpetual brain fog and hypoglycemia so severe I fainted frequently. My career as a fashion model had been cut short as a result of out-of-control psoriasis. While in school, my addiction to sugar lured me to the candy machine and away from class. Trying to keep my blood sugar up, I would binge on bread and chocolate. Eventually, the vicious cycles of food cravings sunk me into a depression. Neither my family nor my doctor took my health issues seriously. After a fainting episode in a bagel shop, I forced my parents to take me to the doctor. Instead of checking my hormones or considering what I was putting into my body to cause these reactions, the doctor prescribed, of all things, birth control pills.

My metabolism changed. The combination of the birth control pills, my hormonal and blood-sugar imbalances, and adrenal exhaustion caused me to pack on the pounds, which of course, as a model, worsened my mental state and caused a further helpless slip into depression. After showing up to a job in Hawaii covered in psoriasis welts that would cost the magazine thousands of dollars to cover in airbrushing, it was clear my modeling days were over. Then my boyfriend confessed he was no longer attracted to me. The downward spiral pulled me under in every part of my life, from the ability to make a living to the emotional capability to have a relationship.

Then I met someone who opened my mind to a completely new way of thinking that not only healed my body, but also became a career. That person was a naturopath and a certified nutrition consultant (CNC). She recommended fumaric acid, a metabolic acid widely used in Europe as a holistic treatment for psoriasis. She also ran blood panels and hormone tests and gave me a list of foods I was to add and avoid. There were no medicines involved. She insisted that I get off the birth control pill. I figured I couldn't lose and tried her program.

Two weeks into the new regimen, my psoriasis cleared completely. Five pounds slipped off my body without me trying to lose weight. My brain fog lifted and my confidence rose. My depression began to lift as well. For the first time, I was getting to the root cause of every symptom I had and I sensed living holistically would become my path in more ways than one.

In the meantime, once my extra weight was gone and my skin clear, I signed with the largest and most prestigious modeling agency in the world, Ford Models. I actually had to get a whole new portfolio because, to my amazement, I looked younger than I had in my early twenties.

The Regenerating Body

With my body and career going strong, I realized that I wanted nothing more than to help other people experience the kind of miracle I had. Inspired by the CNC naturopath who changed my life, I became a CNC and made it my mission to help people lose weight, increase their energy, have younger skin, and reverse the degeneration of their body—or at least that's what it is on the surface. What I really do is increase people's conscious awareness and transform their lives with nutrition. In my holistic nutrition practice, we're helping transform thousands of people all over the globe. I believe that those people, in turn, will help others and all of us, through our ripple effects, will be contributing to positive change for the planet.

Most people don't know this, but every ninety days or so we have an almost entirely new body. Scientists have confirmed that 98 percent of the atoms in our bodies were not there a year ago. The human body is unfathomably intelligent—how amazing that it rebuilds 98 percent of itself in about three months! Blood cells die and are replaced. Red blood cells live from 90 to 120 days, while white blood cells and platelets don't even make it that long. One of the jobs of the liver is to filter out dead red blood cells. Brain and nerve cells also regenerate, although the process takes longer. This is one of the reasons we can forget things; the replacement process isn't perfect. All cells, even bone cells, regenerate. Every seven years, we have a completely new skeleton.

Can you believe that 98 percent of the atoms that comprise your body right now will not be in your body three to six months from now? Where do the new atoms come from? They come primarily from food. So it is absolutely true: You are what you eat! Think about what an amazing opportunity this is. If you've messed up your health over the years, you can start all over and have a new body in ninety days.

Recently, I was speaking to my good friend David Kekich, who is chairman of the Maximum Life Foundation and an expert in aging and life extension. He explained to me that we are only 25 to 35 percent dictated by biogenetics (our genes), which means that as much as 75 percent of our state of health is up to us and completely in our control.

Our thoughts are part of that 75 percent. Attitude and outlook are integral to how we age and the state of our health. We've already thought about 80 percent of the thoughts we have. We just recycle them over and over. Since thought leads to action, you must take control of what's going on between your ears. With every single action you take, you are either enriching your life or damaging it.

I think a lot of us rationalize that living unwell may shave a year or two off of our lives, and that's not that big of a deal. But in reality, how you live, how you manage your stress, what you eat, and whether you see a holistic practitioner or not can make the difference of five, ten, or even twenty years in your life span. And that's just years. All of those factors also affect the quality of those years.

Toward Your Life's Purpose or Away from It

We all know that what we eat impacts how we feel. Most of us also grasp that how we feel impacts how we think. Therefore, it's obvious: What you eat impacts how you think. Did you get that? What you eat impacts how you think. Since thought leads to action, then eating healthy leads to healthy action. And at the end of this equation lies an enriched life. So eating healthy leads to an enriched life. Throw in a dash of right now and we've got the simplest of answers to life's age-old question of how to be happy. Here it is: Eat healthy right now and enrich your life!

Everything in the body is interconnected, each thread woven together in a delicate and intricate lacing. There is a deep connection—some call it scientific, others call it spiritual—between your mind and your body. To change one, you must change the other. Changing what you think is one of the hardest things to do. And yet it's critical for implementing change, taking action in new ways. It all starts with one step: eating healthy now.

Every single bite of food matters. Every single thought matters. If you are thinking positive thoughts, it affects the trillions of cells in your body in a profound way. The cells will actually start to believe you. You must be conscious of what you eat, and you must change your thinking if you want to change your body. When you truly understand this, you begin to gravitate naturally toward what is for your highest benefit and your highest potential.

All food has a vibration in its core. Food that makes your body function the way it is supposed to has a higher vibration, whereas food that drags your body down has a lower vibration. If you fill your body with potato chips and other processed junk, you are filling it with lower vibrations, which do not support your health and well-being.

You have the opportunity today to take a step toward a completely transformed body and consciousness. You can have more energy, be more present, have more confidence, and look years younger. All of this will positively affect every aspect of your life, from your work to your relationships to what you are able to contribute to the world. This upward spiral of well-being goes on and on, and life just keeps getting better.

Most of us are on autopilot when it comes to eating and don't stop to look at our motivation for eating something. We often eat for entertainment, to feel better, or to reward or punish ourselves. Much of the food we put in our mouths is not to fuel our bodies, our cells, and our purpose on the planet.

Unfortunately, most of us spend our lives eating for entertainment and not for the nutrition value, or "energy value," as I like to call it, at the cost of our health, our energy, and our appearance, not to mention the risk of not living to our fullest potential and bringing our greatest gifts to the world.

I've battled unhealthy habits with food my whole life, and I've unconsciously developed a process to check in with myself to keep me in alignment with my path and my purpose. The process goes like this. The first step to changing your body and your mind is to ask yourself about every piece of food that is about to enter your mouth, "Is this for my highest good?" The first answer you hear in your mind is the "right" answer. It only speaks once, and sometimes it speaks softly, but everyone has the ability to tune in and hear this voice. Every answer that enters your mind after the first one is a rationalization, a story you're telling yourself. And some of us have very crafty and creative storytellers inside!

One day recently, in the midst of a long busy day with clients, with appointments booked back-to-back, I ran into the kitchen to grab a basket of strawberries. I paused for just a brief moment to ask my higher self, "Is this food for my highest good?" The answer was no. Within a split second, I started to rationalize and argue with myself in my mind. "But they're organic strawberries. And strawberries are good for you. They have lots of vitamin C." And so on the stories went. But when I got real with myself and asked my higher self again, the answer came "because you're not hungry." I had just eaten thirty minutes before, so I didn't need those strawberries. But I ate them anyway and then I got a stomachache and my energy dropped down a notch. I was also a little less present and engaged with the rest of my clients that day, so I did them a disservice as well.

Our bodies tell us loud and clear what's in our best interests, if we only listen. That's basically what I teach people to do: how to listen to their body's voice and signals. You can go ahead and eat something even if the answer you get from the voice inside is no, but if you do, pay attention to how you feel afterward. Was it worth it? Maybe it was. Only you know the answer to that. Sometimes that piece of cake is worth it to me. I don't eat perfectly all the time, but I know that my body is going to feel my decision for days, even weeks, afterward.

Everything you put in your mouth takes you either further toward your life's purpose or away from it.

Be the Change

My generation is the first generation whose life expectancy is lower than that of our parents. I've learned by watching my family that my fate, and the fate of my health, is in my hands. Just as I chose to change my life from that downward spiral to an upward spiral, I have the choice to keep it going up with everything I eat, think, and do. That upward spiral is what audacious aging, and even dying, is all about.

There is an exponential effect in this approach to life. My upward spiral attracts other upward spirals, and together we create one big spiral of conscious evolution, which is what you are feeling going on in the universe right now as this shift in consciousness gains momentum.

When you choose not to take care of your health, you are doing a disservice to everyone you are supposed to reach with your unique message for the world. Everything that you do has a ripple effect that goes from you out into the world, impacting everyone around you and beyond.

Chapter Eleven ❧

If you believe you are here on this planet to give your greatest gifts to the world, then you have a choice to live your life's purpose, or not. And it all starts with the inner world of your own body and health.

"You must be the change you want to see in the world."

—Mahatma Gandhi

Ram Dass (formerly Dr. Richard Alpert) is a spiritual teacher and best-selling author (notably of *Be Here Now,* published in 1971). As a professor at Harvard in the 1960s, he and colleague Timothy Leary began experiments with psychedelic drugs, which they continued with leading figures of the counterculture after they lost their Harvard positions. He went on to study with Hindu gurus and in other spiritual traditions, which led him to the path of service and compassion about which he writes and teaches. Ram Dass was born on April 6, 1931, in Newton, Massachusetts.

Ram Dass (formerly Dr. Richard Alpert) is a spiritual teacher and best-selling author (notably of *Be Here Now*, published in 1971). As a professor at Harvard in the 1960s, he and colleague Timothy Leary began experiments with psychedelic drugs, which they continued with leading figures of the counterculture after they lost their Harvard positions. He went on to study with Hindu gurus and in other spiritual traditions, which led him to the path of service and compassion about which he writes and teaches. Ram Dass was born on April 6, 1931, in Newton, Massachusetts.

RAM DASS

Embracing Aging

Issues of sexuality, gender, and spirituality have come out of the closet since the Sixties. Because of midwives and hospices, even birth and death are out as well. Aging remains one of our culture's last taboos. Judging from how the old are represented (or rather, *not* represented) by the media, it's fair to say we live in a society that would like to pretend that old people don't exist. Since people typically spend less as they age, advertisers focus their attention on the young, unless they're selling denture adhesives or incontinence pads. A recent study showed that only 3 percent of the images seen in a day of television contains images of older people, and when you notice how these elders are depicted—as silly, stubborn, vindictive, or worst of all, *cute*—you begin to appreciate the not-so-subtle antipathy of a market-driven culture toward the elderly.

We cannot underestimate the media's influence on how we view ourselves as aging individuals. Men get trouble enough from the current obsession with staying young and beautiful, but women suffer even more from this craze. This is because men have traditionally had access to something almost as good as youth: power. Women have been deprived of this access until very recently. A man could be wrinkled and gray, but if he held high social or financial status, his physical losses were offset. Not so for women. Where an older man can be euphemized as "distinguished," a woman is more often called "faded" or "over the hill," and suffers enormous pressure to hide her age, often with painful results. Women now live a full third of their lives after menopause, and yet if you believe our popular culture, a woman who isn't young, shapely, and still capable of bearing children is all but invisible. I have women friends who've gone to great lengths to keep up a youthful front with the help of plastic surgery, and while the results may be superficially satisfying, the impulse to re-carve what nature has created often masks a profound despair. It is as if we are urged to fight, over and over again, a losing battle against time, pitting ourselves against natural law. How ghastly this is, and how inhumane, toward both ourselves and the cycle of life. It reminds me of someone rushing around the fields in autumn painting the marvelous gold and red leaves with green paint. It's a lot of wasted time and energy.

Take the spots I have on my hands. Though I haven't been harmed by them at all, I am harmed by the message I see on TV. "They call these aging spots," an older woman says in a Porcelana ad, "but I call them ugly!" When I see that ad, I become uneasy about a natural process my body is going through. But when I flip that message around in my mind—"They call these ugly, I call them aging spots!"—the illusion is dispelled, and suddenly it's just autumn leaves.

The images our culture generates are designed to make you feel that aging is a kind of failure; that somehow God made a big mistake. If God were as smart as the commercials, people would be young forever, but since God isn't, only the wonders of science and commerce can save us. Can you see how bizarre this assumption is, and how much pain it creates? Pitting ourselves more and more desperately against an inexorable process revealed in crow's feet, stretch marks, and puffiness, we are given two equally doomed choices: to suck in, thrust out, tuck and nip, and build our muscles, all to hold on to a semblance of youth; or resign ourselves in sad defeat, feeling like failures, outsiders, victims, or fools.

The so-called *problem* of aging is trumpeted everywhere we turn. With the great wave of baby boomers moving into their fifties and sixties, the very economic stability of the United States is being called into question. There's the fear that Social Security will go bankrupt as more old people require support. In the eyes of the economists, the aged aren't merely a problem—we're a disaster. And we didn't do a thing!

If we listen to the rhetoric of the economists, politicians, social planners, advertisers, statisticians, and health-care providers, the overwhelming message we're sent is that aging is a great social ill, a necessary evil, a drain on society, and an affront to esthetics. When avoidance finally fails, old age should be coped with as one would cope with a chronic condition—leprosy, say, or an unwanted visitor who unpacks his bags and won't go away. We, the aging, are viewed as a burden instead of a resource. As Betty Friedan wrote in her own book on aging, "The old people begin to look like greedy geezers to the young, because [we're] costing the young so much, in so many ways."

This is a distorted view, of course, and not only a great disservice to the old but also one that inevitably returns to haunt the young. A Chinese story I love points this out beautifully. It tells of an old man who's too weak to work in the garden or help with household chores. He just sits on the porch, gazing out across the fields, while his son tills the soil and pulls up weeds. One day, the son looks up at the old man and thinks, "What good is he now that he's so old? All he does is eat up the food! I have a wife and children to think about. It's time for him to be done with life!" So he makes a large wooden box, places it on a wheelbarrow, rolls it up to the porch, and says to the old man, "Father, get in." The father lies down in the box and the son puts the cover on, then wheels it toward the cliff. At the edge of the cliff, the son hears a knock from inside the box. "Yes, Father?" the son asks. The father replies, "Why don't you just throw me off the cliff and save the box? Your children are going to need it one day."

Unless we see ourselves as part of life's continuity, whether we're currently young or old, we will continue to view aging as something apart from the mainstream of culture, and the old as somehow *other*. In a nontraditional culture such as ours, dominated by technology, we value information far more than we do wisdom. But there is a difference between the two. Information involves the acquisition, organization, and dissemination of facts; a storing-up of physical data. But wisdom involves another equally crucial function: the emptying and quieting of the mind, the application of the heart, and the alchemy of reason and feeling. In the wisdom mode, we're not processing information, analytically or sequentially. We're standing back and viewing the whole, discerning what matters and what does not, weighing the meaning and depth of things. This quality of wisdom is rare in our culture. More often, we have knowledgeable people who pretend to be wise, but who, unfortunately, have not cultivated the quality of mind from which wisdom truly arises.

When we spend time in traditional societies, where the young seek out the wisdom of their elders, we become aware of how upside-down such nontraditional values are. A few years ago I visited a village in India where I had spent a great deal of time. I visited the house of a dear friend, who said to me, "Oh, Ram Dass, you're looking so much older!" Because I live in the United States, my first reaction was defensive; inwardly, I thought to myself, "Gee, I thought I was looking pretty good." But when I paused to take in the tone of my friend's voice, this reaction melted instantly. I heard the respect with which he'd addressed me, as if to say, "You've done it, my friend! You've grown old! You've earned the respect due an elder now, someone we can rely on and to whom we can listen."

In a culture where information is prized over wisdom, however, old people become obsolete, like yesterday's computers. But the real treasure is being ignored: wisdom is one of the few things in human life that does not diminish with age. While everything else falls away, wisdom alone increases until death if we live examined lives, opening ourselves out to life's many lessons. In traditional cultures that go unchanged for generation after generation, the value of wise elders is easy to spot; but in a culture such as ours, wisdom is nowhere near as exciting—or necessary—as surfing the Net. We feel we have to keep running to stay up-to-date, to learn the latest version of Windows or try out that Stairmaster at the gym. I used to have a sign over my computer that read "Old dogs can learn new tricks," but lately I sometimes ask myself how many more new tricks I *want* to learn. How many more of those damned manuals do I want to read in this lifetime? Wouldn't it be easier just to be outdated?

Of course, it's not easy to be outdated—to move into the aging stage with grace and a sense of appropriateness—in a culture that does not value that metamorphosis or provide a respected role for its elders. Through the Omega Institute in New York, I have taken part with colleagues in facilitating "Elder Circles." The oldest people in the group sit in a large circle, and the younger people sit just behind them. We use a talking stick, a custom adopted from a Native American tradition, and as they are ready, members of the inner circle can walk to the center, take the talking stick, return to their seats, and share their wisdom with the rest of the group. By custom, they begin their remarks with "And..." and end them with "I have spoken." This is an opportunity for people to share their own wisdom and to contribute it to the collective group wisdom. Many people flower in the richness of this process, as the group becomes aware of how each person holds some part of the complex mosaic that is elder wisdom. At the close of a circle, people have often said, "This is a role I'm totally unfamiliar with, because nobody's ever asked me to be wise before." It's impossible not to be moved by the poignancy of such a remark, as regards both the aging person and the culture deprived of such a precious resource.

If the situation is going to change, of course, it will be because we, the aging, work to change it. We cannot expect the young to beat down our doors, begging for our wisdom, reminding us of our responsibility to society. As older people, we will have to initiate the change by freeing ourselves of this culture's bias, and remember the unique things we bring to the table. As wise elders, we are capable of cultivating the very resources that our endangered world needs if it is to survive healthy and whole: qualities of sustainability, patience, reflection, appreciation for justice, and the humor born of long experience. These qualities are in short supply in our society.

Since the first baby boomers turned fifty in 1996, the opportunity has existed to right this imbalance and infuse our culture with elder wisdom. The American Association of Retired Persons (which one can join at age fifty) is already one of the most powerful lobbies in the United States. Numbers are power in a democracy, and the question we must ask ourselves now is, How do we want to use the power? Now that aging is coming out of the closet, how can we work toward increasing our culture's wisdom without hampering its devotion to progress? How can we work to reverse the "aging onus" that traps so many elderly people in the badly tailored suit of an outdated identity, blocking what they have to offer?

This is our predicament, then: to regain our roles as wise elders in a culture that has traditionally denied the need for wisdom, or the ability of the old to provide it; to envision a curriculum for aging with wisdom as its highest calling, and to use it as a means of enlightenment—our own, and that of the people around us. But it is futile to try to change the outside world without beginning with ourselves—as futile, said an Indian master, as trying to straighten out a dog's tail. It is futile as well to look for our "selves" without understanding how the self is defined by our culture, and by what we consider reality to be.

Doug Dickson is vice president of Discovering What's Next, an innovative community-based model for guiding midlife adults as they explore and embark on their next life stage. Formerly vice president of New Directions, a career management firm for business executives and professionals, he led initiatives in entrepreneurship and alternatives to traditional retirement. He helped create the Life Planning Network, a national professional association for coaches and other practitioners who assist clients in designing purposeful lives as they age. Doug Dickson was born on September 8, 1946, in Bangor, Maine.

DOUG DICKSON

Becoming Audacious

Audacious aging doesn't just happen. For most of us, it takes time, effort, and intention. It starts with a pang of dissatisfaction with the way things are, builds to an awareness of possibilities not previously conceived, and leads ultimately to a new perspective on who we are and what we have to offer.

Sure, there are some for whom audacious opportunities seem to just fall out of the sky. But in fact, these people have usually enabled or instigated these opportunities, whether knowingly or not, through actions, behaviors, and attitudes that are in themselves audacious.

Audacious opportunities arise for most of us through deliberate effort, triggered by a sense that our lives could be more fulfilling, more purposeful, more enjoyable, or of greater consequence. The path forward from this vague realization can be arduous, but if it's not taken, our energy can be sapped and our spirit diminished.

For the past dozen years, I've specialized in helping people (mostly in midlife) move through various life transitions, often linked to employment. Most are high achievers, people at the pinnacle of their chosen professions. By any measure, they are successful, accomplished, often financially secure, and should be content with their lot in life. But still they strive for something more.

What triggers this need to look beyond the status quo and to reassess the trajectory of one's life? What moves people to seek new directions, new challenges, new ways to contribute, and new ways to create value in later life? Gerontology pioneer Gene Cohen (see his chapter in this book) refers to an "inner push" that signals a readiness to move forward in one's life. Developmental psychologist Erik Erikson (who coined the term "identity crisis") and others describe a drive in later life toward "generativity," a growing interest in transmitting wisdom to the next generation. Whatever the label, there is for many people an itch or an urge that impels them at midlife to look beyond, to explore, to reach out in new ways.

This urge can also be triggered by outside factors. Changes in health or family circumstance, the loss of a loved one or job, or a decision to retire from a successful career can push people to ask, "What's next?" Sudden, unexpected change can awaken long-dormant dreams, restore lost perspective, and raise questions about what's important in life, after all. Honest responses to these prompts can put one on the same path to which the inner push leads.

The seeking urge can emerge over time or show itself suddenly. Some of the people I've worked with have long harbored ideas about alternate careers or changes in lifestyle. I've seen lawyers become headmasters, doctors become business executives, and business executives become sheep farmers. In some cases, the transition took place slowly, sparked by a long-held curiosity and requiring months or years of careful preparation. In other cases, usually in response to external triggers such as those mentioned, the decisions about the future were immediate. Though often born of adversity, these triggers change lives. They are storm clouds with silver linings that open the way to opportunities that might otherwise have gone unrevealed or unconsidered.

The Four Challenges

Responding to the seeking urge at midlife involves four challenges: 1) making the break from where you've been, 2) taking time to gain new perspective, 3) acting with courage to explore and pursue options, and 4) staying the course.

• Making the Break

The first challenge is perhaps the hardest: taking that critical, initial step in the direction of change. When I was in my late forties, I was increasingly frustrated in a job I thought I wanted but didn't enjoy. I was earning good money and my daughter's college tuition bills were coming with predictable regularity, so I felt my hands were tied. Besides, I had no idea what my options were outside the company and industry I'd been in for twenty years. I felt trapped—dissatisfied with what I had but afraid that I'd regret leaving it behind. Finally, fate intervened and an opportunity to leave with the financial security of a severance package and the support of outplacement services presented itself through yet another of the corporate restructurings of the early 1990s. I still didn't know where I was heading but I recognized that if I didn't take advantage of what seemed at the time to be a chance of a lifetime, another might not come my way again.

Having acceded to various promotions and other career opportunities as they presented themselves over the years, this was one of the few times I'd taken a step that was deliberate and required a thoughtful examination of options. But I couldn't start exploring until I'd committed myself to moving away from where I was and toward what I would become (without any idea what that might look like). For me, and for many clients I've worked with over the years, letting go was the first big step and clearly the most difficult.

• **Taking Time**

The second challenge in this process may sound counterintuitive: taking time to gain a new perspective on life. Take time to relax, to think and take stock, to separate yourself from the person you were and to reconnect with parts of your world that may have receded along the way. William Bridges, author of *The Way of Transition: Managing Life's Most Difficult Moments,* calls this the "neutral zone," a "nowhere between two somewheres." It gets you ready for what comes next by shifting your perspective and opening your mind to new possibilities.

Taking time doesn't mean you stop doing altogether. In fact, many people tackle projects that have accumulated—cleaning out closets, the basement, or the garage; painting, remodeling, or landscaping. These are all common ways to use time productively while shifting gears. There is a sense of accomplishment that comes with these activities, but they also help you break with the patterns that previously governed your life. I built a cabinet during one transition and a bookcase during another. Each served as a marker during a period when I was otherwise floating unanchored, except for the support of my family and friends.

Travel is another way to enter the neutral zone. A former client packed his car and took off on a six-week tour of the United States, planning his itinerary around visits to old friends, former associates, and family members. Six weeks grew to eight, then ten, and finally twelve, but he returned refreshed, full of new ideas about his future, and ready to move forward. Another client seized an opportunity to help sail a yacht from Boston to Tortola. The focus required by his watches at sea, the absence of distraction, and the abundance of quiet time helped him leave his former self behind.

Reengaging with family is another great way to take a break—getting closer to your kids or spouse, taking a vacation that wouldn't otherwise be possible, coaching a sports team, or assisting in school activities. Being home during the day offers lots of opportunities to see your kids or grandkids, your spouse or partner, your parents, and other family members in places and situations that can build new and stronger connections.

For some, getting into neutral occurs quickly; for others, it takes considerable time. In my case, I started with the idea of a three-month "summer sabbatical." As Labor Day rolled around, it was clear I needed more time, and three months turned into twelve. How do you know when you've spent enough time in the wilderness? You'll develop a sense of urgency about moving ahead (but beware of guilt masquerading as a positive impulse). You'll gain a new sense of focus about possibilities and you'll have at least one good idea to explore. Until you've reached that point, allow your subconscious to grind away. Engage in introspection, talk to friends and family, and be patient—your audacious self will begin to emerge.

• Acting with Courage

Challenge number three is developing the courage to envision, to explore, and to commit to a new course. This is where bold thinking and bold action really count. It is the ingredient that I think most epitomizes the idea of audacious aging and the one most critical to achieving it.

Several years ago, I worked with a client who had run a bank and a very successful real estate investment trust (REIT). Then in his mid-fifties, he was feeling the tug toward something new and different in his life. He had always worked for others, but had long harbored the notion of business ownership. While he was in the process of exploring the purchase of a small business, a former competitor approached him with an offer to build and run another large REIT. Discussions culminated in a trip to the city where he would move if he took the job. The prospective employer wined and dined him and his wife, showed them around the town, and presented him with an extremely lucrative offer. The temptation to slide back to his former life was enormous, greased by the prospect of a huge compensation package.

But as he wrestled with the offer, he couldn't shake the dream of owning the small chain of hardware stores he had been considering. In the end, after long days of conversation with family and friends and long nights of little sleep, he turned down the big offer and pursued small business ownership. This act of courage freed him to think creatively about this next step and he conceived a plan to use the hardware stores as a way to create good jobs, adding a profit-sharing plan and health insurance benefits. His step was lighter, his mood was brighter, and he never looked back. Today, he has added a store to his chain, proven the wisdom of investing in his employees, and runs the business three days a week, which gives him time for his family and for church and community projects. Giving back has become his mantra and he's hoping this will carry through in the business after he turns it over to his daughters to run.

Another client left the world of high-tech engineering to return to an earlier passion. When her company needed to cut back after the dot-com bust, she knew her salary as head of product development was equal to that of several engineers in her department. She volunteered to restructure the unit, placing it in the hands of capable younger staff and orchestrating her departure from the firm. In her early sixties at the time, she had hoped to work another several years. But upon reflection, she saw an opportunity to reconnect to an earlier interest in sculpture, which she had set aside while working full-time and raising a family. The urge to create had surfaced again and the courage to leave her technology career opened the door to another one. Today, she is an award-winning sculptor with a national reputation. She also teaches others to sculpt and serves on the board of a local art center and museum.

Both of these individuals were able to look ahead with enough clarity to recognize that more of the same would not be enough. They didn't know precisely what would take the place of their current opportunities, but a strong sense of possibility gave them the confidence to take the leap. They scouted the options, narrowed the field, and chose a course. It sounds a lot easier in this telling than it was in real life, but each was successful in sizing up the odds and working to surmount them. In the end, each realized a dream, living a life that is both full and rewarding. And neither can imagine what their lives might be like had they not made the change.

Courage can be facilitated by the prospect of options. Most people don't have the luxury of an indefinite break in the action while options are conjured, considered, and culled. So what guides the process of exploring and deciding what comes next? In my experience, there are five themes that characterize the kinds of options people explore:

1. They go back to unfinished business, like the woman who shifted from engineering management to sculpture.

2. They examine peak experiences to determine what made those experiences special and how they might be reclaimed in a different way or form.

3. They look at ways to give back, to leave a legacy, or to make a mark.

4. They take on something entirely new, in the form of a personal or professional challenge, adventure travel, creative expression, learning opportunities, or new fields of interest.

5. They seek greater engagement, whether in their communities, with their families and friends, through professional, civic, or nonprofit affiliations, or even on an international scale.

Chances are, your audacious self is rooted in one or more of these themes. In fact, hybrid versions of these ideas are more common than not. The owner of the hardware stores started with the notion of something entirely new—buying and operating his own business—but he coupled that with creating good jobs (giving back) and allowing more time for community and church work (engagement).

It is typical for people living audaciously in the second half of life to have a greater range of commitments than before. A colleague with whom I sit on two boards splits his time among consulting to businesses on innovation, writing a book, painting, and hatching a new business. The time he now spends in these four areas is equivalent to what he once spent during his professional career in a single job. In the course of a month, the time he devotes to these commitments waxes and wanes, but all remain in focus for the long term. Keeping them in balance with other pursuits, such as the two boards we share, his family and friends, and travel and entertainment, requires an extreme ability to juggle that comes from experience as well as diligence.

This juggling act is what Dave Corbett, founder of New Directions (where I worked for ten years), refers to as the "portfolio life" in his recent book *Portfolio Life: The New Path to Work, Purpose, and Passion after 50.* He defines this as a collection of interests and involvements, kept in balance over time. It reflects the whole person, not just a sliver or two. For most of us, making space for the parts of our lives that were previously suppressed, denied, or postponed requires significant effort and a huge helping of courage.

• **Staying the Course**

The final challenge is persistence, the commitment to stick it out, carry it forward, and make it work despite obstacles. This is important because a) becoming audacious takes time, and b) it's not always the easiest route. The path of least resistance, as noted earlier, requires little or no change—and change can be demanding of body, mind, and spirit. Under a good head of steam, the barriers inherent in change can fall, but it takes time to stoke the fire and build the pressure needed to create that head of steam. Maintaining focus, adopting a resilient posture, and adjusting to challenges as they arise are all determinants of success.

Persistence works best when we're fully engaged. When we apply the full measure of our physical energy, emotional intensity, intellectual capacity, and spiritual strength, we fill out the promise of our potential. Cut back in any one of these dimensions and we list or lean, like a hot-air balloon that is losing its air supply. Age offers the advantage of experience, from which we learn to align and employ these dimensions in powerful ways to achieve our goals.

The beauty of this synergy of body, feelings, mind, and spirit is that each contributes in distinct ways to decisions and outcomes. Each imparts a different texture and range—inputs of a sensory, sentimental, rational, or intuitive nature, perhaps—that work together to create richness and equilibrium. We can tell when all four dimensions are engaged. Our lives achieve a certain rhythm and we're centered, purposeful, and truly enjoying ourselves. In this state, persistence feels effortless. Even when obstacles emerge, the challenge of overcoming them can be fun.

Our culture asks that we live with disproportionate emphasis on education, career, and childrearing in the early stages of our lives. But the audacious opportunity we have as we age is to bring those elements into better balance with the range of other interests that define who we are as individuals. Identifying the pieces, fitting them together, and then harmonizing them into a coherent whole leads to audacious aging. To age in this way depends on our ability to act on the urge for change, to take time to see the possibilities, to pursue them with confidence and courage, and to persist despite hitches and hurdles.

Larry Dossey, MD, author of *Prayer Is Good Medicine* and *The Extraordinary Healing Power of Ordinary Things,* among other books, has profoundly influenced the recognition in the conventional medical field of the role of mind and spirit in health, notably through his research on prayer and what he terms "nonlocal mind" (mind not confined to the brain and body but spread infinitely throughout space and time). A former editor of *Alternative Therapies in Health and Medicine,* he is executive editor of *Explore: The Journal of Science and Healing.* He was born in 1940 in Groesbeck, Texas.

LARRY DOSSEY

CHAPTER
14

The Power of the Ordinary

In health care today, we are headed in a narrow direction with our focus on high-tech, very expensive approaches. The simple things in life are regarded as perhaps interesting or occasionally helpful in promoting healing, but irrelevant when ranked against high-tech intervention such as DNA manipulation, drugs, and surgery. In my view, this is putting the cart before the horse. I believe there are simple things in life, which typically go unnoticed, that can contribute enormously to our health and longevity. These things are usually free, cause no side effects, and don't require someone in a white coat to administer them. I call them treasures hidden in plain sight.

In my recent book, *The Extraordinary Healing Power of Ordinary Things*, I discuss fourteen of these treasures in plain sight. Some of them may seem outrageous, such as the value of forgetting or the value of dirt, but that is one of the reasons I included them—the fact that they will catch people's attention and get them to stop and think about what the value of forgetting or the value of dirt might be. Other hidden treasures that have healing power for us are optimism, novelty, mystery, risk, tears, unhappiness, doing nothing, music, plants, bugs, hearing voices, and miracles (the spontaneous occurrences we call miracles). Research reveals profound evidence that these simple treasures are extraordinarily influential in our health and longevity.

The value of some of these treasures is fairly sensational. People might surmise, for example, that the benefit that optimists enjoy over pessimists is a better quality of life, but the benefits go far beyond that. Optimism actually extends your life span. Research has shown that optimists live several years longer than people who do not have an optimistic attitude. One study looked at the difference in longevity of people with diagnosed heart disease depending on whether they were optimistic or pessimistic. Within a year after the diagnosis, those who were pessimistic had eight times the risk of dying compared to the optimists.

Beyond the Comfort Zone

Compelling research examined the behavior of approximately fifteen thousand American women to determine why some of the women as they got older aged mentally and lost their cognitive skills, while many did not. The researchers were satisfied that some of this had to do with exercise, diet, and weight management, but they were surprised to discover that the women who preserved their mental faculties as they got older were those who engaged in behaviors that were mentally challenging. The behaviors they were able to single out were simple things like working crossword puzzles, reading books, and playing board games. In other words, it seemed to be one of those examples of "use it or lose it." As they got older, the women who engaged in these mentally challenging exercises had mental faculties far beyond women who did not engage in these activities, all other factors being equal.

These simple mind exercises are the most basic example of the activities we can undertake to help maintain our well-being as we age. Mystery, novelty (new experiences in life), and risk taking have even greater benefits. If we want to take precautions to keep our mental acuity as we get older, these ought to be on the drawing board. Activities or experiences with these traits take us out of habits, ruts, and routines, and stretch us both mentally and emotionally. The activities can be quite simple and don't have to cost anything. Unfortunately, introducing such challenges on a regular basis is still not in the health strategy of most people. We attend to our blood pressure and cholesterol, avoid smoking, and try to eat a healthful diet, but we fail to attend to the simpler and equally important health and longevity factors of mystery, novelty, and risk taking.

It requires some work and effort to push ourselves beyond our comfort boundary. Learning a new language is one of the ways we can do this. There are abundant other resources around us that can help us create mystery, novelty, and risk in our lives. We have only to be willing to look outside our usual box of experience.

The activity or experience need not be exotic. I recently took up something that I have always had a fascination with but never done: bread baking. The challenge of the new was made more challenging by the extra tricks required to bake bread successfully at the nearly eight thousand feet altitude at which I live. I took some lessons, and it turned into a hugely fulfilling experience.

We can let our imaginations run wild to discover the experiences that will carry us outside our everyday lives. I have seen older people take up things that we associate with young people, like flying kites. Where I live, there is a kite-flying club for older people. It's such a pleasure to see them get outdoors and frolic, laugh, and play as if they are fifty years younger than they are.

Researchers and biological scientists are fascinated by whether it is only humans that seek novelty and risk taking or whether there is evidence of these impulses in other species. Studies have established that we are not the only ones. For example, a strain of rat that researchers of aging have studied demonstrates two subdivisions within the strain. One strain of these rats holds back from running a new maze, whereas the other strain of rats takes on a new maze with gusto and appears to love the challenge of running a new pathway. As it turns out, the rats that rise to the challenge of running a new maze live 50 percent longer than the rats that hold back. That is a cute little affirmation that there is something in the biology of mammals that needs to take on new challenges and benefits in terms of longevity from that experience.

Almost everything in our culture goes against stretching into the new. We want to be comfortable and happy; for most people, being comfortable means staying in the familiar. There are all sorts of sociological, psychological, and cultural incentives to staying where you are, but the opposite is better for your well-being. The benefits of audacious aging come not from being comfortable and staying with what you know, but from exposing yourself to a little discomfort, to that which challenges you, seeking out the treasures hidden in plain sight. There is a phenomenon that occurs with these treasures; that is, they augment each other. For example, most people who introduce novelty into their lives, challenging themselves with new experiences, wind up being more optimistic and fulfilled than people who stay in habits, ruts, and routines.

I have been fascinated to discover that risk taking and getting out of the ordinary habits of life actually benefits immunity. Studies out of the University of Tennessee have shown that the immune systems of young men who have been in trouble with legal authorities and who, for example, have shown too much aggressiveness in life, gotten into fights, and wound up in jail, are much more active than the immune systems of their well-behaved counterparts. That fascinates me because it suggests that there is something about risk taking and drifting out of the ordinary, the predictable, and culturally and socially approved habits that benefits the immune system. I am not advocating that people break the law, but I am saying that moving out of ordinary ways of behaving benefits certain aspects of our physiology.

Unfortunately, my observation of people in my own age group is that, as they get older, they tend to narrow their interests and boundaries, they often become dull and boring, and it is difficult to nudge them. In my travels and lectures at medical schools, I rarely find someone over the age of fifty who is willing to engage the evidence of distance healing and who can openly confront the data surrounding prayer research showing that people do have the ability to make a difference in someone's physiology through their compassion, love, and prayers delivered from afar. This is the most immediate way in which I see people narrowing and staying in their habits, ruts, and routines.

Stepping Off the Conventional Path

Sometimes we don't make a conscious effort to move out of ordinary ways of behaving, but the events of our lives take us there. That is how I moved beyond my comfort boundaries in the field of medicine. I confess that I was relatively conventional. The first major nudge that pushed me in a different direction happened during my last year in university. I was finishing a degree in pharmacy at the University of Texas in Austin and preparing to enter medical school that fall when I came down with what turned out to be acute appendicitis.

Like a dutiful student, I turned myself in at the university health center. I was given an emergency appendectomy, and it was a horrible experience. I did not get to meet the surgeon ahead of time; he simply didn't think it was necessary. I did not get to meet the anesthesiologist; he was simply too busy. I woke up in terrible pain, not knowing what the diagnosis was. I was scared, alone, filled with anxiety, and hurting like crazy. Then something simple transpired. A nurse came by, held my hand, and said, "Larry, don't worry, everything is going to be fine."

It was as if someone had flipped a switch in my brain and body. All the pain went away almost immediately, as did the anxiety and fear. I didn't know what had happened, though I knew it was a profound moment. I didn't know what healing was—that word was not in my vocabulary—but the moment was seared into my memory and has stayed with me ever since. It was a dramatic early episode in learning that very simple things can radically alter our sense of being, our appreciation of pain, and our health.

An appendectomy is regarded as a medical intervention. At that time, the hand-holding and reassurance wouldn't have fallen into that category. But now research is showing that, in fact, these things are medical interventions. I don't care whether people call it the placebo response or bedside manner—those are just words—but there is something profound that happens in the body during such moments as I experienced, and much of my work since has been to unravel these kinds of phenomena.

I recall when biofeedback burst upon the scene in the late 1960s. For the first time, we had evidence that achieving a certain mental posture or thought could make a meter move on a gadget that measured your skin temperature or blood pressure. Biofeedback enabled me to finally resolve the terrible migraine headaches from which I had suffered since grade school. None of my medical training had shown me how to do that. My profound biofeedback experience gave me insight into the power of the mind to change something physical.

It's interesting to look back and see where we've come from. I was so impressed with the power of this particular therapy that I formed one of the first biofeedback laboratories in the state of Texas in the early 1970s. The reaction from my colleagues was mixed horror. Actually, many people at the time thought that biofeedback and using your mind in these ways was just a little short of satanic. We've come a long way since then. Today, nobody raises an eyebrow over things like meditation and relaxation, but that wasn't the case a mere thirty years ago.

Yes, You Can Change

After the publication of my book on the power of the ordinary to heal, I discussed at medical schools and hospitals around the country the value of optimism. I constantly encountered the objection that there was no need to discuss this because people are the way they are by birth; you're either born an optimist or a pessimist, the argument went, and you can't change that. There is strong evidence refuting that belief.

One of the leading researchers in this area is Dr. Martin Seligman, a past president of the American Psychological Association. He introduced the concept of "learned optimism." For fifteen years or so, Dr. Seligman has conducted research with young children, college students, and adults showing that, by using certain psychological techniques, one can shift one's outlook from profound pessimism to optimism. In addition, the research reveals that as people go through these training programs, their physiology changes, with improvements in immunity and reduction in stress hormone levels.

The old complaint that we are by nature predisposed and therefore stuck with our optimism or pessimism doesn't hold up anymore. The outlook for anyone who wishes to change is quite good. The method that Dr. Seligman recommends has to do with "cognitive restructuring," which is a systematic way of shifting your reactions to certain things that have happened in your life. This may sound mysterious, but it really isn't; almost anyone can master it. So people can change—that's the good news.

It is important to cognitive restructuring to choose your friends carefully because pessimism is catching. If you surround yourself with optimists, however, you're likely to catch optimism instead of pessimism. Reading about how people maintained an optimistic sense during some of the darkest times in the twentieth century or at other hard periods in human history also helps foster optimism.

We are so blessed in this country. Most of us are well fed, clothed, and sheltered. Most of us have comforts that the great monarchs throughout history never even envisioned. Somehow, all of this isn't enough to prompt optimism. That baffles me. We have forgotten how to focus on our blessings. To remember, it helps to back up and look at the big picture. When we consider the rest of the world, we realize the advantages we have. Travel, especially in the Third World, also helps restore perspective, as does volunteering in a soup kitchen or doing work for Habitat for Humanity or other community organization. Seeing how hard some people have it makes it more difficult to be pessimistic about our privileged lives.

I've written several books on the virtues of compassion, love, and prayer in helping people get well. One of the models of consciousness that I've evolved over the years, along with quite a number of other researchers, has been this idea of nonlocal mind, nonlocal consciousness, which implies that some aspect of who we are is infinite in space and time. If you reason through the implications, you come out with a model of consciousness that says that at some point, at some level of consciousness, we are immortal. If the certainty of immortality isn't enough to arouse a little optimism, I don't know what it will take!

Dominick Dunne is a bestselling novelist and investigative journalist who writes in the tradition of Scott Fitzgerald and Truman Capote. As his subject is often the privileged who believe they are above the law, his TV show, *Dominick Dunne's Power, Privilege and Justice,* covers the criminal entanglements of the rich and famous, including the trials of O. J. Simpson and Claus von Bulow. With high cachet among celebrities, he is a special correspondent for *Vanity Fair* magazine. Dominick Dunne was born on Octber 29, 1925, in Hartford, Connecticut.

DOMINICK DUNNE

I Want to Drop Dead on the Tarmac

I am in my eighties and I've never worked harder. I have a monthly diary in *Vanity Fair* magazine that is widely read. I am shortly to finish my next novel, called *The Solo Act*, and I have a weekly television series called *Dominick Dunne's Power, Privilege and Justice*. I'm doing them all. There are two documentaries being made about my life for French Television and Australian Television.

Now that I'm in my eighties I don't care about a lot of things that used to bother me. I used to always back down to male authority figures, because my father was so mean to me as a kid. It's women like Tina Brown who have helped me find myself. But I'm unafraid now that I hold my own—totally. I say to myself, "Screw it! I'm eighty!"

There's something very freeing about being eighty.

I'll tell you what shocks me the most today. I think the reason I've stayed so young is that I have a lot of young friends. I encourage young writers. I learn from them and they learn from me, but it shocks me that even successful young people—I'm talking people in their thirties—don't read newspapers. Reading newspapers is an hour and a half of every morning for me. That's a very important time for me. I read three newspapers. I always have, all my life, every single morning. It stuns me that people get all their information from television. There's nothing wrong with that, but I think they're kind of missing out.

In 1983, the night before I left for the trial of the man who murdered my daughter, a journalist friend, Marie Brenner, invited me to her house for a Tex-Mex Sunday dinner. There were about eight or ten of us in the kitchen. I sat next to a young English lady and an English gentleman. The English lady was not quite the glamorous Tina Brown that we now see. I had a wonderful time with her at dinner—just a terrific time. She was fascinated by Hollywood. The next day, which was the day I was leaving, I got a call from Marie Brenner saying,

"Tina Brown wants to have lunch with you." I said, "Oh, Marie, I can't." Marie said to me, "Do it!" I believe in these orders in life.

I met Tina, without a clue as to what she wanted to see me about. We didn't have a minute of pleasantries. I sat down and she said, "You know you shouldn't waste all those Hollywood stories that you have at dinner parties. You should be writing that for a magazine." I said, "Tina! I just wrote my first novel and it was dumped on in the *New York Times* and they made fun of it. I wouldn't know what to write." She said, "I could teach you." Then she told me that she had just set the deal with Sy Newhouse to become the editor of *Vanity Fair*. She said, "Last night, we all knew where you're going today." At that time in my life, I was so raw that if anybody mentioned my daughter's murder, I would start to cry. Tina said, "I've read a lot about trials, but I've never read about a trial written by a participant." She said, "Keep a journal and when it's over, you come and see me."

I did exactly that, and writing the journal helped me get through the worst experience of my life. When it was over, I gave her my journal, and she turned me over to an editor. That was my first magazine piece ever, called "Justice." The week before the issue came out—the first all-her-own issue—Tina Brown took me out to lunch again, and she said, "Next week, when this issue hits the stand, every magazine in New York is going to be after you, but you're mine." I had been down and out for a lot of years after Hollywood. It was the first time anyone had shown the slightest interest in me. I owe Tina everything. She worked with me. I love her. I had lost confidence in myself—had totally lost it and never expected to get it back—and she gave it back to me, or made it possible for me to find it again. Then she would say to me, "Put yourself in the story. I want you in the story."

Graydon Carter, the current editor of *Vanity Fair*, is a great editor, too. He can read an article and say, "It lacks this. You've got to get this. You've got to build up this area." He can give you overall notes like that, and he's invariably right.

On my tenth wedding anniversary, Lenny, my late ex-wife, and I gave a dance. It was a black-and-white ball. It started at ten o'clock at night, and we had a set designer redo the whole inside of our Beverly Hills home. It was like the Ascot scene in *My Fair Lady* that Cecil Beaton had done. We had backdrops outside of the windows, lights in the house, and everything. There was a kind of a rule...the fire people had come and told us how many people we could have, and we had to say no houseguests. Truman Capote called—of course we had invited him—and he said, "I have to bring these two people from Kansas. He's the D.A." It was Alvin Dewey, but Truman's book *In Cold Blood* hadn't come out yet, and Alvin Dewey was not yet famous for solving the murder of the Clutter family. Anyway, he brought them and they were great. Truman was like a star. He was at the peak of his fame. It was before the drinking got to him and everything. What people don't know about him is that he was a great dancer. He danced with all the movie stars...wrote us the most wonderful note. And then he gave his own black-and-white ball for Kay Graham at the Plaza Hotel and didn't invite us.

My first successful novel was the second novel that I ever wrote and it was called *The Two Mrs. Grenvilles*. My agent and my editor both had said, "This is wonderful." I had been down for so many years, I didn't expect anything. Then one night, I had been at the magazine late and the elevators were closed and I took the freight elevator down. A young woman I didn't know got on the elevator, and she said, "You're Dominick Dunne." I said, "Yes." And she whispered, "I loved your book." Then I thought, "Hell!" Her comment meant so much to me, because your friends rally around, your agent and your editor praise you, but what she said was so real.

"I loved your book." I thought, "My God, I did it."

The turning point in my life? I was producing an Elizabeth Taylor movie called *Ash Wednesday* in the Dolomites of Italy. I was over there for a year. Elizabeth Taylor took a dislike to the writer and he got sent home. I used to drink in those days and do more than drink. When I was loaded at a party in Italy, I said something that was funny at the time, but was mean. It was repeated in the *Hollywood Reporter* two weeks later. I had made a joke at the expense of the writer's wife. She was a very powerful agent. It hurt her feelings when it was repeated. Sometimes you can say something that's funny, but it doesn't work on paper. When I got back to America, I knew it was over for me. I stopped getting invited to dinner parties and all that stuff.

So I just left Los Angeles. I drove up to Oregon. I got a flat tire in a little town called Camp Sherman in the Cascade Mountains, and I took a one-room cabin for the night and I stayed six months—with no telephone, no television. It was the most incredible experience of coming to terms with yourself—the silence. I'd always been a party person—going out to parties constantly, and there I was in total isolation. That is where I started to write, in that little cabin. You can't bullshit anymore. I used to say, "Oh, she ruined my career because she's..." Baloney! I picked her to ruin my career. It was an incredible experience.

When I was up there, Truman Capote wrote me a letter. I was stunned to get this grand letter from 870 United Nations Plaza on this great Tiffany stationery. It was sent to the general store. It was amazing what Truman had done. He heard that I had dropped out of my own life, and it was a letter of encouragement and admiration for what I had done. He ended it by saying, "But remember this. That is not where you belong. When you get what you went there to get, you must return to your life." At that time when I'd begun to feel peace for the first time in quite a few years, I really was thinking of living there forever. What he pointed out was there was a purpose in going there. When I went to Truman's funeral, two years later, I thought if he'd only done what I did, he wouldn't be dead. His alcoholism killed him.

I think about age. I have two sons and a granddaughter, and I think about their lives after me. I'm in that phase now where I hope I have a wonderful, big funeral. Jerry Wald was at the funeral of a man he detested and they said, "Jerry, why are you here?" And he said, "I just wanted to be sure the son of a bitch was dead."

I'm an active participant. I'm not a bystander. I used to be a bystander in life. Today, every day is full for me. I don't know how to relax. I write every day. I'm about to go to France for the Cannes Film Festival and I'm going up to Monte Carlo while I'm there to check on a celebrated murder case. The [Edmond] Safra murder utterly fascinates me—that billionaire who was murdered. And the male nurse is coming up for another trial. I'm going to try to see him in prison. When you're working like that, of course you embrace life. I see these guys who are even younger than me and they're all on walkers and they've got a maid in attendance. I think, "I don't want to live like that." I want to drop dead on the tarmac.

Ken Dychtwald

Daniel J. Kadlec

Ken Dychtwald, PhD, is a psychologist, gerontologist, and author of numerous bestselling books, including *Age Wave* and *Age Power*. A leading visionary on the longevity revolution, he lectures widely, advises major global corporations and organizations, and appears often in print and broadcast media, including the *Today show, 60 Minutes,* and *Good Morning America*. He was born on March 27, 1950, in Newark, New Jersey.

Daniel J. Kadlec is an author and award-winning journalist whose work appears regularly in *Time* and *Money* magazines. A former editor and columnist at *USA Today,* he was also a contributing editor at CNN. His third book, coauthored with Ken Dychtwald, is *With Purpose: Going from Success to Significance in Life and Work*. He was born on September 17, 1956, in St. Louis, Missouri.

Ken Dychtwald & Daniel J. Kadlec

Welcome to the Power Years

Do you long for a life without work or pressure in which your days are spent baking for the grandchildren or playing eighteen holes of golf in the morning, followed by a leisurely lunch and afternoon of bridge, then cocktails, a delicious early dinner, and a good movie? After all, that's how it worked for our grandparents and parents, isn't it? We grew up surrounded by this model of a leisure-filled later life.

Please forget everything you've been told. It's not your obligation to go away just because you're getting older. Nor is it your birthright to cede all responsibility to your community and humankind so that you may lead a life of leisure in retirement. Of course, you may choose these paths if you wish, but in our view that would be a mistake. Certainly there is no guarantee that you'll be able to afford a carefree romp through later life or even that you'll enjoy it if that's where you can afford to wind up. Reinventing yourself and *repowerment*—ramping up life where and when you choose and in ways that excite you, not winding down into obscurity—is the mold-shattering, exciting new stage that will come next for our generation.

While we've had our heads down toiling away these past few decades, spending more time that we might have envisioned at work and raising our children, the world has changed enormously. As we all know, the Internet, global trade, medical breakthroughs, and more are speeding up the pace of life even as life itself is being extended, posing new challenges in our careers and families. It's vitally important for each of us to appreciate just how different things really are and will become as we move into the next stage of life, a stage that we—the eighty-four million North Americans born between 1946 and 1964 as well as hundreds of millions more maturing adults around the world—will redefine as *the power years.*

The majority of our parents worked for one company all their lives. When their careers ended at age sixty-five, the norm was that they got a nice party and a gold watch and happily hopped on board a slow cruise into the sunset. Forty years of toil behind and the kids now grown, both Dad and Mom were done. They floated over the horizon, eagerly retreating to a life of leisure.

For their employers, it was a great deal. They got to bring in younger, more energetic, and less expensive labor.

For a lot of reasons, many of us won't have the same options that our parents had. For one thing, government and employee-sponsored entitlements have questionable futures, and the idea of early retirement, or even for many of us the idea of retirement at sixty-five, took a quantum leap backward when the global stock market bubble burst in 2000, eroding much of our savings and more than a few of our dreams.

Demographic trends threaten to foist an unprecedented labor shortage on the world economy. Companies of all sizes and shapes are going to want us to stick around longer and will be willing to provide us with a great deal more flexibility to do so. Meanwhile, our careers have been far more mobile. We've bounced among three, four, five, or more employers, often in as many cities, and we won't have been with any one of them long enough for a gold watch, much less the pension and wall-to-wall retirement health coverage that our parents might have been blessed with.

The slow, lazy cruise that our fathers and mothers eagerly signed up for turned out to be a little too slow and lazy. Look hard enough and you'll see that many of our parents have begun to rebel against the idea that they should fade away; they're going back to school and back to work, taking up writing or painting and otherwise reengaging with a society they had dropped out of. Throughout this book we will lean on the experiences of what we can call Ageless Explorers, the growing number of leading-edge adults of our parents' generation and some from even further back, to illustrate the changing nature of the power years.

These years present a unique opportunity for us. The notion of staying in the game longer, of not having to step aside at a set age, will liberate us, setting us free to lead the lives we want to lead by staying engaged, vital, and youthful as long as we like. Opening before us is a whole new stage of life squeezed between our primary career years and a steadily retreating old age. Just as we moved from adolescence into adulthood three or four decades ago, we are not pushing into a whole new period of discovery and personal growth—what we call *middlescence*—as more and more of us make the most of the many fruitful decades that lie ahead.

Our generation is coming to realize that we will have numerous decades to live past the age commonly thought to be the time to stop working. What we do with that time will set us apart from all previous generations.

As we step over the threshold into maturity, we will transform the stage of later life known as retirement into something that squares with our generation's desire to work, play, and love on our own terms, staying young in mind and body, and engaging in new pursuits without becoming bogged down with too many numbing obligations. With greater energy and drive, higher expectations for our later years, and a greater willingness to repeatedly reinvent ourselves that any previous generation, perhaps we'll reshape work into something that we can do three days a week, or eight months each year, or seven years per decade. And with extended longevity, why wait until maturity for a long break? Why not take time off along the way? Instead of being stuck on a one-career path for life, why not go back to school, learn some new skills, and reinvent ourselves again and again?

What we're naming the power years has also been called by some our *third age*, a concept derived from the European tradition of adult education. This view holds that there are three ages of man, each with its own special focus, challenge, and opportunities. In the first age, from birth to about thirty, our primary tasks of life are biological development, learning, and survival. During most of human history, the average life expectancy wasn't much longer than the end of the first age, and as a result, the entire thrust of society was oriented toward these basic drives.

In the second age, from about thirty to sixty, our concerns focus on forming a family, parenting, and work. We apply the lessons we learned during the first age to these responsibilities. Until very recently, most people didn't live much beyond the second age. But with today's longer life expectancies, new generations of youthful, open-minded, and high-spirited men and women are not interested in fading into the sunset at sixty.

A third age, which spans the period from sixty to ninety (and longer), is unfolding ahead of us. This is a less-pressured period in which we can further develop our intellect, imagination, emotional maturity, and wisdom. This is also a period when we can give something back to society based on the lessons, resources, and experiences we have accumulated over a lifetime. We need not be social outcasts, but instead can assume the role of a living bridge between yesterday and tomorrow, and in this way play a critical role that no other group is as well suited to perform.

If the past fifty years of boomer evolution have taught us anything, it is this: as we enter each new life stage, we keep what we like and replace the rest, like remodeling a house.

With the right insight and planning, we'll be able to merge what we most enjoy in our youth—energy, freedom, flexibility, health, and personal growth—with the good things that come with age, things such as experience, perspective, wisdom, and depth. One thing is clear: as our massive numbers ultimately catch the wave, the ripples will stretch far and wide.

The Seven Reasons These Are the Power Years

1. We'll be living longer and healthier.
2. The cyclic life plan (cycling in and out of careers) will replace the outmoded linear model.
3. We'll have a big—and growing—pool of role models.
4. We'll be wiser about what matters.
5. We'll have new freedoms.
6. We'll still have clout in the marketplace (advertisers will need to break free of their addiction to youth).
7. We'll be open to change.

five children would have lost their forty-nine-year-old mother. The morphine overdose that killed me that day was a hospital error.

I know what it is to be dead. It is a visceral knowing without words and without "memory" in the usual sense of the word. Death is infinity and ultimate safety. I have been there, beyond embodiment, way out beyond consciousness and unconsciousness. There is no fear there. There is no sadness there. It is only the living who are fearful and sad.

Development Does Not Stop at Midlife

Another misconception that supports the idea of aging is that once humans reach middle age, development stands still. In actuality, every moment of living gifts us with vast networks of experience that manifest simultaneously in body, mind, and spirit. Life experience patterns our spiritual, emotional, and physical beings simultaneously. Living is a continuum of growth, change, and expansion.

We are familiar with other developmental stages. In infancy, trust and safety are developed. In the "terrible twos," toddlers experiment with independence (I think two-years-olds are wonderful!). Then follow the phases of early school years and middle and late adolescence, each developmental phase having its own tasks and goals. During early adulthood, the task is to establish stability and form long-term love relationships.

And then there is the midlife crisis, which includes andropause and menopause signifying a downward spiral of age. Men and women become restless in careers, and relationships become stale, shoulders hunch, bellies ooze over belts, memory declines, brains fog, and attachment to routine solidifies. Advertisers have a heyday now with the aging baby boomers, creating cures for imaginary illnesses such as vaginal dryness, leaky bladders, and, yes, the dreaded ED (erectile dysfunction).

How audacious it would be to teach our preschoolers that being twenty-one is nice, but that seventy or eighty is when we are at our best. Imagine if movies and advertisers, make-believe games and storybooks taught children to see life on Earth (getting older) as a continuum, along which we continue to deepen, ripen, and develop, from the first to the last day of life.

Imagine children playing with Granny and Pops dolls at least as often as they played with Barbie and Ken. Barbie's tiny waist and enormous perky breasts defy physics; a real woman with Barbie's proportions would not be able to stand up. The Granny doll has soft breasts that offer comfort; Granny's boobs are utterly huggable. Kids playing with these dolls know that Granny breasts have been shaped by babies she has nursed, and that her wide hips offer a graceful perch where a child can ride. The Pops doll is muscular and capable. Each Pops doll has a different little potbelly. His shoulders are perfect for riding on, for seeing over the crowd. Both Granny and Pops have beautiful little wrinkles near their eyes and these doll faces are smiling and wise, with mischievous knowing in their expressions. Both dolls wear pants that have marvelous pockets with secrets and magic in them.

Children would collect the outfits and the storybooks telling of the adventures and experiences of Granny and Pops. While Barbie and Ken giggle and go on dates and choose gowns for the prom, Granny and Pops tell fabulous stories about mysteries they have solved, they travel the world to help build schools and houses, and they learn something new every day.

From my work as a rule-defying physician, I understand that it takes at least half a century to grow up and grow wise. At fifty, a brand new developmental phase begins. It is a time of new vision and of a new ability to savor pleasure and manage grief. It is a time to develop wisdom and cultivate spiritual evolution for ourselves and the world.

Instead of viewing the second half-century of life as an incredibly rich time of profound changes, many people see it as a time of undesirable results from hormonal shifts. Our cultural attitude (our expectation of what "aging" inevitably means) combined with our complete ignorance of the care and maintenance of spirit, body, and mind and an inability to decipher the message of the so-called symptoms we experience are what give middle age and beyond such a bad rap.

The Gift of Embodiment

We deteriorate because we are never taught to embrace and cultivate the gift of embodiment.

Before the mid-1980s, the idea of a mind-body connection was not part of medical or even public discussion. Reductionist medical science had established the idea that we are a series of linear systems or components. Organ systems (circulatory, pulmonary, reproductive, and nervous systems) were reduced to organs (heart, lung, blood vessels, ovaries, testicles, brain, spinal cord, nerve cells), which were reduced to tissues cells and eventually biochemicals.

I recall the heated debate among physicians over whether behavioral patterns (very little sleep, intense desire for achievement,

Hendrieka "Hennie" Fitzpatrick, MD, medical director of Integrated Health
Medical Center in Santa Fe, New Mexico, is a pioneer of European biological
medicine in this country. Biological medicine, which focuses on eliminating
the causes of symptoms, is especially effective in the treatment of chronic
and degenerative diseases and complex health problems that are difficult to
diagnose. She teaches biological medicine to physicians nationally. For
the past two decades, she has also been teaching sensuality and
sexuality to teenagers and conducting rites of passage for teens.
She was born on May 15, 1955, in Baltimore, Maryland.

Hendrieka Fitzpatrick

Move Over, Barbie and Ken

To be audacious is to be empowered and independent, spirited and energetic, original and bold. Sadly, not many people think of these characteristics when they think of aging. If you ask teenagers about aging, they will use words like shriveling, limping, confused, wrinkly, and feeble. They are just voicing the view of aging that most of us in this society hold.

Aging is a concept created by our culture. Under the current paradigm, we are destined in our later years to feed, fuel, and finance the drug industry and medical specialists and subspecialists who "treat" age-related illness. Under this paradigm, aging leads us inevitably toward debilitation, dementia, physical pain, and stiffness. This occurs as part of aging because we are ignorant of what holistic health or holistic living means.

Since I am a physician, I can best describe this ignorance from the perspective of health care. In our medical system, physicians learn physiology and then use this knowledge only to identify a symptom and give out a drug to suppress the symptom. Medical language is obscure and serves to protect the notion that symptoms are mysterious. Most of the illnesses that prevent audacity at the middle and the end of life have "unknown etiology" (that means that doctors do not know why they happen).

The truth is that nothing, absolutely nothing spiritual, emotional, mental, or physical, is of "unknown etiology." In this chapter, I will provide a brief overview of three obstacles to cultivating audacity: fear of death, the view that development stops at or before midlife, and ignorance of the mind-body connection.

No Need to Fear

First, most people in our culture are unfamiliar with death and are therefore afraid of it. We discourage children from asking questions about death. We do not care for others until death and so do not witness death. We do not wash and dress the dead body of a loved one, as people in other cultures do.

Additionally, in the world of medicine, death signifies the ultimate failure. When your physician determines "there is nothing left to do" and death is imminent, you are discharged from your physician's care.

I have always been a rule breaker. In fact, try as I might, I can never get the rules straight. In keeping with this tendency, I created an independent major in college and studied medical ethics even though I was "pre med." In the prevalent dis-integrated study of pre med, ethics is not part of the curriculum.

I remember my excitement when I volunteered to be on the ethics committee of the local hospital shortly after I began working as a physician. These meetings turned out to be deadly (pun intended). A group of stodgy male physicians gathered once a month to discuss solutions to "ethical" problems that arose in patient care. These problems always involved settling disputes among family members over end-of-life care for someone dying in the hospital.

One day, as the committee was planning the agenda, I enthusiastically suggested that at the next meeting we discuss our thoughts and feelings about what happens to someone at death. I assumed that everyone struggled with the interface of physician and individual in considering the great mysteries of life.

As soon as I had made the suggestion, ten solemn, old pairs of eyes turned to gaze at me with unabashed disdain. After an uncomfortable and lengthy silence, the chairman informed me in a monotone that I had breached a major rule in the practice of medicine. I was kicked off the committee.

From this comes the image that people of a certain age are sucked kicking and screaming toward an unknowable void. And if the physician, family member, or nursing home staff realizes the time is near, they disappear.

Years later, an experience I had after routine surgery took away whatever fears I myself harbored about death. The surgery had gone well and I was in my hospital room. My sister was just leaving after a visit. Thankfully, she decided to say good-bye one more time, even though she knew I was sleeping. My body lay eerily still and was the color of death. My limbs had begun to curl into a decerebrate posture (which indicates cessation of brain activity or a malfunction in the brain). Had she not turned to look at me, had she not started CPR, my five children would have lost their forty-nine-year-old mother. The morphine overdose that killed me that day was a hospital error.

I know what it is to be dead. It is a visceral knowing without words and without "memory" in the usual sense of the word. Death is infinity and ultimate safety. I have been there, beyond embodiment, way out beyond consciousness and unconsciousness. There is no fear there. There is no sadness there. It is only the living who are fearful and sad.

Development Does Not Stop at Midlife

Another misconception that supports the idea of aging is that once humans reach middle age, development stands still. In actuality, every moment of living gifts us with vast networks of experience that manifest simultaneously in body, mind, and spirit. Life experience patterns our spiritual, emotional, and physical beings simultaneously. Living is a continuum of growth, change, and expansion.

We are familiar with other developmental stages. In infancy, trust and safety are developed. In the "terrible twos," toddlers experiment with independence (I think two-years-olds are wonderful!). Then follow the phases of early school years and middle and late adolescence, each developmental phase having its own tasks and goals. During early adulthood, the task is to establish stability and form long-term love relationships.

And then there is the midlife crisis, which includes andropause and menopause signifying a downward spiral of age. Men and women become restless in careers, and relationships become stale, shoulders hunch, bellies ooze over belts, memory declines, brains fog, and attachment to routine solidifies. Advertisers have a heyday now with the aging baby boomers, creating cures for imaginary illnesses such as vaginal dryness, leaky bladders, and, yes, the dreaded ED (erectile dysfunction).

How audacious it would be to teach our preschoolers that being twenty-one is nice, but that seventy or eighty is when we are at our best. Imagine if movies and advertisers, make-believe games and storybooks taught children to see life on Earth (getting older) as a continuum, along which we continue to deepen, ripen, and develop, from the first to the last day of life.

Imagine children playing with Granny and Pops dolls at least as often as they played with Barbie and Ken. Barbie's tiny waist and enormous perky breasts defy physics; a real woman with Barbie's proportions would not be able to stand up. The Granny doll has soft breasts that offer comfort; Granny's boobs are utterly huggable. Kids playing with these dolls know that Granny breasts have been shaped by babies she has nursed, and that her wide hips offer a graceful perch where a child can ride. The Pops doll is muscular and capable. Each Pops doll has a different little potbelly. His shoulders are perfect for riding on, for seeing over the crowd. Both Granny and Pops have beautiful little wrinkles near their eyes and these doll faces are smiling and wise, with mischievous knowing in their expressions. Both dolls wear pants that have marvelous pockets with secrets and magic in them.

Children would collect the outfits and the storybooks telling of the adventures and experiences of Granny and Pops. While Barbie and Ken giggle and go on dates and choose gowns for the prom, Granny and Pops tell fabulous stories about mysteries they have solved, they travel the world to help build schools and houses, and they learn something new every day.

From my work as a rule-defying physician, I understand that it takes at least half a century to grow up and grow wise. At fifty, a brand new developmental phase begins. It is a time of new vision and of a new ability to savor pleasure and manage grief. It is a time to develop wisdom and cultivate spiritual evolution for ourselves and the world.

Instead of viewing the second half-century of life as an incredibly rich time of profound changes, many people see it as a time of undesirable results from hormonal shifts. Our cultural attitude (our expectation of what "aging" inevitably means) combined with our complete ignorance of the care and maintenance of spirit, body, and mind and an inability to decipher the message of the so-called symptoms we experience are what give middle age and beyond such a bad rap.

The Gift of Embodiment

We deteriorate because we are never taught to embrace and cultivate the gift of embodiment.

Before the mid-1980s, the idea of a mind-body connection was not part of medical or even public discussion. Reductionist medical science had established the idea that we are a series of linear systems or components. Organ systems (circulatory, pulmonary, reproductive, and nervous systems) were reduced to organs (heart, lung, blood vessels, ovaries, testicles, brain, spinal cord, nerve cells), which were reduced to tissues cells and eventually biochemicals.

I recall the heated debate among physicians over whether behavioral patterns (very little sleep, intense desire for achievement, emotional rigidity) could actually create a physical illness: coronary artery disease or peptic ulcers. Medical science resisted the idea that behavior was a cause of "real" clinical disease.

Eventually, science could no longer deny the reality of a mind-body connection. Now, the concept of a mind-body connection is obsolete because the word "connection" implies the possibility of disconnection. Mind, body, and spirit are not only connected; each is integral to the living matrix.

Each human being is an elaborate ecosystem. We are in constant relationship, interaction, and flow. We are interdependent, complex, organized, and patterned by the experiences of the mind, emotions, and spirit. We are embodied for a good reason. Our physical bodies are resilient, tough, and very forgiving.

Along with eliminating the mind-body connection from your way of viewing health and life, eliminate the old concept of a "symptom" as an indicator of disease, aging, or death.

Every cell in our body can and does regenerate in a cyclical and reliable fashion, but only if we take responsibility for the care and nurturance of our entire selves—body, mind, and spirit. Symptoms are actually welcome messages from our magnificent internal milieu, alerting us that we are not giving some aspect of ourselves the care it needs. Symptoms require interpretation, rather than the suppression that is the conventional medical approach. Become well educated in translating or deciphering "symptoms." They are the ultimate language of the body, mind, and spirit. Every cell, tissue, and organ is constantly regrowing and regenerating in response to spiritual, emotional, and physical information from the internal ecosystem.

Understanding rather than suppressing symptoms is the new model for audacious aging. At any moment from your first to your last breath, your body is doing its best job in the context of the micro-environment.

The New Paradigm

The most audacious of us need to create an entirely new understanding of self-care, particularly for the developmental phases that begin after fifty.

There are myriad self-help books, classes, exercises, and approaches to transcend barriers to well-being through mind and spirit. These excellent guides offer provocative ways to develop audacity. Likewise, there is astute advice about maintaining your physical body with herbs, homeopathics, orthomolecular supplements, diet, and exercise.

But here are the facts: No psychological, spiritual, somatic therapy, or energy work will succeed without interpreting physiological messages that coincide with spirit/emotional change. Likewise, physical health is not enough for audacious living.

Forget about mind-body connection; that idea will misguide your audacious nature. Replace the idea of mind-body connection with the idea of an internal environment or ecosystem. In any sustainable ecosystem, there is absolute dynamic interaction at every level. Thus, mind, body, and spirit are all reflections of our internal ecosystem, which in the new paradigm is a single, inseparable entity.

Spiritual growth or understanding cannot occur without a simultaneous biochemical patterning and vice versa. For example, even the most elaborate balancing of DHEA, estrogen, testosterone, and growth hormone will not restore hormonal balance unless you also balance your cortisol levels, thyroid hormone levels, immune mediators, and mood biochemicals. Likewise, hormones will not remain in balance if you are worried, isolated, or always rushing. In fact, loneliness causes estrogen deficiency, thus loneliness can be a factor in hot flashes and osteoporosis.

Laughter and play not only put you in a good mood, but can also enhance your digestion, improve mental clarity, decrease hypertension, eliminate inflammation, and strengthen your immunity. These improvements can be demonstrated by standard lab testing. Children know this. Adults think of laughter and play as what you do in your free time. From a health and audacity standpoint, it would be better for you to stop brushing your teeth or showering as often instead of considering play as the activity to eliminate when your schedule is tight.

Here are other examples. We agree that suppressed anger is a cause of depression. No antidepressant nor somatic, energetic, or emotional therapy on Earth will resolve that depression unless your biochemistry is balanced simultaneously. Likewise, balancing neurotransmitters such as serotonin, DL-phenylalanine, GABA, theanine, or taurine alone is not sufficient if you do not have balanced intestinal flora, normal thyroid function, and normal cortisol levels and diurnal cortisol rhythms. In the new model, if psychiatrists, even those set on only dispensing pharmaceuticals, would add in testing and rebuilding intestinal flora, even antipsychotic drugs would be more effective.

Liver toxicity from preservatives, heavy metals, and pharmaceutical residues always coincides with the development of spiritual angst, and liver toxicity (which can be measured in lab work by SGPT, which indicates liver enzyme levels) is a necessary cofactor for developing diabetes. This point is important. Even if you are morbidly obese and sedentary, if you spend an hour a day in a mindless playful activity and detoxify your liver, you will not develop type 2 diabetes. So your spiritual work will help detoxify your liver and lowering your body toxicity will allow spiritual breakthroughs otherwise not possible.

Not only does liver toxicity prevent fully realized spiritual breakthroughs, but it also causes the accumulation of fat. No wonder we get fatter as we "age." Instead of regarding fat as an enemy and a nuisance, realize that body fat is your body's wise way of storing toxic residues in a place where this toxicity does not poison you. Body fat is the body's best effort at dealing with our toxic environment. And to complete this complex interaction, that stubborn abdominal fat around our otherwise audacious middles has endocrine activity.

If you are lonely or uninspired, you will never be able to balance your hormones. You will suffer from signs of low thyroid (maybe weight gain and fatigue). If you correct one or the other (e.g., you either take thyroid hormones or cultivate a meaningful relationship, but not at the same time), you will still be plagued by measurable fluctuations in hormones, signs of low thyroid, and the deep physical fatigue of depleted adrenals. Lack of motivation will not easily be replaced in such a microenvironment.

If you are really exploring your past issues with the best therapists in the world, even if you are doing somatic therapy, psychotherapy, and elaborate energetic therapy, if you do not have enough serotonin, enough estrogen, and a healthy amount of cholesterol, you will never achieve spiritual clarity. Even if you take hundreds of dollars of supplements and see the best nutritionist who prescribes a diet for your exact blood type, even if you are the perfect weight and physically fit, you will not feel vibrantly well if your intestinal flora is out of balance (which is very common even if you take the very best probiotics on the market).

Your Gut Feelings Are Right!

Intestinal microflora provide a good example for understanding our interdependent internal milieu. Our intestinal systems house billions of bacteria. There are far fewer cells that make up "you" than there are bacterial cells housed in your intestine. These bacteria link each of us to the earth herself as well as to the first cells that emerged into life from the primordial bog centuries ago. Through spiritual practice, we connect to the universal whole. Intestinal bacteria are a physical embodiment of the same.

We know that dysbiotic flora ("dysbiotic" means out of biological balance) growing in our intestines creates digestive complaints: gas, bloating, belly pain, constipation, and diarrhea. These bacteria also directly determine your sense of emotional well-being. Gut flora actually put you in a good or a bad mood. Dysbiotic flora also creates metabolic by-products that cause bad moods such as anxiety and depression. In fact, most of the serotonin you make is made in your gut if your gut is healthy.

Developing these connections further, the large intestine meridian (or energy channel, in traditional Chinese medicine) represents what you take in and absorb and what you need to let go of. The gut houses an entire nervous system that operates independently from the brain and spinal cord. Gut feelings indeed provide an alternate form of guidance associated with intuition and "inner knowing." Imbalanced gut flora prevents proper digestion and absorption of nutrients, which in turn triggers systemic inflammation that can lead to autoimmune disease, coronary artery disease, and stroke Dysbiotic flora prevents the proper conversion of vitamin D metabolites, which is a cause of joint pain and inflammation as well as osteoporosis. Dysbiotic flora creates an excess of the estrogen metabolite associated with the development of breast cancer.

So you can see that every symptom, yearning, mood, and spiritual revelation is connected to every other. Our physical bodies, our spirits, and our emotional growth emerge and develop on a continuum from birth to death and then perhaps to birth again.

All of us, but particularly experts in the fields of psychology, somatics, spirituality, and energy medicine need to cooperate with biological physicians to provide a truly holistic medicine of the future. And people seeking the help of such experts need to join in shifting the paradigm as well. In so doing, we will become audacious and we will not age. Instead, our roots will strengthen, our blooms will flower brightly and fully, and our fruit will ripen. We will become joyful, wise, and spirited. Enjoy each moment, cultivate connection on every level, and be excited!

Nikki Giovanni is a world-renowned poet, writer, commentator, activist, and educator. Early in her career she was dubbed the "Princess of Black Poetry." She is now listed as a "National Treasure" and one of Oprah Winfrey's twenty-five "Living Legends." Among her myriad honors and awards are Woman of the Year (*Ladies Home Journal* and *Ebony*), the Rosa L. Parks Woman of Courage Award, and the Langston Hughes Medal for poetry. The author of more than thirty books, she is a professor at Virginia Tech. Nikki Giovanni was born on June 7, 1943, in Knoxville, Tennessee.

Nikki Giovanni

Riding a Rainbow

I'm a big fan of aging. People talk about going back to their twenties; I wouldn't even go back to my forties. I love being in my sixties. The sixties are like riding a rainbow. You learn more and understand so much more about your place in the world and how the world actually runs. Everything makes a lot more sense.

I've been called outspoken in my life, but I never thought of it that way. I was just going forward with what I knew to be right. A lot of that came from the two fabulous women who reared me—my mother and my grandmother. I conduct my business as they conducted theirs. Grandmother was very outspoken, which meant she said what was on her mind. One of her messages to me was "Just tell the truth and let it fall." Because of that I've always been comfortable with accepting what comes my way and not worrying about what doesn't. Their support of me for being myself and speaking the truth was also an important part of this. Both of them were big believers in me and that was a huge help.

Some people might view the way I got my career started as audacious, but they don't know the reason I wanted to have my first book party at Birdland [the fabled jazz club in midtown Manhattan]. I had borrowed the money to pay for the printing of my first collections of poetry, *Black Feeling, Black Talk* in late 1967 and *Black Judgement* in early 1968. Nobody had ever had a book party at Birdland. Lloyd Price was one of the owners of Birdland, but I met with Harold Logan, who was his silent partner. I told him I wanted to have a book party there on a Sunday. The club was closed on Sundays.

"So you want to rent the club," he said.

"Oh no, I don't want to rent the club," I said. "I don't have any money, Mr. Logan. I'm a poet. I want to have it here because my mother's a jazz lover; she loves Bird and she loves Billie Holiday. So I'm not asking you and then I'm going to leave and ask somebody else. I want it at Birdland, where George Shearing stands, you understand?"

He was looking at me like, "What the hell is this girl talking about?" Then he said, "Well, Giovanni, I'll tell you what. If you bring me a hundred people, you can have the club. Ninety-nine people and you'll owe me five hundred dollars."

That was real money back then, but I said, "You got it," and we shook on it.

Birdland used to be on Forty-fourth, before they moved, and I walked upstairs, saying to myself, "Oh, my god, I just shook hands with a man that kills people for a living."

But I didn't have a problem asking Logan. I wanted to do something that Mommy would enjoy. It was that simple. The only thing that could happen is that I could fail. And I'm sure Mr. Logan would have had something ugly happen to me had I failed. I had no doubt about that. Or I would have found the five hundred dollars. But I knew that I was not in over my head as to what I thought was possible. I wasn't scared of failing. I've never been scared about that. If you can't embrace failure, you can't be a writer.

I called my sister, Gary, because I needed some help and I couldn't afford to pay for it. She's extremely well organized and helped map out everything. We absolutely packed Birdland. My next-door neighbor and good friend Morgan Freeman read for me. Barbara Ann Teer read for me. Larry Neal read. It was wonderful. Harold was pleased. I was pleased. We made the second front in the *New York Times*, the New York page, with a big picture. And we made the front page of the *Amsterdam News* and of *Muhammad Speaks*.

The success of the event brought me a lot of publicity. Phil Petrie, who was working at William Morrow, invited me to lunch with the vice president and they said they'd like to publish the books. I said, "Great, because publishing is a capital intensive business, and I'm not in business. I'm a poet." I told them the amount I needed as an advance, so I could pay back the money I had borrowed from my grandmother and other people to publish my books. The vice president told me they didn't give that kind of advance for poetry. So I thanked them for the lunch and the offer but told them I couldn't sell the book because it was all I had to pay back the people who had helped me. "I'm going to pay them back or I'm going to go down," I said, "but I'm not going to sell them out and tell them I don't have their money."

Four days later, Phil called me and said, "You got it."

I wasn't trying to hold them up. I wasn't trying to do anything but take care of the people who had taken care of me. I've always done that and I always will.

So that first event wasn't all about publicizing me. It was all about love. I was explaining that to a young man I'm mentoring. I told him, "You cannot let other people's priorities be yours." As for me, my priorities are simple. What I love I look out for—it's that basic.

Listen and Learn

People sometimes ask who my role models were. That's a term I really hate. It's one of those terms that's in the lexicon, so we're stuck with it. Look at Harriet Tubman. She didn't do what she did because she had a role model. There wasn't anybody doing what she did; she didn't see it anywhere. We live by our imagination; we don't live by what we see. We in America try to dumb people down with the concept "If you can't see it, it can't be done." That doesn't make any sense. If you can't see it, that's every reason to do it.

The phrase "influential people" works better. Influence is something that's been around forever and will always be. In my case, aside from Mommy and Grandmother, one of the influential people in my life was Sister Althea, my sixth grade teacher who is a nun. I met her when I was ten and we have remained friends. She still spends Thanksgivings with me. Another was my eighth grade teacher, Alfreda Delaney. She was a good friend and a strong believer in my writing ability. I enjoyed writing, but I wasn't sure I was really doing it. She assured me I was, then said, "But you're handwriting is so poor, you have to take typing." I'm not good with physical things like that, but I took typing. You couldn't tell those old ladies you couldn't do it—and God knows that's why we love them. When they said do something, you said, "Okay, I'll do it."

I am close to the two of my mother's friends who are still alive. I visit with them, correspond with them, and talk with them. My mother and that generation had great friendships. They showed me how important it is to love your friends.

So you try to do what the old ladies did because they did it right.

My grandmother was a club woman—the garden club, the book club, the flower club, the Court of Colanthe, and the Deltas. I learned from her that good leaders have to enter into the realities of other people. In other words, we have to listen to understand what's important to another person. If we can enter into another reality, then we can make a change. Eldridge Cleaver had that statement, "You're either a part of the solution or a part of the problem." That was never true. You're part of both. That's why I tell my students that it needs to be "we can," not "you should."

I used to watch some of my colleagues, if I can use that collegial term for the sixties, become frustrated with the people. They would be organizers and they would become frustrated. You can't be frustrated with the people. You have to learn. And I still do. I listen to the people. It's one of the major reasons I'm a big fan of hip hop. When hip hop started coming up, a lot of people my age rejected it. They didn't like the cadence, they didn't like what the rappers were saying, they didn't like the way they dressed. And I thought, what are we missing here? Some of the most creative minds of the next generation are involved in this music. We have to find out what it is.

A lot of people ask me if it's really true that I have a Tupac Shakur tattoo [top-selling hip hop artist and social activist, murdered in 1996]. Well, that's not something you'd lie about! I have a "Thug Life" tattoo, which is what Tupac had tattooed across his stomach. He used to say, "I'd rather be with the thugs than the people who are putting them down." [By thugs, he meant people who came from oppressed backgrounds but made something of themselves despite their early lack of opportunity.] I have that on my lower arm because I wanted to share it. I wanted a public tattoo because the loss of him was so great. How you could not admire the passion and the genius of Tupac Shakur is beyond me. The loss of him is only comparable in white America to the loss of John Kennedy Jr. They were both saying the same thing: we can make a difference here. I mourned both of them.

The Boulder of Love

If asked for words of wisdom on how to approach life at any age, I would say that the key is to say yes, say yes to everything. Don't always be second-guessing yourself, finding reasons why something won't work even before you try it. Possibilities cannot occur without yes. So you have to say yes. Especially because so many people tell you "Don't."

Audaciousness comes in refusing to be silenced. People especially want to silence women. We have had in the world infibulation, the sewing up of the labia of a girl or woman. I saw a sculpture of a woman with her mouth sewn shut. And I thought, "Yeah, that's really what they want to sew up." The vaginal area is a substitute for the mouth.

If you live long enough, though, which I'm happy that I have, all the truth you spoke and maybe got criticized for comes to pass and then you're seen as a sage.

I'm very optimistic about the future of human beings. There is progress in the human condition. The progress is never going to be what you would like when you start off as a young person and you're really committed to change. You want to see things get better, but you want them to get better soon. But things don't get better soon. Things get better incrementally, so what you have is a revolution so that the evolution can take place. That's a hard concept for kids. I was like that. You want to see the change that you're trying to bring about, but you're not going to see it in that way because the change is rising water.

In my view, what you want to do is good work while you're here. You cannot look to tomorrow. You have to do it today. And of course, if you're an old revolutionary like me, you realize you have to teach the kids. American kids are being dumbed down and I'm really tired of it. Everything cannot be Clifford the big red dog. There have to be some good stories, and we have to tell them.

I'm working on a poem about Sisyphus, which will then be a children's book. What we've heard about Sisyphus is wrong. Yes, he was pushing the boulder up the hill, but it wasn't a punishment. He was pushing that boulder out of love. The gods bless you with a boulder to push. It may be hard, but you have to push your boulder up the hill. You do it because you love what you're doing.

That doesn't mean you forget to have fun. Audacious aging means that you're still enjoying yourself, that you're still finding things that are joyful, even when your circumstances might seem to make that difficult. I have a dear friend who has multiple sclerosis, for example, and she is audaciously and wonderfully alive because she is still enjoying her living.

As for me, I am the first Giovanni to make it to the age of sixty-five. There is nothing as wonderful as growing old.

Lori Grace, MA Psych, LMT, is an election reform and environmental activist, an antiaging specialist, and an authority in Tantra. She has had a private practice dedicated to teaching Tantra for over a decade and been conducting Tantra workshops for fifteen years. She also teaches communication and conflict resolution, particularly utilizing Compassionate Communication (Marshall Rosenberg's system, known also as Nonviolent Communication). She was born on November 14 in New York City in the 1950s.

LORI GRACE

CHAPTER
19

Living on the Edge

Throughout my life, I've lived on the edge in a number of ways, which other people might call audacious but which I was simply drawn to do. The latest edge to which I was led has very high stakes for the whole United States, and by extension, the world.

It began in 2002 when I saw the film *Unprecedented: The 2000 Presidential Election* and learned the details of how George Bush got elected in 2000 through election fraud, notably in Florida. As I watched the information unfold about the padding of the Florida list of felons barred from voting, the purging of people from the voter rolls in Democratic districts who had a name even remotely similar to an entry on the felon list, tabulator fraud, and the complicity of government officials including Florida governor Jeb Bush and Florida Secretary of State Katherine Harris, I felt a terrible sinking feeling. The movie urged me to find out more about the issue and then do something to help.

I began to work closely with Beverly Harris of Black Box Voting, the nonprofit elections watchdog group. I was an initial investor in the making of the HBO documentary *Hacking Democracy,* which is about her work and the work of others in investigating voting irregularities. Upon learning that votes can be shifted from a distance via computer, I knew that the 2004 election was at risk. This understanding coincided with the information a friend put on my desk about Diebold, one of the companies that makes electronic voting machines, attacking the website of Beverly Harris because she had published what they had put on an international file server for a few days: a how-to manual for getting into their vote tabulator. All that was missing was the password, which I later found had been widely distributed to Diebold employees. Additionally, in 2003, Walden O'Dell, the chief executive of Diebold in Ohio, pledged in a fund-raising letter for the Republican Party to help deliver the state of Ohio to Bush in 2004.

The Audacity of Grace

by Cliff Arnebeck
Attorney specializing in public interest election litigation
Chair of Legal Affairs Committee, Common Cause Ohio
National cochair and attorney, Alliance for Democracy

Lori Grace provided significant moral and fund-raising support for Citizens for Secure Elections–Ohio (CASE). CASE made a big difference in helping to secure the 2004 Ohio election, which was at the center of determining the outcome of the 2004 presidential election. CASE helped make sure Ohio had mostly paper ballots that could have been checked to detect electronic and other forms of fraud. As it was, some 1.5 million ballots were destroyed after the election. That in itself is evidence of fraudulent conduct. Susan Truitt, an attorney and founder of CASE, was a key public speaker in helping to build public support for corrective action against the fraud in the 2004 Ohio election.

Lori has also played an important role in bringing people together in ways that have enhanced the election protection movement. The best example of this is her connecting of cyber security expert Stephen Spoonamore with election protection processionals in Washington DC and Ohio. Lori always follows through, as she did in this case by assisting these new combinations of people in finding the resources they needed to advance their cause of protecting the integrity of the 2008 presidential election. She had done the same kind of thing in helping bring the late Ohio congresswoman Stephanie Tubbs Jones (she died in August 2008) together with California's Senator Barbara Boxer to enable the historic challenge in the United States Congress to the corrupted 2004 Ohio Electoral College vote.

Though the battle for election integrity was tough, it was successful in the 2006 and 2008 cycles in preventing Karl Rove's methods from destroying our democracy. Lori is clearly one of the heroes in that struggle and success.

During the Bush years, I thought about emigrating to another country because I was so dismayed at his policies. This was a painful thing over which I cried. When I was growing up, I felt so proud to be an American. I believed that Americans don't torture people, that Americans are fair, that we stand for truth, liberty, justice, and

the American way. Now I was seeing all these policies I didn't like being put into place based on stolen elections. I visited New Zealand, Canada, Belize, and Costa Rica as possible places where I might live. But I came back from these trips loving my own country and mourning at the idea of leaving it.

After watching the election being stolen again in 2004, I had no more thoughts of emigrating. I took a stand for honesty and integrity. I view my election work as a form of patriotism. I come from a strong Republican family. Although I am a registered Democrat, I can see and feel the humanity on both sides. Happily, most people from both sides can agree on the need for honest elections.

What I discovered from working on this issue is how embedded the problem of election fraud is in our system, with voting machine companies that want to control their corporate profits and election supervisors and secretaries of state who want to defend their choice of voting machines and look good for the next election or appointment. In addition, other kinds of politicians, even presidential candidates, want to avoid looking at election fraud because they want to keep encouraging people to vote and make campaign donations. Added to that are the media corporations who avoid covering election fraud because they want the Republican and Democratic parties to buy ads. Nobody is willing to talk about the issue because, in a country based on corporations and proprietary information, everyone worries about losing their job or their profits.

Is Your Vote Being Counted?

Here is what I learned that I'm dedicated to informing people about. Every American citizen needs to know this.

Whether you vote electronically or by paper ballot, your vote is counted by a tabulator. In California, where I live, many people use absentee ballots to be sure they're voting on paper. You fill out this paper and you have a sense of confidence that your vote is going to count. After it is fed into an optical scan tabulating machine, the machine scans your ballot and records it on a memory card (storage device) or sends it electronically, especially outside of California, to a major tabulator at another location, just as electronic votes get sent. Election results can be tampered with at the optical scanner level, at the memory card level, and at the main tabulator level. In the case of memory cards, there have been instances in which a memory card was being driven to the main tabulator and another memory card was substituted along the way. Or the memory card can be rigged from the very beginning, as it was in Volusia County, Florida, where

Beverly Harris of Black Box Voting found minus 16,000 votes installed in the card for Al Gore.

Changing the results on the tabulator is the most efficient way to rig an election. A highly skilled computer person can communicate with a tabulator that is across the country and program the tabulator though sending a worm or a Trojan horse to flip votes or add or subtract votes and to disappear without a trace. It's very difficult to identify a problem with the tabulators because the company holds the source code as proprietary. The voting machine company won't let anyone, not even election supervisors, look at the source code, although it is officially kept in a jointly held escrow account. Whoever has access to the source code has a great chance of affecting election results.

Stolen Elections

Various investigators and whistleblowers have exposed the details of election fraud. Almost every whistleblower who has reported electronic voting machine fraud has lost business or their job, been taken to court, and endured great economic hardship after reporting what they had observed. Additionally, one investigator of a vote-flipping program organized by Bush and Congressman John Feeney of Florida, Ray Lemme, died in an "apparent suicide" in 2003. Two other people involved with our election system have also died under mysterious circumstances. One is a man named Athan Gibbs, the inventor of a new voting machine that provides a voter-verified paper audit trail, who was killed in a car crash in 2004, and the other, in 2008, Mike Connell, a Republican IT man of major proportions who worked for Karl Rove and the Bush family.

In May 2008, a highly distinguished Republican security expert, Stephen Spoonamore, dismayed by the apparent dishonesty he saw in the McCain campaign, told Velvet Revolution, an organization involved in tracking election fraud through mobilizing whistleblowers, that the 2008 presidential election appeared to be already rigged for McCain to win in six states. Mike Connell, the CEO of New Media Communications, who had been doing IT work for Karl Rove and the Bush family since 2000, was working with McCain and Rove, McCain's campaign manager on the 2008 presidential election. Spoonamore suspected that Rove, together with Connell, had organized the stealing of the 2000 and 2004 presidential elections as well as the disappearance of the 16,000 e-mails related to the controversial U.S. attorney firings in 2006.

On the Friday and Monday before Election Day 2008, in a Ohio lawsuit headed by attorney Cliff Arnebeck (see the accompanying piece by him), a Ohio federal judge compelled Mike Connell, after he had resisted two subpoenas, to appear in court to testify on the programs that he had set up to give Ohio to the Republicans in 2004. Spoonamore had written for this lawsuit two affidavits about what he had seen happen in Ohio in 2004 that helped the judge compel Mike Connell to appear in court.

Velvet Revolution had also been in communication with an anonymous tipster in the McCain campaign who was dismayed with the dishonesty he saw as well. He confirmed Spoonamore's suspicion that six states had been already rigged since at least May. The tipster also said that Rove was very uncomfortable that Velvet Revolution had been tracking Mike Connell for a year and a half and that Spoonamore had decided to reveal what he had seen in the presidential election of 2004. Although Mike Connell denied in his deposition that he had anything to do with affecting the election results of 2004, Rove reportedly decided over the weekend before the election not to activate the rigging that had been set in place because even conservative polls showed Obama ahead of McCain by more than 3 percent.

In May 2008, when I learned from Spoonamore, who I had met in 2006, that six states were rigged, I might not have taken it completely seriously. But when the tipster confirmed that six states were indeed rigged, I sadly closed my private practice to work full-time on this issue because I did not want to live in a country with yet another stolen presidential election.

The tipster also shared with Velvet Revolution that Rove had told Mike Connell that he and his wife would "be very sorry" if he did not take complete responsibility for everything that had happened in the 2004 election. The first threat involved getting both Mike Connell and his wife into jail and sending his kids to foster homes. The second threat, delivered later, involved "physical danger."

On December 19, 2008, Mike Connell, an experienced pilot, died in a plane crash in good weather in his fully instrumented Piper three miles from landing at his hometown airport. He had turned back from recent flights twice before due to suspicious things he noticed in his plane.

Safeguarding Elections

Because of these events and others on which I had firsthand information, I was too frightened to go public on these issues. I was well aware of the deaths that had occurred and the attacks on whistleblowers' lives. I was also advised not to say anything as it might hurt our efforts in bringing Rove to justice. So until recently, I worked entirely behind the scenes. (My work on this issue is entirely volunteer.) At this time, though, I am reaching out to other Americans to help make our elections more trustworthy. I do not like seeing the trustworthiness of our elections depend on a few private and under-funded citizens every other year. Burnout is very possible.

It is clear that citizens need to become watchdogs of their elections. In fact, highly suspicious information has emerged about the passage of Proposition 8 (banning gay marriage) in California in the 2008 election. There are huge differences of 25 to 35 percent between the exit polls done by a reputable nonprofit polling organization, Election Integrity, and the vote totals announced by ES & S, America's largest electronic voting machine company, which is owned by funda-mentalist Christians. This might have been prevented had there been many publicly supported exit polls taken in the state rather than only a few. California did not get much attention from Election Integrity because it was not considered a swing state. By contrast, in Ohio in that same election, vote manipulation was substantially lower due to citizen activism and participation. Other states can have this too. We need many citizens to be behind creating honest elections.

I began presenting on these topics in October 2008 through my organization Sunrise Center (www.sunrise-center.org) and have since expanded to other groups and gatherings in both California and Hawaii. I am open to presenting elsewhere as well. Here is a beginning prescription I'm promoting to election officials, politicians, and the general public to counteract election fraud:

1. Paper ballots.

2. Prohibiting tabulators from sending election data over the Internet.

3. Using only software certified by the Election Assistance Commission.

4. Publicly supported and audited exit polls (i.e., not propri-etary, in which the polling company is not required to reveal how they arrived at the vote totals).

5. Supervised manual recounts of 1% or, preferably, 3% of the total votes (as a random sample to check percentage differ-ence between winning and losing candidates or initiatives).

6. A responsive as opposed to resistant response from election officials when a citizen or candidate calls for an investigation of an election.

7. Reasonably priced recounts. If a candidate calls for a recount, raising the price of the recount eliminates a candidate with limited funds. A citizen can call for a recount of a proposition, such as Proposition 8 in California, but the recount costs are exorbitant.

You can investigate the issue of election integrity for yourself. Good sources of information are www.electiondefensealliance. org, www.openvotingconsortium.org, www.velvetrevolution.us, and www.bradblog.com. They are all run by private citizens and definitely need your financial support as well.

The Edgy Path

Though election work was something completely new for me, I had lived on the edge in other ways before, as I mentioned.

As a young woman, I felt very emotionally blocked. Seeking solutions, I got involved in the human potential movement, earned a bachelor's and then a master's in forms of psychology, and started running my own classes in dance therapy, which expanded into bioenergetics and Gestalt therapy. I also felt very sexually blocked for a variety of reasons. Tantra yoga helped me liberate my sexuality, and after extensive study, including in India, I became a Tantra teacher. Tantra is a spiritual path that enables you to weave different parts of the self together, interconnecting with a beloved partner, with all of community, and ultimately with all of life. It's very important to know about the spirituality in Tantra; the practice is not just a sexual strategy. A lot of people come to it for healing in that area because we're so wounded in our culture, but it is truly a spiritual path, for connecting to oneself, to others, and to God/spirit.

Then I had a child and I had to be private about my work because sexuality is not an open subject in our culture and I needed to protect my son. In our culture, there is not an archetype for a sexy single mother. In our culture, a sexy single mother is frequently seen as someone who neglects her children because she is out "messing around" or is possibly even carelessly exposing her child to sexual situations, contributing to the delinquency of a minor. There is not an image of a sexy single woman, much less a teacher of Tantra yoga, who is also very dedicated to her children. Again, I was out on the edge, doing something different, which made me vulnerable. There were people who made trouble for me during that time, but my son and I survived.

In my private practice, I had discovered that communication was as much a problem in relationships as sexuality was, so I studied different systems of communication. In 1999, I began working with Marshall Rosenberg's Nonviolent Communication (also called Compassionate Communication). I found that particular system the most heart-centered and the easiest to learn and to teach. I liked that it had a wide view of the world. Marshall was teaching all over the world, helping people learn how to communicate, and creating peace at all different levels. I also liked that the teachers of this method weren't charging a lot for their work. In looking for a system and an organization involved in social change, I wanted something that was affordable for a lot of people. In integrating Compassionate Communication with my Tantra teaching, I found that the amount of peace, joy, efficiency, productivity in work environments, and closeness with others all increased. It had that effect in my life as well.

At that point, many of my clients were older than I and were going through hormonal shifts. I began to study aging and the shifts that happen hormonally. I developed alliances with holistically oriented physicians who were using nutritional strategies, which I had always been interested in, and bioidentical hormones (those that are biochemically identical to the hormones in the human body) to slow biological aging in both men and women.

From this I learned that if you believe that the changes going on in your body are just part of "normal" aging, then you will not look outside the box to the view of "That may be normal, but I have no interest in 'normal' aging. I have an interest in optimal aging." For instance, in 2002, I started developing osteopenia, according to a dexa (bone density) scan. Osteopenia is beginning osteoporosis. I was already exercising, lifting weights, and taking a calcium-magnesium-vitamin D supplement, that is, already following a lifestyle to protect against bone loss. Unfortunately, I also have some mild genetic factors for bone loss. When I learned that I had osteopenia, I used bioidentical hormones and the same supplements I had been taking before to treat the condition. Two years later, a dexa scan revealed that I no longer had osteopenia. In fact, my bones are stronger in some places than women aged twenty-nine and younger. If I had gone to an ordinary doctor, I would have gotten Fosamix, the conventional drug that produces inferior bone material and has side effects.

In another example of in-the-box versus out-of-the-box thinking, one of the signs of declining estrogen levels in women, and in men, is depression. The conventional strategy is to prescribe an antidepressant (usually a selective serotonin reuptake inhibitor [SSRI] such as Prozac), which doesn't deal with the underlying hormonal cause.

In my case, from a baseline test of my neurotransmitters, I learned that my serotonin level was down, just as it is in a lot of women my age. In me, it manifested as lower quality sleep and some anxiety. I started taking the amino acid tryptophan and vitamin B6 on a regular basis. A year later, I repeated the test and my neurotransmitter levels were excellent. Instead of taking a drug that actually interferes with the uptake process in the brain, I gave my body the food it needed to make more serotonin.

As a result of my antiaging research and personal experience, I espouse quality testing and the use of bioidentical hormones. Hormones are very powerful systems so I encourage working with an overseeing physician who is educated in testing and in nutritional and hormonal methods for creating better balance and health. Many doctors don't know about bioidentical hormones. Again, we're dealing with the corporate world. Our pharmaceutical companies are in bed with our medical schools and continuing education for physicians.

The Audacious Cassandra

My research led me to the next edge. I was increasingly aware of the fact that I was teaching breathing exercises and the air people were inhaling was contaminated with toxic substances. Around that time, I saw a slideshow by Al Gore about all the implications of the state of our environment. I applied to study with Al Gore and I became one of his one thousand foot soldiers giving presentations on global warming. I also started teaching about green lifestyle changes to live more simply on the earth. I was already an environmentalist and aware of many of the issues, but this added a new level of commitment and action.

I couldn't keep teaching Tantra and working in the personal sector without taking the broader world into consideration. When the very government that was making it even worse for us to have a clean planet had been brought in through stealing, I felt impelled to act. I began to work for more integrity in our elections. If I had chosen to continue teaching people only about Tantra yoga when I had the awareness of what was going on, including our stolen elections and global warming, I would have felt like Nero fiddling while Rome burned.

My role throughout my life seems to have been to explore frontiers and come back to report to others on what I find. Sometimes, particularly with the issues around the elections, I've felt like

Cassandra warning people about the Trojan horse and not being believed. That, too, seems to be part of the role. Nonetheless, it has been incredibly exciting to explore new territories and to see the changes in people and their lives through the work I've done.

Lena Horne—legendary singer, actor, and activist against racial injustice—
began her career at the Cotton Club but soon moved on to Café Society
(another New York nightclub that featured black performers but which, unlike
the Cotton Club, welcomed black audiences). Though the first African American
to sign a long-term contract with a major Hollywood studio, she was never
given a leading role because of her race. She became an outspoken critic of
Hollywood's color barriers and was blacklisted in the McCarthy era for her
political views. Lena Horne was born on June 30, 1917, in Brooklyn, New York.

LENA HORNE

Several Lifetimes in One Life

Never paid much attention to film work, except when I was working with Vincent Minnelli. My film work was so truncated and limited because of the prevailing racism. I preferred cabaret work because I could communicate directly with the audience. I realized it first at Café Society in 1940. I felt that I was in control as a performer for the first time.

At the age of two, I became the youngest lifetime member of the NAACP. Naturally, I didn't know what it was all about at the age of two, but I have horrible memories of being in the South with my mother, who toured as an actress.

I grew up attending integrated schools in Brooklyn with mostly white teachers. I liked some of them so much—Mrs. LeBaron, my art teacher, and Mr. Young, my tough Latin teacher—that I wanted to be a teacher. My grandmother had been a teacher so she encouraged my ambition. She stressed education above all. She died before I went into show business—she would have been horrified! But teaching and show business aren't necessarily that far apart. We remember great teachers the way we remember great performers. I've forgotten most of the names I knew, but not the names of my favorite teachers.

As an adult, Café Society became my civil rights training ground. Barney Josephson, who ran the place, wouldn't let me sing "Sleepy Down South," for example. And I met Paul Robeson and Walter White, who had been friends of my grandmother. They both explained to me that I couldn't work just for myself, but for so many other people. They told me I didn't have the luxury of white performers, of working for my personal success alone—but I had to think about sharecroppers and Pullman porters.

I didn't rebel, because the family lesson had already been instilled in me. I was used to being obedient. It hit me hard during the Second World War, when I saw for myself how horribly black GIs were treated—worse than the enemy. I was kicked out of the USO for refusing to sing at a camp in Arkansas where black GIs were forced to sit behind German POWs to see the show. That was a big moment for me, because it made me wonder what we were fighting for.

Blacklisting after the war was another difficult time. It seemed to me that civil rights activist were being targeted—that it was "subversive" and "un-American" to want black people to be treated like human beings and citizens.

The civil rights movement of the 1960s was only another part of the process, though certainly the most powerful. I was with Medgar Evers in Mississippi two days before he was murdered. I must say, after that I almost gave up hope. Obviously, many things have changed for the better. But entrenched inequality still exists, especially in economic and educational opportunities.

I believe that the whole anti-affirmative action movement is a way to return to racism and Jim Crow. Racism is imbedded in America. Alabama just voted [in 2004] to keep its Jim Crow laws on the books.

Unfortunately, I am no longer optimistic about things getting better for the people that Paul Robeson and Walter White told me I was really working for. The saddest thing is that there are no more great civil rights leaders, because it seems the people really can't do it by themselves.

The advantages in old age? I could have answered that in my sixties, when I was most happy as a performer, and when my grandchildren recognized me as a performer.

Am I looking for something new? Yes, I'm always looking to see new things in people—especially politicians.

Advice for the young? Realize that you will live several lifetimes in one life. You may be one person at twenty, another at sixty, another at eighty.

Nancy Wilson said, "Everyone sees Lena Horne as a beautiful, sophisticated lady, but there is a fierce lioness in this woman." Well, I'm old and I'm still angry. And if there is a "lioness" inside, it's because not everybody had a grandmother like mine.

Jean Houston, PhD, is a scholar, philosopher, researcher in human capacities, and author of twenty-six books, including *A Passion for the Possible and Jump Time: Shaping Your Future in a World of Radical Change*. She is also the founder and principal teacher since 1982 of the Mystery School, dedicated to human development and cross-cultural, mythic, and spiritual studies. Since 2003, she has been working with the United Nations Development Program, training leaders in developing countries worldwide in the new field of social artistry. She was born on May 10, 1937, in New York City.

JEAN HOUSTON

CHAPTER 21

The Journey
of Transformation

W e are living at a new edge in history. This is the great turning point, and what we do will make a profound difference as to whether we live or whether we die. As a cultural historian, I have to say there is nothing so far as we know in any of the arenas of human history that compares with this time. It is indeed as if we are the people on the edge of history, where what we do will not only make a difference, it will have to do with the continuance of our species, of all other species, and of much of the life on planet Earth. We have no choice but to be audacious. We must risk in decision and action as well as go deep into ourselves to find the ideas and the patterns of possibility to bring into this time.

The audacity required of us today is a level of courage, a level of compassion we've never had to have before, and a sense of being able to experience the new. Most of us live five to ten to a hundred times the amount of sheer experience of our ancestors of a hundred to a hundred fifty years ago, but even with that, most of us are unprepared for this time. What is required of us at this turning point is a great deal of constant learning and constantly being available to the unexpected, which means available in ways that people haven't been before.

We are going to have very long lives. Adolescence doesn't end till you're thirty-one or forty. You don't know a darn thing till you're about fifty-five or sixty. The years after that are the years in which you can bring your humanity to bear upon the great issues of our time. And I think that people of a certain age have to be reempowered to do so.

I've worked in over a hundred countries and in many indigenous cultures where people of a certain age are honored; having the breadth of life and the depth of life, they are felt to know more. In societies in which time is accelerated, however, the people of a certain age are treated as though they belong to the nineteenth century. That is changing, but so many people are living past a certain age now. When they were few, they were honored. Now that they are many, we're in that great parenthesis where we have lots of people and we don't know what to do with them because if at seventy, eighty, and even ninety, you feel your life and your energy full within you, what do you do with it?

It's not unlike the story in Parsifal, one of the Grail stories, where Parsifal crosses a bridge and the bridge ends right in the middle of the lake. What is he going to do? Suddenly, the bridge swings back over to the next shore. Many people are at the place where evolution says they're supposed to be dead or they're supposed to be calming down. They are neither, and if they're put off in little sunny coves with golf courses, it doesn't work. If they're made to just take care of the grandchildren all the time, it doesn't necessarily work. So this bridge is swinging over to the other side with people having had so much more experience than anybody has ever had in human history and they can't just be dumped. There need to be new professions and new ideas—and the new professions are not just volunteerism.

In the late 1960s, I helped create with my best friend, Gay Luce, something called SAGE, Senior Actualization and Growth Exploration, where people who were well in excess of eighty began to appreciate their bodies again, to begin to tell their story, and to begin to take on new life purposes. We found that given the stimulus, given the lure of becoming, given restoration to the love of life, they came back in remarkable ways. We need new patterns and new paradigms for what life beyond seventy is.

The new paradigm needs to include lifelong education; that means both learning and teaching. Grandpersons as educators are very important in this time because so many people who are well over fifty, certainly well over sixty, find that they have been through more history for the human race than their own grandparents could have ever known.

Many years ago, Margaret Mead [Margaret Mead was a mentor and close friend] and I developed a program with Carol Tice in Michigan to create teaching-learning communities in schools, where grandpersons, and some of them were really pretty grand, became educators. So a man who was in his eighties went into the school and he had a generalized affection for and availability to all the children in ways that the harassed twenty-five-year-old teacher did not. We asked, "What can you do with these children?" His answer was "Well, I can teach birdhouse building." So he taught them birdhouse building, and suddenly these children felt seen and loved. It made an enormous difference. Then there was this tiny ninety-year-old

Chinese lady who taught Chinese to great big black kids. They were about three feet taller than she and it was marvelous watching the interaction. She offered a capacity for loving everybody and having time for the young people. It's a different order of time and timing that comes in with aging.

Myth and Mystery

To age audaciously today is to have a breadth of life previously unknown in human history, and at the same time to have access to your own depths, so that you can bring both inner and outer ecologies to bear upon issues. There is a rising of the depths all over. The psyche has been breached. In any kind of renaissance or radical time of renewal, which we are in, the psyche is always breached and the symbols of the unconscious are up there either to be expressed musically, esthetically, and scientifically, as in the European Renaissance, or to be repressed and feared and explode.

Studying the mysteries gives us perspective on our human condition—our past, our present, our emergent future—that we don't get from ordinary education. There are all kinds of mysteries, not only the mysteries that we think of as esoteric. There are the mysteries of the depths and complexity of the body, of the brain, of the mind, of the soul, of purpose, and of destiny, and the mysteries that are contained in the genius of so many different cultures. In my work, we combine the cognitive understanding of these things with a great many experiential processes, exercises that grow the mind, the body, and the spirit in ways that allow for the stimulus of who and what we are to become, what we really yet can be, because we are a process. Then each person can take this into the world and apply it in new ways.

When I work in many cultures, I try to find what is each culture's key or core myth, and then weave developmental processes on at least four levels—sensory and physical, psychological, symbolic, and spiritual—to enhance growth in the individual and in the community. People will go much further and deeper if they are growing within the matrix of the story, especially a mythic story, than they will if it's just a didactic series of exercises. The myth gives us very large story, which a lot of people lack, especially as they get older because the story changes. A myth gives you a journey, it gives you a ritual of transformation, it gives you stages in the process of becoming, it allows you to confront every possible shadow. It really gives you, in an intense coded way, the entire human comedy and the human dilemma. A myth is something that never was but is always happening. It's part of the coded DNA of the human psyche.

Mythic story is also key to the connection of people around the globe, especially because the story is shifting universally. It's no longer the lonely young hero battling his toxicities to get to the beloved. It's men and women together; it's all ages; it's all cultures and races; it's the Earth herself who is the beloved.

The Rising Feminine

I've been enormously blessed in knowing some of the great elders of the time: Margaret Mead, Pierre Teilhard de Chardin, Buckminster Fuller, Arnold Toynbee, Aldous Huxley, and great theologians such as Paul Tillich, with whom I studied. I've always been drawn to the elders. Because I appreciated them, they hung out with me and talked to me, from the time I was three. I had an experience at three years old that has always stayed with me. It was at a July Fourth parade, in Indiana, I think. There were still a few old Civil War veterans in their bleached-out gray and blue uniforms—by that point, they all liked each other. A very old man, probably well up in his nineties, who had probably been a very young soldier in the Confederate army, came up to me. He was very tall and spindly. He reached down and shook hands with me, and he said, "Young lady, you're shaking the hand that shook the hand of my Pappy, and my Pappy shook the hand of Thomas Jefferson."

My high school was five blocks from where Eleanor Roosevelt lived in Manhattan. She held at her house and elsewhere gatherings of young people who were presidents of their High School General organizations. I was there often and she would talk to us about the United Nations, about getting involved in international work. Once she turned to me and said, "My dear, I rather suspect you're going to have a very interesting professional life, but, my dear, remember, women in this time who are out in front can expect to get trashed." She didn't use the word "trashed," but it was something like that. Then she said, "Remember, my dear, a woman is just like a teabag. You put her in hot water and she just gets stronger."

Actually, the only time in my life that I experienced my gender as an issue was during the whole Clinton debacle when the discussions Hillary and I were having in the White House were made into something they weren't. Talking to Eleanor Roosevelt was just a little role-playing game. [Jean and Hillary were pilloried in the press for, among other things, trying to talk to the dead.] Half my professional life was taken out almost overnight as a result of what was made out of that simple role-playing. If my name had been spelled "Gene" and Hillary had been "Harry," I don't think any of that would have happened. It was the fear of the female, the rising feminine, especially Hillary who has so much power. What are these women up to in the solarium of the White House? What are they talking about? What are they plotting? What mysterious mysteries are they into that the men don't know about? I think it was the fear of the female who is unknown and the fear of the mystery of the feminine in a patri- archal society.

But that's the only time in my life I've ever run into it. The men among the great elders I knew were too wise and too deep to regard a woman in a cavalier fashion. Paul Tillich, for example, was always in awe of women. Jonas Salk kept talking about the survival of the wisest, of the wise women. Of course, the biggest change in human history is right now, with women slowly but surely rising to full part- nership with men in the whole domain of human affairs.

One of the things I find all over the world is that it is women of a certain age who by and large are the ones making a difference. They're out there leading the projects; they're forming the volunteer associations; they're taking the initiatives, especially with regard to the millennium development goals. They are not afraid; they are past worry about getting wounded or having their souls hurt. They're out there making the difference and they bring the young people along with them.

They are practicing social artistry. Social artistry is the bringing of the same kind of passion, commitment, and focused skill that an artist brings to his or her materials, but in this case the materials are the social canvas. This is absolutely what is required at this time in human history. In 2007, I received a mandate from Dr. Monica Sharma, director of Leadership and Capacity Development for the United Nations, to train ten thousand people all over the world in my work in social artistry who in turn will be required to train a hundred million people.

I have hope about the outcome of this crucial time in our history because when I go into a society or a culture, I'm generally there or back and forth for a period of time, so I get to see what is really going on. I see not only the rising feminine, but also people getting together in ongoing teaching-learning communities, volunteer associations, and widespread understanding of the great passion play of the earth at this time—the need to join together in greater wholes. It's this interwoven world that we've never had before. That and having an opportunity to, in a sense, take depth soundings of the psyche of so many different peoples and places have given me hope and a kind of perspective on the great shifts of history. I just don't believe that the human experiment is going to end in a flash of light anytime soon. But there's no question that we are at the great either/or of history right now. It's not for nothing that people talk about 2012 and the next few years being the time of decision.

Lisa Schuetz Kuimjian is a graphotherapist and certified graphologist. She has dedicated her life to investigating the neuroscience of thought and the reading of the energy of thought through scriptural (drawing or writing) movement. She is currently pursuing graduate studies in Jungian psychology at the Saybrook Institute (Saybrook Graduate School and Research Center). She was born on February 10, 1958, in Milwaukee, Wisconsin.

Lisa Schuetz Kuimjian

Reading the Energy of Thought

What we think, we become.

—Buddha

A man is but the product of his thoughts. What he thinks, he becomes.

—Mahatma Gandhi

For thousands of years in recorded history, all the great theologians, scientists, and philosophers have agreed on one point and possibly only one point, which is: What we think about, comes about. Our thoughts are the creative energy behind what we manifest in our lives. Unfortunately, an estimated 98 percent of daily functioning and thinking is unconscious, reflexive action, otherwise known as habit. Many of us are unknowingly living a life that isn't of our making, a life created by internalization of the worldviews of our parents and the mass culture in which we live.

Given that our thoughts determine what we manifest in life and that most of what we think is unconscious and unintentional, we cannot begin to change our lives until we discover the content of our thinking. Sadly, when most people tune in to their unconscious thoughts, they discover that the majority are self-defeating patterns of thinking, or what I call "thought energy." As long as our thought energy is self-defeating, we will not be able to create what we truly want in life. Only when we become aware of our self-defeating thought energy can we begin to reprogram it to support our greatest potential rather than undermine it.

Though many people associate aging with purely physical events of the body, the more important aspect is the call to life's greater task of finding where it is that our spirit lies. Aging entails more that adding years to our lives; it requires that with each passing year we become a fuller expression of who we are meant to be. Living an optimal life necessitates growing and evolving so that our emotional age matches our chronological age. By consciously taking responsibility for how we think and navigate through life, we are able to engage life to the fullest. It is in this full engagement that the body, mind, and spirit thrive, and we live and age audaciously.

To wake up to our unconscious patterns so we can move toward full engagement, we need a method of objectively assessing our habits of thought. Since the body and mind are inextricably linked, we can use our physiology both to understand and to change our psychology. This approach is the basis of biofeedback and other self-directed modalities such as dance therapy, art therapy, and the brain-wave entrainment called neuroacoustics. These methods work by utilizing the plastic nature of our brain, that is, its inherent ability to reorganize itself in response to new situations or changes in environment. This quality of the human brain is called neuroplasticity.

Graphotherapy (also called graphocybernetics) is another self-modification method that utilizes the brain's neuroplasticity. Graphotherapy is the application of graphology (the science of handwriting) to psychological problems. It is based on the existence of a bidirectional relationship between the hand and the brain, which means the brain communicates with the hand and vice versa.

All Is Revealed

Graphic gestures, which include handwriting, doodles, and drawings, are records of thought energy. These expressive gestures offer unfiltered, uncontaminated information about our subconscious drives, innate temperament, and possible neuroses or energy blocks. We can "read" this energy for diagnosis and manipulate it for the purpose of healing.

The piece of paper on which an individual writes represents that person's world. Thus how we put strokes on paper mimics how we see ourselves in the world and how we move through it. Handwriting is basically "brainwriting." How we express ourselves on paper originates not from our hand but from neural impulses from our subconscious. Our movements on paper give us direct information into the organization of our brain and the state of our energy field, that is, the energy state of our emotions and thoughts.

We can use the bidirectional relationship between body and mind to gain insight into ourselves and others. In fact, most of us already do this in everyday life in the reading of voice quality and body language such as facial expressions, gait, gesticulation, and posture. Handwriting is one of the many expressive gestures that humans make and it is one that supplies a permanent record, a snapshot in time of the state of balance or imbalance of our body, mind, and spirit.

A flexible, integrated, balanced brain is outwardly evidenced by fluidity and gracefulness in our handwriting and other movements of our body. The quality of our voice and expressive gestures such as facial expressions, gait, gesticulation, and posture also reflect the state of organization and integration in the brain. Thus a velvety voiced singer is sure to have a smooth gait, expressive hands, and a flowing script. A person that walks haltingly and with rigidity is sure to speak in a choppy voice and write with a non-flowing script.

How we adorn and embellish our writing, the extraneous qualities our strokes have, and whether there is balance or imbalance in our stroke formation provide a window into how our brain is operating and the state of balance in the body, mind, and spirit. To sum up the basics of graphotherapy, writing is a series of straight and curved lines that are either moving away from us (expansion) or moving toward us (contraction). Very generally, the goal of the prescribed hand movement exercises in graphotherapy is to create balance between the contraction and expansion or release. When in our handwriting there is balance between straightness and curvedness, balance between expansive movements and contracted movements, balance in the different parts of stroke formation, and a balanced use of space on the paper, we are balanced energetically and emotionally.

Balance indicates adaptability and the ability to see reality, whereas imbalance indicates the opposite as unconscious fears and projections constrict us and cloud our perception. When balance is present, our core motivation is love. With imbalance, our motivation is fear-based. Just as we appear "guarded" when assuming the posture of crossed arms and hunched shoulders, our writing strokes reflect this same contraction of energy. When our stance is outstretched arms and open hands, our handwriting shows expansive, full, rounded strokes.

The Polarities of the Psyche

The psyche is a self-regulating energy system, and as with all such systems, it functions on the principle of polarity. Some of the major paired energies operating within us that we can readily see and interpret from writing are intensity and relaxation, objective/logical/yang and subjective/emotional/yin, and intellectual and physical.

• Intensity

Notice the squeezed appearance and rigid-looking formations in the following writing sample. This indicates tension, "uptightness." The individual may be emotionally inhibited or overly controlled in expression of thoughts and feelings, which results in narrowness of thinking.

• Relaxation

Notice the relaxed look of the following writing sample and the garland shapes at the base of letters. The garland is the most practical, quick, easy, natural, and agreeable way of connecting two letters. Some qualities associated with formations like these are naturalness, friendliness, talkativeness, adaptability, an easygoing nature, and a benevolent personality. Just as the gesture of an open, cupped hand conveys a sense of one reaching out in a friendly manner, this open, cupped-shape connection indicates the same in writing.

If the writing's form looks overly relaxed, as in the following, the person may lack mental control and focus and be highly impulsive.

• Objective/Logical/Yang

In the following sample, notice the small size and clear spacing, which indicates that emotions are kept out of the decision-making process.

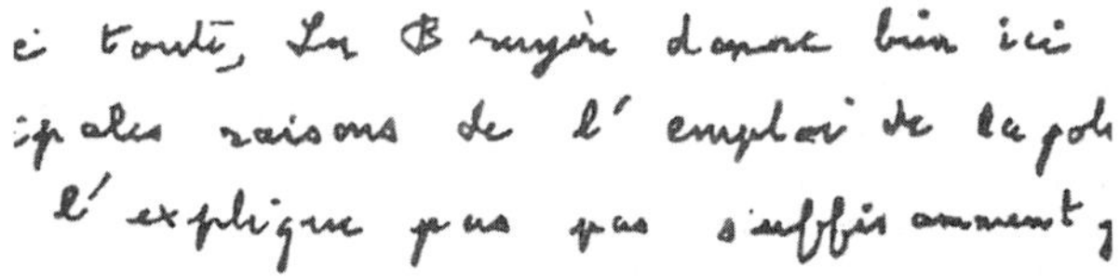

[handwritten sample in cursive script]

• **Subjective/Emotional/Yin**

In the following sample, notice the middle zone size (see the next section on zones) and the crowded spacing, which indicates that emotions influence thinking.

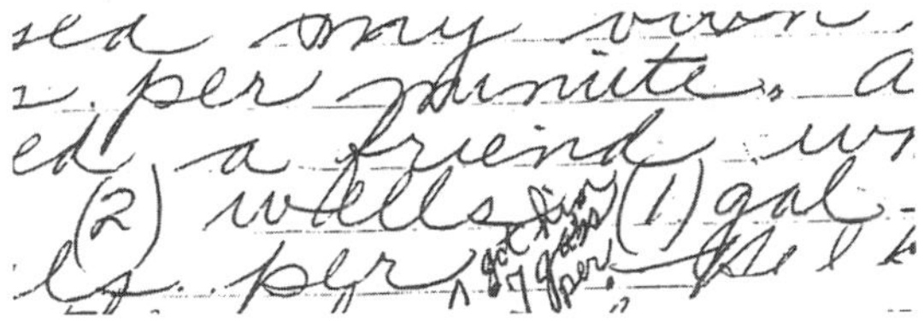

[handwritten sample]

• **Intellectual**

In these samples, notice the emphasis in the upper zone (see the following section) loops of letters *h, d, b, l,* and *k,* which indicates that a disproportionate amount of energy is spent in the world of conscious ideas, intellect, and philosophical ideals.

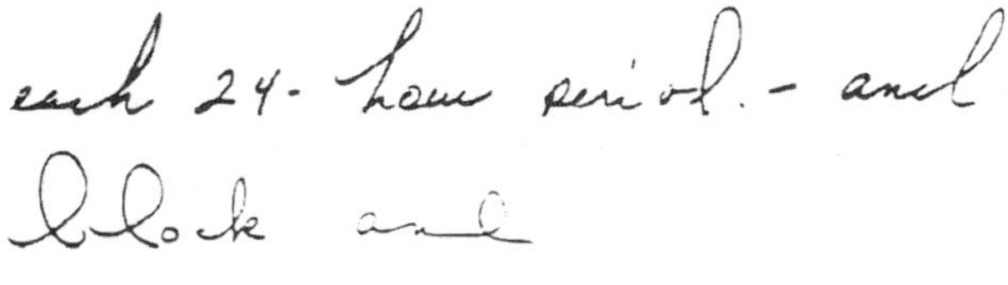

[handwritten sample]

• **Physical**

In the following samples, notice the emphasis in the lower zone loops of *y* and *g,* which indicates the flow of energy into unconscious motives as well as things of a more physical nature. These writers prefer the concrete over the theoretical, are often practical minded, security conscious, and in need of physical activity.

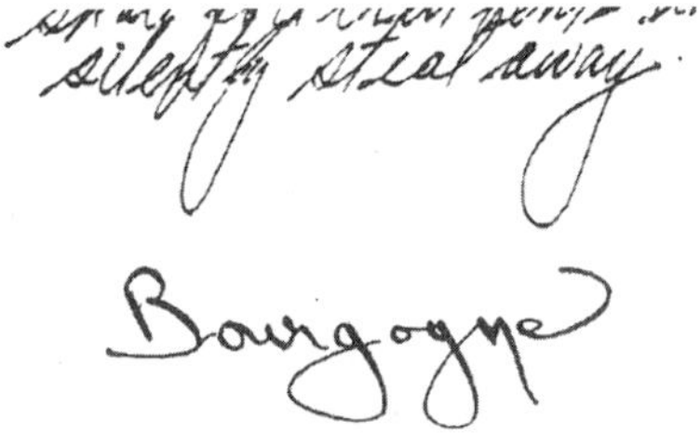

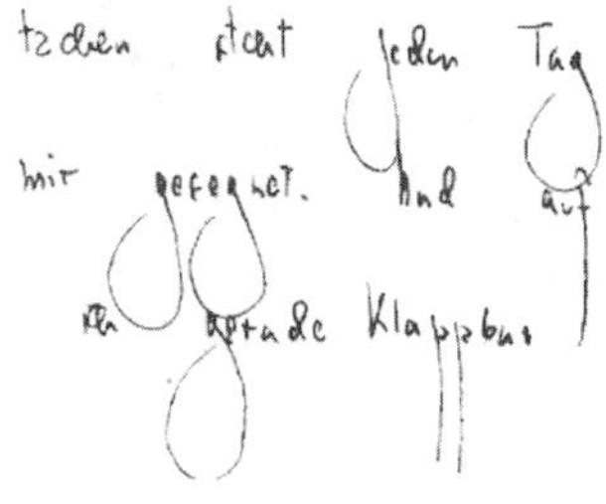

[handwritten samples]

• The Zones of Writing

Spatial zones in handwriting reveal further important information. By looking at how our writing makes use of these zones—lower, middle, and upper—we are able to see where our energy is devoted as well as how balanced or imbalanced that energy is. A major indicator of healthy functioning is the ability of a person to maintain balance between the physical, emotional, and mental/spiritual aspects of life—a balanced life. The following handwriting sample illustrates the different spatial zones and the arena of life with which each is associated.

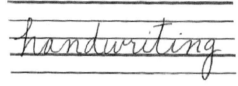

Upper Zone: Intellectual interests, Spiritual awareness, Philosophy
Middle Zone: Everyday routine, Social behaviors
Lower Zone: Materialistic interests, Physical needs, Instincts, Unconscious/subconscious

Balanced use of the upper, middle, and lower zones indicates a balance of energy in the areas of life. An individual who writes in this way is typically able to adapt to various situations and cope with adversity, and is viewed by others as someone who "has it together."

Any zonal area that is overdeveloped or underdeveloped reveals an imbalance in the corresponding area of the writer's life. Excessive energy devoted to one area of life is represented in writing by excessively large, long, or heavy strokes in the zonal area relative to that aspect. Similarly, a denial or repression of any aspect of life is represented by short, tiny, light, or compressed strokes in the writing zone relative to that aspect. An exaggeration in one zone indicates a lessening of interest in one or both of the other zones, or areas of life.

If the upper zone is emphasized at the expense of the other two, the writer is likely a person of intelligence and ambition (someone "reaching for the sky") but not emotionally mature enough (contributions of the middle zone) or physically determined enough (contribution of the lower zone) to carry out her plans successfully. This person can't realistically bring ideas into fruition. This type of zonal emphasis is shown in the "intellectual" sample in the previous section.

An enlarged middle zone at the expense of the upper and lower zones reveals that the writer is overly concerned with himself and his daily activities (see the following sample). This energy is in the area of the ego. This doesn't indicate a strong ego, however, rather, an emphasis on self-survival, the ego's need for recognition. Selfishness

is indicated and this person is literal-minded, that is, not able to deal well with abstract concepts.

The sample shows that this writer's flow of life energy is devoted to everyday, mundane routines. Notice how most of the writing, most of the psychic energy, falls between the green lines. The writing of adolescent girls often exhibits this trait. If seen in a woman's writing, it may indicate that emotional maturity doesn't match chronological age.

(Note: The sample on the right is Princess Diana's handwriting.)

Emphasis on the lower zone indicates an individual who is dominated by survival needs, materialism, sexuality, and the need for emotional expression, which is evidenced in the following handwriting sample in the length and width of the loops on *y*, *f*, and *g*. Notice the relative length of this zone compared to that of the middle zone, as indicated by the red arrows.

(Note: This is a sample of killer Ted Bundy's writing.)

The handwriting of a well-integrated, mature, self-actualized person will reflect that balance in a balanced use of the spatial zones, as in the following writing sample of the venerable French explorer and ascetic Father de Foucauld.

Notice the zonal balance as indicated by the markings in the third line. This writing is an example not only of zonal balance, but of spatial balance as well. Balance, harmony, and lack of unnecessary embellishment indicate a highly evolved, self-actualized personality. People who are answering the call of their lives and living their soul's higher purpose would have these qualities evident in their writing. This harmonious, balanced use of space tells of one who is able to move through life gracefully, coming from a motivation of love rather than fear.

A Tool for Transformation

Our higher Self, our soul's calling, is shown in life by the absence of egoism, pride, distrust, and fear. The Self is revealed little by little as the ego is effaced. The more our internal polarities are lessened, the more evident and real the Self becomes and the less extreme our handwriting movements are. The more our writing loses its large, exaggerated strokes, its loops, and any other unnecessary addition to a stroke beyond what is required to make the letter identifiable, the more simplified and harmonious our writing becomes, while still remaining alive and expressive, the closer we are to our true Self, our authentic being, our essence.

With this valuable energetic insight, this external picture of the subconscious mind along with its self-defeating tendencies of contraction and fear, we can utilize graphotherapy as a modality for transformation. By changing your writing movements, you can change old unconscious patterns that create conflict within you or make you less efficient. As startling as this concept may seem, it is indeed true that consistently repeated writing strokes will affect your unconscious, either in a positive or negative manner. By voluntarily making changes in your handwriting movements, you send a message to your unconscious and the signal, when repeated consistently, will awaken a response and begin the corresponding changes within you the writer.

For example, if your writing is highly contracted, "uptight" writing, as in the earlier handwriting sample, it would be helpful for you to engage in hand movements that aid the release of energy such as:

These types of movement help release tension and constriction. Over time, with the proper series of exercises done with the proper frequency and duration, the release felt in the hand will be mirrored in your psychology by instilling a more relaxed attitude and less mental constriction.

If your writing is overly relaxed, as in the earlier sample, indicating lack of mental focus, graphotherapy would introduce hand movements such as the following:

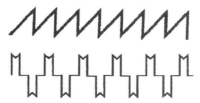

These movements help increase concentration and instill mental discipline. The top movement also has a calming effect due to its monotony. The bottom movement is used to foster control of behavior as well as resoluteness in decision-making. Certain movements impact the brain's organization in specific ways so we are able to address specifically what we need to strengthen or develop.

The following illustrates the happy medium in writing (*after*), which is neither too tight (first *before*) nor too loose (second *before*), and reflects balance within the writer.

Retraining the Brain

Research demonstrates that hand movements can, in fact, retrain the brain. Dr. Rudolf Pophal, a German neurologist and graphologist, has proven through extensive studies that the rhythmic, interactive, repetitive manipulation of thumbs and fingers impacts the brain on both the physiological and psychological level. Repetitive handwriting movements first activate and engage the brain's lower level. This neural data is then transmitted through the emotional brain to the higher brain.

Science is now showing that we can develop our ability to self-regulate via the process of rewiring our brain. Through reprogramming our brain's neural circuitry, we reprogram our thinking. Science tells us that brain structure determines function. Just as we can change the programs on our computer, we can change the programs in our brain. The structure of the computer program determines the end results we can get. The structure of our brain's neural circuitry determines our thoughts, feelings, and behaviors. New neural connections mean new ways of thinking, and as our thinking changes, so do our results in life.

The concept is by no means new. The Greeks devised an ingenious system of *grapho-therapy*, which they used to enhance performance in sports and battle. Leonardo Da Vinci knew the importance of developing ambidexterity to aid his thinking. In 1929, Dr. Pierre Janet and Charles Henry of the Sorbonne in Paris conducted clinical tests on the efficacy of graphic psychotherapy. Dealing principally with alcoholics and correcting bad habits in children, the experiments confirmed that handwriting therapy, intelligently and conscientiously applied, has impressive positive results. In 1950, the Parisian doctor Camille Streletzki reported on the applicability of graphotherapy (known also in France as graphological re-education) in the treatment of depression, insecurity, phobias, fears, inability to concentrate, anorexia, and hypochondria. In Germany, graphotherapy has been used successfully in clinical settings for learning disabilities (including dyslexia) and neuroses in children, anorexia, phobias, stammering, bed-wetting, and antisocial behavior.

The Heroic Journey of the Soul

In the first half of life, we answer to an egoic call to fit into society in an attempt to be safe and comfortable. The second half begins when we hear the larger cry of our soul, our spirit begging for us to become who we are meant to be. No longer do we equate who we are with what we do or what we possess. Rather, we begin to realize something far greater than title or material wealth: the ability to live a life of integrity, which means congruency of mind, body, and spirit.

To live an optimal life we are required to engage in the heroic journey of our soul. Reading our thought energy as contained in handwriting and working with this energy to bring more balance lights the way. This hero's journey, the journey into our wholeness, is the path of audacious aging. By choosing this path, we not only find peace within ourselves but also contribute to peace and a higher level of consciousness in the world.

Patt Lind-Kyle, MA, is a teacher, consultant, and innovator in the use of brain/mind research to teach people meditation and mental tools for transforming their lives and communities. A meditator for thirty-five years, she has followed, through multiple careers, her passion to question, explore, research, and then create programs and methods that enhance the lives of others. Author of *When Sleeping Beauty Wakes Up,* she is currently at work on a new book, *Conscious Mind, Conscious Brain: Mental Tools to Change Your Life.* Patt Lind-Kyle was born on May 4, 1937, in Duluth, Minnesota.

PATT LIND-KYLE

Building Community from the Inside Out

After decades of exploring and creating ways to serve people, I now have an audacious passion for working with individuals and groups in silence. The beauty of sitting in silence is that the brain-mind map is so clear that people readily open to discovering their inner landscape when they start this practice. It is such a joy to see the settling of the mind and an inner resolve as individuals discover how to explore the great potential that exists in each of us. And I still watch in amazement as mental and physical healing occurs naturally when all brain functions are moving together in harmony.

As I look back on my life, the driving passion of it has been service and learning. Formerly a dental hygienist, I became a college professor in the health sciences, then a psychotherapist. In the early seventies, I wanted to understand how people learn so I created a learning center to teach kids and adults how they learn most effectively. Out of my study and focus on learning, I saw that people in corporations were struggling to be themselves, so I built a corporate executive consulting and therapy practice primarily focused on women executives. After years of a personal meditation practice and an astounding six-month long silent retreat, I realized there had to be another way for people to explore their inner world and establish what I call "Home Base" within themselves.

In search of this way, I created an eighteen-month study of women, exploring the difference between ordinary consciousness and spiritual consciousness. Through this research and further study about how the brain works, I discovered that we can functionally and structurally change our behavior, thoughts, and attitudes by changing our mental patterns. I learned that the harmony of the mind and the pattern of our thoughts have a significant impact on our health and mental well-being. I learned how stress interrupts the inner flow of our lives. And through my experiences with others in meditation, I learned how we can build community from the inside out, from our hearts and minds into the world around us.

When we have the opportunity to meditate together, it changes our lives. We build a kind of community that affects the human spirit. When asked what part spiritual community plays in the lives of participants, Buddha answered that the community is the whole of spiritual life, while meditation itself is only half. Group meditation develops a positive environment that opens people to accepting each other in a deep, caring way. As we age, it is so important for us to have meaning in our lives and rich connection with others. This is what happens when you build a community from the inside out.

Illness and Stillness

My journey to building community from the inside out began twenty years ago when I was quite suddenly felled by chronic fatigue. At that time, most doctors were not familiar with chronic fatigue syndrome and could not help me. I had to discover how to heal myself. Through many starts and stops, I discovered how to do so by focusing on the physical, mental, emotional, and spiritual aspects of my life. Though I was not aware of it at the time, I healed myself by following the way the brain works. In my years of study since then, I've come to understand how that healing happened. One of the most important aspects of my healing was using meditation to remove the negative thoughts about myself and help bring my body back into a natural balance. Today as I work with individuals and groups in the silence I know from my own experience that the mind heals the mind. I also know that the silence of meditation increases flexibility, clarity, and positiveness in problem-solving and decision-making. In my journey through illness, meditation also showed me that how I nourish my inner life has a huge impact on my family, friends, and other people I work with or encounter in my life.

Five years after I had recovered from the chronic fatigue, I broke my tailbone in a fall. Three days later, an enormous amount of energy began shooting through my body. It came in the form of a roar, heat, and excited intensity. I felt as though I was being turned inside out and rewired. A friend described this electric experience as kundalini energy surging up my spine. This is a yogic view of how the body, brain, and mind are rewired to experience a different state of consciousness.

As the months passed, my tailbone healed and my energy began to rebalance itself, with the care of a wise woman and master of energy. As I emerged from this experience, I found that I was a different person. A major shift in my perception of reality had taken place and I struggled to integrate what had happened to me. I spent hours meditating at home every day and attended meditation retreats. I couldn't seem to get enough of nurturing that inner world within me.

At the end of my first three-month silent retreat, when it came time to "break silence," one of the participants said, "It feels like we are all patients in ICU recovering from open-heart surgery." She spoke what the rest of us were feeling. Indeed, what a heart-opening experience and process of inner development it had been.

After other retreats, I embarked on a six-month silent retreat. In a little trailer on the grounds of the retreat facility, I cooked my own food and set my own schedule. This allowed me to let go of my patterns and just let myself be. I began to live in a peace that, as the Bible says, "surpasses all understanding." I lost the strain of striving and felt released from the need for purpose. I settled into a simple acceptance and had the awareness that in every person—beneath their tension, anxiety, and pressure—lies this incredible source of peace and happiness.

The retreats raised my curiosity about how our internal mental states work. I wanted to know what interrupts and invades our naturally peaceful mind, and shifts us back into the state of being tense, resistant, and discontented. I also wanted to know what allows the mind to periodically and naturally fall back into a state of peace.

Some of these questions were answered when I was serendipitously introduced to a neurofeedback monitoring technique called the Brain Mirror. Based on electroencephalograph (EEG) technology, it provides a way to measure and monitor mind states. I was excited to have found a tool that could be used to identify what happens in the brain during meditation and how the brain-wave patterns integrate mind and brain. Via the change in brain waves, this tool could also show me when and how my mind became busy, fearful, or stressed.

I bought one of these systems and began using it to explore what the brain did when in different mental states. I also began to study neuroscience, the study of the molecular, cellular, physiological, and psychological processes of the brain and nervous system. Through this study and what I had learned from meditating, I understood that with the right instruction people can discover how to control their mental states and clear the dysfunctional patterning in their brain structures. The brain and mind can work together to heal themselves and release the individual into creativity, presence, and lucidity.

Through this study, I began to understand what I discuss in the following sections.

Flow between the Inner and Outer Worlds

As the human brain evolved, it added new levels to the old: First was the reptilian brain, followed by the mammalian brain; next, the new brain or neocortex formed; and finally, one hundred thousand years ago, the prefrontal lobe arrived. Every evolutionary shift has changed the way we perceive who we are and how we experience the world in which we live. Almost every aspect of human experience, including love, memory, dreams, and our predisposition to religious thought, can be traced to one of these brain centers and the mental states they induce. In fact, the brain's inherent transformational process can serve as a model or guide for training our mind to be less intense and busy, and free from chaos, fear, pain, and inner wounds. We can train our mind to move into a silent, peaceful landscape of unbelievable possibilities. We can consciously train the mind to shift its movement from busy to quiet, from reactionary to calm and accepting, and from sensations to awareness of the body. The most recent evolutionary brain center, the prefrontal lobe, makes this conscious choice possible. It is like a conductor who orchestrates all the centers of the brain. This conductor oversees the activities that take place in each brain area, and integrates the whole. This integration stimulates the development of our mind and has a profound effect on our experience of the external world. In this relatively newly evolved brain, it is possible to consciously focus and fully engage in whatever we are doing, to ride the energies of all the brain centers, and to become highly creative.

There is also an inner and outer brain-mind interaction that keeps us energized and enlivened. This is a state of consciousness that follows an energy pattern that circulates throughout the brain and body. This flow moves directionally from the reptilian brain (which interprets the external world) to the prefrontal lobe (which orchestrates the internal world). Carl Jung termed this flow between the inner and outer experience of reality "synchronicity," which is beyond the physical world's experience. This flow has been the focus of many spiritual traditions and is best represented by a sense of being alive or joyful.

Is the Switch to Your Inner World Turned Off?

Most of us find that our experience of flow is easily disrupted. Scientists say that this fluid integrated state is difficult to maintain because of a fundamental flaw: The brain was not redesigned after the addition of new brain centers at each stage of its evolutionary development, leaving us with a somewhat inelegant design. What we find when we examine the brain is that one layer of gray matter has been plopped on to another layer, and then the next on to that layer, moving from the primitive system to the more powerful one. The result is communication flaws that affect the natural energy flow circulating in the brain. These imperfections become quite pronounced with the communication connections between our internal awareness and the way we interact with the outer world. These flaws can cut off the communication between the outer world experience and our inner world response. This creates an imbalance that disrupts the flow of energy, in our brain-mind system.

Because of these design flaws we are limited in our ability to flick off the mental switch when life is counterproductive for us. For example, when we are attacked physically or verbally, we often fight back to protect ourselves and stay in the conflict, ignoring the inner voice that tells us to stop escalating or to leave the destructive situation. In fact, rather than listening to this inner voice, we usually press harder to match the force of the situation. We pay less attention to our inner resources than to the outside world. We find it difficult to turn off the switch when an action is having the opposite result of what we desire.

We can take the idea of not listening to this inner direction a step further and look at how we become so driven and stressed in our daily lives. We all seem to be caught up in our fast-paced society with little time for our loved ones or ourselves. We are constantly on the go, with a cell phone in one hand and a PDA in the other. In fact, many of us drive, walk, and sleep with them. When we are in so-called relaxation, we are filling our time with movies, television, and computers. We are always connected with the outside world but find little time to reflect, be quiet, and find connection to our inner selves. The switch to our inner world is off, and we don't know how to turn it on. The Buddha called this condition suffering. Today we call it stress, which is being out of balance, with no time to rest and reset the very system that will bring us back to a natural flow.

The brain gives us support as we become aware of the need to make a change and flip the switch. Herein lies the magnificence of the brain's fine wiring system. The neuronal pathways (the brain's wiring system) can be altered and changes made in how we feel, think, and behave and how the body responds to stressful situations. Yes, it takes effort and some training, but these flaws can be rewired in the light of conscious awareness and disciplined practice. At birth, we have an immature brain, and it takes a long childhood with extensive parental nurturing followed by many life experiences to develop the brain.

The Brain Can Evolve

Remember the old adage, "You can't teach old dogs new tricks"? Well, it just isn't true. We are not stuck with our "old" brains. Our brains exhibit a high degree of adaptability to change. Scientists call this neuroplasticity, or how the brain can change the size of its structures and also their functions by strengthening the neuronal connections between different areas of the brain.

Research conducted by the Harvard Medical School found an increased thickness of the brain in the area of the prefrontal lobe in those who meditate regularly. The thickness in this area indicates an increase in brain function, primarily in concentration and memory. Thus, meditation influences the neuroplasticity of the brain by increasing the brain's function and structure. Other research has shown that meditation decreases depression, reduces high blood pressure, reduces stress, and improves the immune system. All of these conditions have a direct influence on the aging process.

We can change our brain structure, increase brain cells, and modify neuronal pathways through our life experiences. Meditation and mind-training work is at the heart of making positive changes in every area of our lives. Brain studies conducted at the University of Wisconsin indicate that people who meditate are rewiring their brains, with the outcome of a more positive and compassionate mind. From current research with Tibetan monks in meditation, we know that all levels of consciousness in an advanced meditator function at a high rate of efficiency and integration.

The brain's nerve cells are the saviors of our evolution. They are constantly in networking mode, with their one hundred billion neurons at work. If these neurons were lined up, they would extend for more than two million miles. Neurons have an amazing ability to communicate and interact with other neurons.

It is the brain's plasticity that gives rise to the human mind. Through neuronal networking processes, the mind expresses our thoughts, translates sensations, and creates memory and our perception of who we are in the world. By training our mind through meditation and other mental practices, it is possible to alter the brain's neuronal connections and circuitry responsible for emotions, behaviors, and perceptions. This actually changes the structure of the brain and the way it functions. As we alter the brain circuitry, we are changing our mind or literally reshaping the nature of our mind.

To evolve and change your brain/mind requires engaging in some mental training practices. In this way, you can change your habitual patterns, reduce stress reactions, and alter your attitudes and emotions, and shift your outlook on life from negative to positive.

The Inner Community Grows Outward

A few years after my six-month meditation retreat, I had a dream in which I saw people throughout the country sitting in circles—with their families, at work, in community centers, in nonprofit organizations, in medical schools, wherever there were people needing to be together. I saw that in each circle people were being transformed as they integrated their brain/mind through meditative practices. From the practices they shared, they created a deep connection to themselves and each other. The circles of people began to open the flow of their lives and create a supportive community that gave them stability to meet life challenges and have an impact on their larger communities.

I woke from this dream very excited. From meditation groups I led and years of working on my own brain flaws with the support of others, I knew that circles of people working together in this way have a positive impact on others in the circle members' lives, as well as the organizations and institutions with which they are connected.

The dream led me to speak to community, church, educational, and business groups about what I had learned about shared silence and its healing power within people and between people. I then created circles within these communities.

My dream has come to life in deeper and wiser communities that grow from inside each person out to form in that person's external world—wherever people come together. What is gratifying is that these circles eventually become self-sustaining.

I am reminded of Sara, one of my consulting clients who is the president of an executive leadership consulting firm. One afternoon, she barely made it to the airport to catch a flight. She felt stressed out and harried as she got to the gate. Then, as she took her seat on the plane, she spotted a woman she knew a few rows ahead of her. Sara was stunned because she had recently fired this woman and was in a bitter lawsuit with her for a million dollars. This put her stress level over the top and she wondered if she could handle the two-hour flight. As she buckled up, Sara remembered that she had my Beta Relaxation CD on her iPod. She turned it on, put the earphones in her ears, and went into a peaceful mental state for two hours. She told me later that if it hadn't been for the relaxation meditation, she would have "lost it." Her stress response had become too intense to push down. At the end of the flight, she was calm and centered enough to be gracious to the woman as they disembarked. By choosing to be calm rather than nervously fretting, Sara was also being gracious to herself. The circle of community begun within begins to express itself naturally out in the world.

In the variety of organizations—health, church, and business— that I talk with about creating community from the inside out, I first present to the entire organization the brain-mind background and how stress negatively impacts all of us. Second, I invite people who are interested in learning the meditative practices and the mental tools to form a mind-training circle in their organization or group. Third, I meet with them for their first session and give them the initial mental training tools, a meditative practice, written material, and a practice CD. Finally, I help them set up a regular meeting schedule to meditate and work together, and I return monthly for six months to give them new practices and tools. After that, I return periodically to review their progress and update them with further practices and tools.

I've worked in monthly sessions with one group for more than three years. The group members come from a variety of professional fields and lifestyles. Their strong commitment to circle is from deep respect for and genuine interest in each other, which allows love to be palpable among them. This type of group is not the same as a support group that untangles life issues. These twelve women work silently together to investigate their own consciousness, from which the group's energy field forms and has, in turn, a direct impact on each one of them. Amazing results have occurred. Physical issues and mental wounds have healed, awareness on healing repressed emotions has emerged, and insights on the next steps in a person's life have arisen. Individuals report that they are more capable on a day-to-day basis of handling stressful events with ease and little or no reaction.

One friend, a psychiatrist and professor at a medical school, sees the important application of all this to doctors in training. They need to learn how to work with their mental states to relieve their increasing stress, she says. And they need to discover the process of giving and receiving real support from each other if they are going to be capable of genuinely caring for themselves as well as their patients. My friend is excited about creating within her training process with medical students the circles I've modeled.

Now, at my audacious age, my vision is to train a cadre of teachers who will take this work out into our communities. Our brains are evolving and learning how to interface inside our own brain/ mind. Circles of supportive people who are willing to sit together and be open to the potentialities of silence will speed up this process and increase the evolution of connection between us. People sitting together in silence to know their own inner landscape gradually create trust in self and in each other. In this way, we build a community of heart from the inside out.

Both science and the spiritual discipline of meditation have brought to us a richer, more exciting understanding of how to expand our minds. This expansion can be true for all of us, if we but commit to it, whatever our age.

Bruce H. Lipton, PhD, author of *The Biology of Belief,* is an internationally recognized authority in bridging science and spirit. A cell biologist by training, he taught cell biology at the University of Wisconsin School of Medicine and later conducted pioneering research at Stanford University. His breakthrough studies on the cell membrane presaged the new science of epigenetics and have made him a leading voice of the new biology. Bruce Lipton was born on October 21, 1944, in Mount Kisco, New York.

BRUCE H. LIPTON

Aging: Belief or Biology

A character of all multicellular organisms in the biosphere is that their life progresses through a defined series of sequential stages that collectively define a life cycle. In the animal kingdom, the life cycle stages are: conception, development, maturation, decline, and death. Though death may be inevitable, the duration of an individual's life span is an unknown variable.

As a linear time line, the whole life cycle represents a process of aging. The conventional usage of "aging," however, is generally associated with the phase of the life cycle defined as decline. The period of decline is characterized by a loss of physical and mental function, decrepitude, and infirmity, all traits of "growing old."

The human aging period is of variable duration. Some individuals experience a long, protracted period of decline, while others are fortunate enough to have a vibrantly healthy life and then pass peacefully in their sleep, essentially without experiencing any infirmity.

Must a period of degeneration, "aging," precede death? Can we get old without aging? According to conventional biology, the answer is no. To understand that answer from a scientific perspective requires a little insight into the nature of biology and our bodies.

Immortal Cells and the Community

When life was first created on this planet, natural death did not exist. "Primitive" single-celled organisms, such as bacteria, fungi, algae, and protozoa (e.g., amoebae and paramecia), were immortal. Cells would grow until they reached a certain size; they would then divide, forming two daughter cells, which in turn would repeat the cycle. If unicellular organisms would age and die, then they would not provide a sustainable lineage. Think of it this way. The amoeba you see under a microscope today is technically the same cell as the original amoeba that existed more than three billion years ago. Now that's the kind of aging we can live with!

In the course of evolution, single-celled organisms increased their survivability by teaming up with other single cells to form communities. These primitive assemblies, known as colonial organisms, are afforded two fundamental life-enhancing benefits: 1) Efficiency enhances survival. Communal life is more efficient as exemplified by the adage "Two can live as cheaply as one." 2) Awareness is one of most important contributing factors to survival. Community offers individual cells increased awareness. Every cell possesses awareness and has access to the collective awareness of all the other cells in the community.

Though they live as a "community," colonial cells still behave as independent single-celled organisms. If the cells of a colonial organism are dispersed, every cell can survive on its own. When a dispersed colonial cell divides, its daughter cells stay in close proximity, forming the seed of a new colony. The population of the colony increases through the continued cell divisions of the daughter cells' progeny. Large communities frequently fragment and each of the fragments enlarge until they too fragment.

Over time, the populations of the colonies grew so large that they could only sustain themselves by having constituent cells take on specialized jobs. Rather than all cells being the same, cells began to differentiate and express specialized functions such as muscle, bone, skin, and nerve. There was, however, a profound cost for this evolutionary advancement: The acquisition of a differentiated state interferes with the cell's ability to divide. As these cells mature, rather than undergoing mitosis and producing more progeny, they age and eventually die.

The continuous loss of differentiated cells would inevitably lead to the death of the community. To sustain survival, multicellular communities maintained a population of cells that do not differentiate and therefore retain their ability to divide. These "immortal" cells, called stem cells, maintain a continuous cycle of growth and proliferation. Stem cell progeny are the equivalent of "embryonic" cells, and when needed by the community, they can differentiate into any of a body's specialized cell types. Stem cell populations provide for a renewable source of differentiated cells. Stem cell populations are needed to sustain the life span of multicellular organisms, including human beings.

Body cells have different life spans. Some cells, such as those lining the gut, only live three days; others cells, such as neurons and some classes of immune system cells, survive for decades. The human body loses billions and billions of differentiated cells every day due to aging and normal attrition. Stem cell progeny continuously replenish the body's differentiated cell population. Feasibly, stem cells should allow humans to survive indefinitely. Since stem cells are the equivalent of embryonic cells and continuously replace older cells, we may rightfully ask, "Why do we age and die?"

Insight into the answer to that question was first provided by the experiments of microbiologist Leonard Hayflick who in 1962 followed the reproductive fate of single cells in a tissue culture dish.[1] His results revealed that normal human and animal cells in culture have a limited capacity for replication. The results suggest that animal cells are not immortal.

In his studies, a typical cell would provide for fifty to sixty normal cell divisions, a phenomenon known as the "Hayflick limit." As the number of cell divisions approaches this limit, the subsequent daughter cells begin to express life-threatening dysfunctions and a decline in vitality. Each additional division further diminishes the cell's ability to survive and, inevitably, its death leads to the extinction of the cell line. Hayflick's research focused attention on the finite cellular life span as the fundamental source of aging. He suggested that cellular immortality, a key feature of tumor cells, was a pathological abnormality.

According to Hayflick's findings, stem cells will maintain the normal health of the body until they have exceeded a certain number of cell divisions. After that time, stem cell progeny become dysfunctional. Body tissues and organs populated with these "aged" cells go into decline and manifest the characteristics of aging. Inevitably, the dysfunctions become so great the body cannot sustain life processes and dies. Based on his observations, Hayflick and his associates vehemently condemned "anti-aging medicine," criticizing both the feasibility and desirability of human life extension.

Scientists initially attributed cellular aging to defects in the replication process that introduce mutations into the genes. DNA copying errors contribute to a loss of cell function that is physically expressed as aging. Molecular biologists have subsequently discovered, however, a set of specialized enzymes that comprise a system for DNA repair. These enzymes function as proofreaders that read the gene's code and correct mutations that are accidentally introduced into the DNA. Repair enzymes catch almost all errors that occur in the replication of DNA. Consequently, this repair mechanism would presumably serve as a means to prevent the hypothesized loss of stem cell function.

---

1. Hayflick, L. (1965). "The limited in vitro lifetime of human diploid cell strains." *Experimental Cell Research* 37:614–636.

More recently, scientists have attributed cellular aging to altera-tions in a very specific region of the DNA helix called the telomere.[2] Telomeres are extensions on the ends of the DNA molecules that resemble the plastic tips that cap the ends of shoelaces. When a shoe-lace loses its plastic tip, the threads comprising the lace unravel and become frayed, making the shoelace dysfunctional. Similarly, when the DNA double helix loses its telomere cap, the DNA helix unwinds (i.e., frays), compromising the integrity and structural stability of the DNA.

Researchers discovered that every time a cell divides, a short length of each telomere is lost during the replication of the DNA helix. After a certain number of cell divisions, the telomeres would be lost, which in turn leads to destabilization and dysfunction of the genes. Telomere research supports Hayflick's findings that an organism's life span is determined by a specific number of cell divi-sions, by directly linking telomere length to the number of potential cell divisions.

Molecular genetic research has recently undermined this hypoth-esis. It has been found that cells possess an enzyme identified as telomerase that extends the length of telomeres. When activated, this enzyme would presumably maintain telomere length and allow cells to divide forever.[3]

Though challenged, science still favors the telomere story of aging since it conforms to the conventional belief that genes control our traits. Unfortunately, acceptance of this belief acknowledges that in regard to aging, we are victims of forces outside our control and must accept physiologic degeneration as an unforgiving fact of life.

An Aging Story We Can Live With

And now for something completely different—an aging story we can live with.

The story of cellular senescence just described is very much the same story of aging I was teaching medical students back in the early seventies. My research on cultured stem cells at that time, however, provided a radically new understanding of the mechanisms that control life. In my experiments, a single stem cell would be isolated and placed into a culture dish. The cell would subsequently divide

---

2. Verdun, R. E., and Karlseder, J. (2007). "Replication and protection of telo-meres." *Nature* 447:924–931.

3. Zhao, Y. M., et al. (2008). "Cell cycle dependent telomere regulation by telom-erase in human bone marrow mesenchymal cells." *Biochemical and Biophysical Research Communications* 369:1114–1119.

and form two daughter cells. These cells divided and formed four cells. Over several days of reproducing, there were thousands of cells in the dish.

The unique character of all the cells in the culture dish was that they were genetically identical, having been derived from the same parent cell. The cell population was split into three different portions inoculated into three culture dishes. Each dish was fed growth medium containing a different chemical composition. For a cell, growth medium represents the "environment" in which it lives.

After several days, the fate of the cells was profoundly altered. In one culture, the stem cells became muscle; in the second dish, they became bone; and in the third dish, the cells differentiated as fat cells. The point is all cells were genetically identical when introduced into the culture dish, so the genes did not control their differentiated fate. Their fate was controlled by the environment, a finding in direct conflict with the dogma that genes control life.[4]

When cultured cells are fed a less than healthy growth medium, they get sick and begin to die. If the medium is replaced with a more supportive medium, the cells recover their health and thrive. This research emphasizes that the environment controls the genetics and the health of the organism. The profound joke is that human beings are, in reality, skin-covered Petri dishes containing over fifty trillion cells. The fate of cells in the human body, like that of the cells in a culture dish, is directly influenced by the environment in which they live.

This work presaged today's most exciting new field of science: epigenetic control. The conventional model of genetic control literally means "control *by* genes." The meaning of epigenetic control is profoundly different. The difference is emphasized in the Latin prefix *epi*, which means "above." For example, epidermis means the layer above the dermis, the skin. Epigenetic control literally reads as "control *above* the genes."

By 1990, science had clearly established that "When a gene product is needed, *a signal from the environment*, not an emergent property of the gene itself, *activates expression of that gene*." (italics, mine) The profound essence of molecular biologist H. F. Nijhout's quote is simplified by reading just the italicized phrases, "...*a signal from the environment...activates expression of that gene*."[5]

---

4. Lipton, B. H. (1977). "A fine structural analysis of normal and modulated cells in myogenic culture." *Developmental Biology* 60:26–47.

5. Nijhout, H. F. (1990). "Metaphors and the role of genes in development." *BioEssays* 9:441–446.

Simply, the new science of epigenetic control is the study of how environmental signals control genetics and cell behavior.

Over the past fifteen years, leading edge science has revised its prevailing belief that genes control life. Unfortunately, these revisions are only recognized at the level of research scientists. The new insight on environmental control of genes through epigenetic processes is only now entering into public awareness.

Masters of Our Fate

The significant difference between the older conventional version of genetic control and the newer insights of epigenetic control is that the former emphasizes that we are "victims" of heredity, while the latter reveals we are actually masters of our fate, for we are free to change our environment and consequently change our lives.

As described in my book *The Biology of Belief: Unleashing the Power of Consciousness, Matter, and Miracles,* the human brain is the interface between the environment and the genes of our cells.[6] In response to environmental stimuli, the brain adjusts the composition of the body's tissue fluids, the equivalent of "growth medium" for our body's cells.

In the exact same way, the growth medium constituents regulate the genetics of cultured stem cells, and brain regulated chemistry of the blood and tissue fluids regulates the genetic expression of the cells that comprise our tissues and organs. Neurological perceptions are translated into biochemical cascades that control the genetics and behaviors of our cells. When we change our perceptions, our "beliefs," we change our body chemistry and epigenetically influence the fate of our cells.

Conventional medical practice is scientifically outdated since it still adheres to the notion of the primacy of genes in controlling our traits in health and disease. This perspective fosters the image that our fifty-trillion-celled bodies are genetically controlled mechanical vehicles. By contrast, epigenetic science profoundly modifies that belief. Though it still acknowledges the body as a vehicle, epigenetics introduces the concept of a driver—the mind. The perceptions of life we hold in our minds control our biology via epigenetic mechanisms. Through this process, the mind creates a biological response that complements our perceptions or beliefs about life.

An individual with good driving skills can maintain and enjoy good performance of a vehicle throughout its lifetime. Bad driving

---

6. Lipton, B. H. (2005). *The Biology of Belief.* San Rafael, CA: Mountain of Love Productions and Elite Books.

skills are responsible for most of the wrecks that litter the roadside and fill junkyards. The influence of a driver's skill holds true for any vehicle, be it an automobile or a human body.

Employing good "driving skills" in the management of our behaviors and the maintenance of our vehicular bodies offers an opportunity for a healthy, happy, and productive life. Inappropriate and dysfunctional behaviors, in addition to a neglect of bodily maintenance, stresses our cellular "vehicles," interferes with their performance, and ultimately provokes a breakdown.

Are you a good driver or a bad driver? Before you answer that question, realize that there are two separate minds that provide the body's controlling "central voice." The (self-) conscious mind is the thinking you; it is creative and expresses free will. It is the mind that has all your wishes, desires, and aspirations. The self-conscious mind is the one that hopefully visualizes a life filled with health and happiness.

Since almost everyone holds a conscious desire of vitality and wellness in their minds and the mind is supposed to control our biology, you may rightfully ask, "Why are we so plagued with ill health, disease, and the decrepitude of aging?"

Good question. The answer lies in this fact: Neuroscientists have found that the conscious mind controls our biology less than 5 percent of the day; 95 percent of our life is actually under the control of programs in our subconscious mind.

The subconscious mind is an entirely different entity from the conscious mind. It is a record-playback device that is a million times more powerful information processor than the conscious mind. The subconscious contains a database of reflexes and learned perceptions that are directly downloaded from our life experiences. Recorded as stimulus-response programs, automated subconscious behaviors are expressed as "habits." Habits free the conscious mind from spending valuable processing time on repetitive behaviors that range from standing and walking to driving a car.

Most subconscious programs are acquired, "learned," and are used to automatically adjust the biology and behavior of the body without the observation or participation of the conscious mind. That's why it is referred to as the "*un*conscious" or "*sub*conscious" mind.

The subconscious mind is not a seat of reasoning; it is strictly a stimulus-response device. When an environmental signal is perceived, the subconscious mind reflexively activates a previously programmed behavioral response—no thinking required. The subconscious mind is a programmable autopilot that navigates the vehicle without the necessity of observation or awareness by the "pilot," the conscious mind.

In contrast to the conscious mind, which has your wishes and desires, the subconscious mind's programs are primarily beliefs copied from observing others. The meaning of this awareness is profound and sobering: "We" control our lives less than 5 percent of the time, while other people's programs control our biology 95 percent of the time. We are essentially living other people's lives.

The dual-mind system's effectiveness is defined by the quality of perceptual programs stored in the subconscious mind. Essentially, the person who taught you how to drive molds your driving skills. For example, if you were taught to drive with one foot on the gas and the other on the brake, no matter how many vehicles you own, each will inevitably express premature brake failure.

Youth-ing Ourselves

From the perspective of "new-edge" science, the character of an individual's aging is primarily a reflection of their subconscious beliefs and not their genetic history. As discussed in *The Biology of Belief,* the EEG activity of the brain through the first six years of life reveals that a child's mind is primarily engaged in a hypnotic trance. Consequently, whatever the child experiences or learns during this critical period of development is directly downloaded into the subconscious mind.

These acquired developmental perceptions represent the fundamental beliefs that essentially control the biology of an individual for the rest of his or her life. This conclusion is supported by recent medical studies revealing that the propensity of experiencing a disease in adulthood is determined by environmental influences during the periconceptual, fetal, and infant stages of life.

During this important period of development, a child downloads into its subconscious memory a program of aging by observing the physical character of people in its community. An infant readily connects infirmity and physical degeneration as a pattern associated with aging. More important, the subconscious programming of aging is further emphasized because it is linked to one of the most important facts of life any human learns—mortality. Aging patterns take on a profound significance in our minds because they are associated with death.

The perception that our mental and physical abilities must fade as we age is a notion that we now accept as fact, though it is patently not true. The new science suggests that we age according to our beliefs. When we "feel" we are too old to do something, we commit to an aging program and the brain will ensure that our biology matches our beliefs. Does this new science suggest that we can eliminate, or at least profoundly limit, degenerative changes associated with aging? Absolutely!

A fabulous experiment revealing the ability to "youth" ourselves by changing our perceptions was provided by Harvard psychologist Ellen Langer.[7] In 1979, Langer selected a group of elderly men from a retirement community and ran them through a battery of tests to evaluate their mental and physical parameters. The group was then taken on a retreat to a lodge where the clothing, food, magazines, music, memorabilia, and even the conversation were from 1959, twenty years earlier. After spending just five days in this environment of "altered" time, the participants went through the same tests they took before the retreat. The tests revealed that with just a few days of mentally "living" in the past, these men dramatically reversed their physical and mental traits and had test results similar to subjects who were twenty years younger. By simply changing their environment, people can actually reverse aging!

When we align our subconscious programming with our conscious desires, we become the masters of our fates rather than the "victims" of our programs. Historically, it has been a tedious and time-consuming process to effect changes in limiting or sabotaging subconscious programming. Fortunately, a new variety of rapid and efficient reprogramming processes are available to rewrite limiting programs, such as those we acquire about aging. For a listing of effective behavioral reprogramming methodologies, as well as more detailed information on this new science, visit www.bruce lipton.com.

---

7. Langer, E. (1989). *Mindfulness*. Reading, MA: Addison-Wesley.

Carolyn Matzinger, MD, has built her career around the premise that a deep, individual connection between doctor and patient is vital to medical treatment. In her private practice, she combines cutting-edge diagnostics and therapeutic modalities in anti-aging medicine with the personal attention missing in health care today. With specialties in internal medicine and anti-aging, regenerative, and functional medicine, she is a Diplomate of the American Board of Internal Medicine and the American Board of Anti-Aging Medicine. She was born on September 29, 1961, in Lockport, New York.

CAROLYN MATZINGER

Increasing Your Health Span

With all the advances in modern medicine, the number of diagnostic and treatment techniques available is greater than at any point in history. Disease management with prescription drugs is the norm and the life span of the average American is at an all-time high. With all of the studies, technologies, and medical breakthroughs, why aren't Americans healthier?

One answer lies in the most common response to another question: Has your physician ever discussed with you strategies to improve your health—*when you were healthy?* Most people's reply is no. This lack of foresight in our health-care system reflects a disregard of the huge difference between optimal health and not being sick.

Stop to consider your life span. Now factor in how many "good years" you want to have. Your "health span" is the number of quality years of life. On your current path of managing your health, what do you think will be the quality of your health in ten, fifteen, or twenty years?

Keep in mind the advancements in medical technology. For example, if you have a stroke and lose your ability to swallow, you will have a feeding tube inserted and will probably be placed in a nursing home. This is living, but not quality living. If your lungs become nonfunctional, you will be put on a breathing machine, lie flat for twenty-four hours a day, and develop bedsores. No one would consider this quality living.

Modern technology can keep you alive and increase your life span. Are you willing to trade quantity of life versus quality of life? Treating illness lengthens your life span; treating health lengthens your health span.

CHAPTER TWENTY-FIVE

"Just Give Me a Pill."

Like most physicians, I completed medical school and residency training eager to save lives and make a difference in health care. As a young graduate, my assumption was that everyone wanted to be happy and healthy and would be willing to do whatever it took to achieve optimal health. It only took a short while of being in private practice to realize that was not the case.

Conventional or Western medicine aims to treat the symptoms a patient is experiencing, not necessarily the underlying cause. As a result, the more symptoms a patient is having, the more pharmaceutical medications the patient will be prescribed. The more drugs a patient is taking at one time, the greater the likelihood of drug interactions and adverse reactions. The more pharmaceutical medications you take, the harder it is for your body to eliminate the drugs properly. This increases the likelihood of adverse drug reactions.

This did not sound to me like a healthy way to treat patients. I soon discovered, however, that the majority of patients would rather take a pill to treat their illness than adapt to healthy lifestyle changes. For example, I would counsel patients with diabetes and hypertension to follow a healthy eating program appropriate for their condition and be sure to exercise regularly. They would complain that lifestyle changes were too hard. Rather than taking the time to work toward optimal health, they would ask me just to increase the medication dosages.

I vividly remember one young woman. She was only in her thirties, but was overweight, suffered from hypertension, and had high stress. She was already taking two different blood pressure medications and her blood pressure was still elevated. During one doctor's visit, I spent approximately forty-five minutes counseling her regarding healthy eating, exercising, and taking time for herself to manage her stress. We ended our visit with a discussion about being accountable and responsible for her health and her life in general. Weeks later, her husband came in for a checkup. When I inquired about his wife, he told me she no longer wanted me as her physician. My conversation about how she had to be responsible for her actions greatly upset her. Rather than choosing a healthy lifestyle, she chose another physician.

I spent the next twelve years in a conventional internal medicine private practice, and grew increasingly frustrated with the mainstream approach to health care. Treating symptoms without getting to the root of the illness was commonplace. Watching patients succumb to laziness regarding their own health, overmedicate, and refuse to grasp the deeper issues of personal health care was a daily occurrence.

Accountability and Responsibility

A colleague introduced me to the specialty of anti-aging and functional medicine. Anti-aging medicine is aimed at the early detection, prevention, treatment, and reversal of age-related decline. The anti-aging model changes or slows the process of aging. Functional medicine focuses on understanding the fundamental physiological processes, the environmental inputs, and the genetic predispositions that influence health and disease so that interventions focus on treating the cause of the problem, not just masking the symptoms. From this model of medicine, I created the unique style of medical practice that I currently have.

The foundation of my medical practice and belief in optimizing health are personal accountability and responsibility. It is my belief that each individual creates his or her own existence. There are no victims.

Every human being has challenges in life. From these challenges, we discover our courage within. If you are unhappy with your life, you have the internal power to change it. If you are not satisfied with your health status, you have the internal power to change it. How is this possible? Your thoughts dictate your words, your words define your actions, and your actions become your reality. We all know people who are constantly complaining; they have multiple aches and pains and various health issues. They are generally negative and are mentally draining to be around. These individuals are choosing to be negative, and that is the reality that they are creating for themselves both externally and internally.

The energy you put out in the universe is the energy you get back. If you are thinking, speaking, and projecting positive thoughts, health, and happiness, that becomes your reality. This is Universal Law.

The following examples illustrate the role of accountability and responsibility in maintaining health. Patient A is told by an oncologist that he has cancer and only has six months to live. He accepts the diagnosis, does nothing for his health, and dies within six months. Patient B is also told he has cancer and only six months to live. He seeks alternative forms of treatment, maintains a positive attitude that he will recover, takes control of his illness, and lives for several more years, cancer free.

On a more personal level, my son, Harley, is almost five years old. At eighteen months old, he was diagnosed with a rare genetic condition called Angelman's syndrome, which is characterized by seizures, mental retardation, severe developmental delays in language and motor skills, a vocabulary of only four words throughout the individual's lifetime, and a host of other medical issues. Conventional medicine had nothing to offer, aside from seizure medication. I was not about to settle for that! My family and I took control of the situation, constantly projecting positive energy, and sought out alternative therapies. Harley's progress has dramatically improved in many areas of development and he is seizure free. He is currently projecting vowel and consonant sounds, the beginning stages of speech.

Adding to Your Health Span

What does it mean to be healthy? My definition of optimal health is: mental, physical, and spiritual well-being. The three go hand in hand. The goal is to increase your health span, not just your life span. Your health span increases when you have strength, vitality, happiness, creativity, contentment, and spiritual satisfaction. No one wants to live with chronic illness, cognitive impairment, or depression.

While there are many lifestyle modifications you can implement to increase your health span, perhaps the best place to begin is learning to love yourself. Loving yourself is an ongoing, lifelong process. It does not happen overnight and the journey is different for everyone. When I speak of loving yourself, I am referring to honoring your individual divine spirit, owning your greatness and your magnificence! As you begin to love yourself, you have less self-doubt, you trust yourself more, you embrace your courage, and you discover inner peace and satisfaction. You will notice that as you love yourself more, you increase your capacity to love others and for others to love you as well. As you love and honor yourself, you naturally become more accountable and responsible for your actions and you realize that maintaining your health is up to you.

There are other key areas to attend to in managing your health, particularly what you eat, pH balance, supplements, water, exercise, sleep, and stress reduction. Many people have pointed to these as health factors, but they bear repeating since so many Americans continue to ignore them.

First is a healthy eating program. I do not use the term "diet." This word has strong emotional connotations for most people. It is important to manage your eating habits. A healthy eating program varies according to specific medical conditions and diagnostic laboratory results (cholesterol profile, vitamin deficiency workup, and hormonal status).

To maintain a healthy pH balance within your body, eat more alkalinizing foods and limit acid-forming foods. An overly acidic body is at risk for numerous disease states due to a weakened immune system. Examples of alkalinizing foods are carrots, broccoli, peppers, apples, and pears. Examples of acidifying foods and beverages are corn, oatmeal, bread, beef, turkey, sugar, coffee, beer, and wine. You can eat foods that are acidifying; the key is to eat more foods (approximately 80 percent) that are alkalinizing.

Your nutritional status is the vital foundation of your health, so it is important to take appropriate nutriceutical supplementation to maintain it. It is equally important to take supplements that are customized for your particular needs as determined by your health conditions and your individual nutritional and hormonal status. Antioxidants, amino acids, specific vitamins and minerals, coenzyme Q10, and omega-3 fish oils are the basic supplements that individuals living in industrialized nations require.

An underrated part of health care is the quality of drinking water taken into the body each day. Public drinking water and most wells around the country are loaded with contaminants and free radicals. I recommend adding to the water you drink the water treatment products from the company Monatau. These products function to neutralize free radicals and help maintain an alkaline pH balance in the body. Remember, an alkaline pH balance is required to support a healthy immune system, which will prevent illness and numerous medical conditions.

A personalized exercise program is the next item on the health list. The benefits of regular exercise are well documented. As every person has different needs and goals, one exercise plan does not fit all. There is plenty of information available to help you design an appropriate exercise program if you don't already have one.

Adequate sleep is essential for optimizing your health status. When you are sleep deprived, your body goes into a state of inflammation. Inflammation leads your body to age prematurely and increases the production of free radicals. Free radicals also lead to premature aging and are the cause of numerous disease states. Inadequate sleep suppresses the release of specific hormones, which in turn causes hormonal imbalance. These are just a few effects of sleep deprivation.

Stress reduction is vital to obtaining a balance in health and life. Sustained stress has numerous detrimental effects on your body, including: elevated cortisol levels, which can cause abdominal obesity; increased risk of diabetes mellitus and hypertension; and increased risk of cognitive decline and memory loss. Chronic stress also weakens the immune system, which can lead to major illnesses and chronic health conditions. Chronic stress also suppresses the release of human growth hormone (the body's youth hormone).

While the previous measures are essential in optimizing your health, you may also want to consider your hormone levels. Hormones are powerful substances that have specific and numerous effects in the body. Estrogen, for example, has more than four hundred functions. It is involved in sleep, memory, mood, the regulation of cholesterol and blood pressure, and the maintenance of muscle mass and collagen in the skin.

Since hormones decline as we age, hormone replacement therapy, when used properly, can offer medical benefits. Estrogen replacement therapy, for example, can result in improvement in all the areas listed here as well as in its many other functions. Hormone replacement therapy means to replace only what is missing, restoring to healthy levels those hormonal cellular stimulants that decline due to disease or dysfunction related to the aging process. It is important to replace hormones with natural or bioidentical hormones, which means hormones that are biologically identical to what your own body makes (unlike Premarin, for example, which is made from *pregnant mares' urine*).

As part of optimizing your health, I recommend that you have your levels of the following hormones measured: estrogen, progesterone, testosterone, DHEA, melatonin, pregnenolone, cortisol, and human growth hormone. These measurements should be performed by either saliva or urine tests. Blood tests are *not* accurate for determining hormonal levels. It is important to measure your thyroid status as well; this can be done by a blood test.

There are other tools that can help you improve your health *before* you become ill. I urge you to be open to the many options available. One that I have found highly useful is the Ondamed biofeedback device, which combines PEMF (pulsed electromagnetic field) technology and pulse biofeedback. It raises the electrical potential of tissues that are in a weakened state, restores normal function, promotes relaxation, and provides an effective, painless, and noninvasive complement or alternative to other pain relief options (surgery, drugs). Ondamed also complements pharmaceuticals, homeopathic remedies, and nutritional supplements. Patients respond more quickly

I still think he would have made a great president. Of course, ego commands me to say that America would be better off if I had been elected in 1972 instead of Nixon.

The press today, with notable exceptions, has let the Bush people get away with a lot that is not in the national interest. I'm not anti-Republican—my mother and dad lived and died Republicans—but what we have under the Bush-Cheney team is quite fraudulent: too many things held in secret, too much sham and not enough substance. And when they do offer substance, it's usually wrongheaded. Witness their war in Iraq, the big tax giveaway, and a mind-boggling national debt, to say nothing of such folly as their opposition to stem cell research in the interest of saving lives.

My faith in the American voter is shaken at times. I still have faith in the common sense of the American people, but they've been misled by our leadership, complicated by too timid a response from the Democrats and the press. I understand why many people are off the track. I think they're inclined to trust the country's leaders, and with bad leadership, you're usually going to get bad results. Voters don't always see beyond the demagoguery and the sham.

With huge issues such as global warming now threatening the world, it is ridiculous to see our leaders playing politics with abortion, marriage by gays, and flag burning. Does anyone believe that some nut burning a piece of cloth or paper with a flag on it is going to threaten our constitutional freedom? And should a bunch of old men and women decide how a desperate young woman handles an unwanted and perhaps dangerous pregnancy? Do genuine conservatives really want the long arm of Washington invading our bedrooms and marital relations?

But I'm hopeful. I think this country has the capacity and the resources for a promising future. So I don't give up on us yet. I've always thought I lived in the greatest country on earth. And we must be great, because we've made such horrendous mistakes and we still survive. It must be our Constitution, our Bill of Rights, and the decency of our people.

I have been married to Eleanor for sixty-five years. That's another reason why we are still young—both of us now eighty-six. We were both twenty-one when we married during my days as a B-24 combat bomber pilot in WW II. I was awarded the Distinguished Flying Cross after completing a full tour of thirty-five bombing missions over Hitler's most heavily defended target. In 2000, I won the Presidential Medal of Freedom, the nation's highest civilian honor. I hold a PhD in History from Northwestern University. I take pride and zest for life from these three honors; from Eleanor and our five children, a dozen grandchildren, and three great-grandchildren; plus my marvelous Newfoundland dog Ursa, an inseparable companion.

Lynne McTaggart, an internationally recognized spokesperson on the science of spirituality, authored the bestselling books *The Field: The Quest for the Secret Force of the Universe* and *The Intention Experiment: Using Your Thoughts to Change Your Life and the World,* and was featured in the hugely popular film *What the BLEEP!? Down the Rabbit Hole.* Also author of *What Doctors Don't Tell You,* she and her husband, Bryan Hubbard, publish a newsletter of the same name and online information on natural medicine. She was born on January 23, 1951, in Yonkers, New York.

and the effects of the treatments are longer lasting. I have personally seen dramatic benefits with the use of the Ondamed device, not only for specific health conditions, but also for routine health maintenance and stress reduction.

Let the Good Years Roll!

When evaluating your health and the number of good years you want to live, be honest with yourself. Self-research is the starting point for everyone. Evaluate your mental, physical, and spiritual health. Determine your personal strengths and weaknesses in all areas of your life. Make a list of incidents in your life that caused trauma and duress. Dig deep to understand if your physical ailments are manifestations of mental anguish.

Putting a health plan into action takes focus and determination. Meet with your physician to get an accurate medical analysis while you are healthy. Work hard to eat right and exercise on a daily basis. Most important, love who you are and the person you want to become. Embrace your current state of health and work to improve it. Keep yourself focused on the small victories and stay positive.

People sometimes ask, "Don't you wish you were twenty years old again?" My reply is an emphatic no! I am at a place in my life where I have inner peace and satisfaction. I have a better understanding of what it means to love myself. If I find myself not in a space of love, I know how to get there quickly. I do not focus on my calendar age. It is not important to me. It is my biological age that determines my health status. I find that as my calendar age increases, my biological age decreases. How is that possible?

As I experience life's challenges (I see all challenges as an opportunity for growth), I gain more wisdom. As I gain more wisdom, I obtain more inner peace and happiness. The more inner peace and happiness I have, the more balanced my health becomes, thus increasing my health span.

Remember, you too have a choice in how you live your life and how you create your existence. It is more rewarding to live your life being accountable and responsible for your actions—and it has the side benefit of giving you a longer health span!

George McGovern wore many hats in his illustrious career, among them history teacher, bomber pilot, congressman, senator, and 1972 presidential nominee. During his presidential bid, the former war hero found his valor under attack. His support of America's withdrawal from the Vietnam War may have cost him the presidency. In his earlier years, McGovern campaigned for Adlai Stevenson during his presidential bid and served as director of the Food for Peace Program under John F. Kennedy. George McGovern was born on July 19, 1922, in Avon, South Dakota.

GEORGE McGOVERN

An Appetite for Life

I used to say when the subject of aging came up that it doesn't matter how long you live, it's what you do with the time you have. But now that I'm eighty-six, I don't say that anymore, because I want to live a long time. And I think that enthusiasm for constructive change is the driving force in my life that keeps me going.

I'm supposed to be retired, but retirement for me means going from working fourteen hours a day down to twelve. I think an appetite for life promotes longevity. Of course, we all know wonderful people with a great zest for life who died young—Mozart, John and Robert Kennedy, and Martin Luther King—so that's no guarantee.

I have never quit caring about what's happening in the world. I try to keep learning, to keep digging, and when the opportunities arise, I keep speaking and writing. I wrote *Out of Iraq: A Practical Plan for Withdrawal Now* (Simon & Schuster, 2006) with William Polk, one of our leading authorities on the Middle East and Iraq. I'm enthusiastic about the book.

I've always thought that a sense of history was one of the indispensable qualities that make a good citizen. In the first Kennedy-Nixon debate, one of the reporters asked each of them to say in one minute the most important quality that commended him to be president. Nixon talked about his experience, and it was a persuasive answer. And then I think Jack [Kennedy] said, "I think if I have any one quality for presidency, it's my sense of history." And the substance of what he said was this: he had the capacity to know what the historical forces were that made America a great country. And he knew the forces in our own time that were most admirable and the ones we had to improve. When he said that, he had me, as an old history teacher, hooked.

I mourn the absence of historical knowledge in many of our young people today. As I travel around the country, I see that history is badly neglected. Many kids think it's dull. You've heard the questions that Jay Leno asks young folks and their incredible answers. Some don't know who was president during the Civil War, or what the New Deal was. Perhaps the "No Child Left Behind" agenda has given history too low a priority. Worse yet, even our leaders seem to be ignorant of history. How is it possible that those who took us into Iraq have forgotten so soon the lessons of Vietnam? And why are the leaders puzzled over the Iraqi insurgency when even an alert high school student knows that the American insurgency of 1776 was created because our forefathers did not want British troops occupying the American colonies?

Are there any advantages to age? Absolutely. First of all, you have corrected wisdom and memory of the long years. You have a little more time, you don't have to work quite so hard to make a living, you have the time to read more, to think more, and to modify some of your earlier opinions in view of more wisdom and tolerance and less fanaticism. Will Rogers warned us long ago: "It ain't what people don't know that's dangerous; it's what they know that just ain't so."

I think older people, with obvious exceptions, should be consulted more on national and international questions. For example, I wish that George Bush the Younger had paid more attention to advice from his father, from Jim Baker, from Brent Scowcroft, or to such veteran senators as Robert Byrd, Edward Kennedy, and Bob Graham. He would have been better off had he listened to some of those older heads. We might not now be floundering around in the Arabian desert and alienating a billion Muslims and Arabs.

During the Kennedy years, there was the Bay of Pigs and the intervention in Vietnam. I was opposed to those things then and have been ever since. But there was an excitement, an enthusiasm, an innovativeness: The Peace Corps, Food for Peace, the Nuclear Test Ban Treaty, Civil Rights, etc. I think we're missing that today. My colleagues in the Senate tell me that politics isn't much fun anymore. No one ever said that about the Kennedy era. It was exciting, it was intelligent, and for the most part it was well directed. I've always thought it would have been better in a second Kennedy term of four years. The Kennedys were quick learners. They were very educable. Jack grew every day he was in the White House. Assassination deprived us of his growing experience and wisdom.

I admired Adlai Stevenson's high intelligence. I admired his eloquence, his humor, his capacity to laugh at the ridiculous aspects of the human condition. He had a sensitivity about issues that was more than just words. Those were the things that drew me to him.

I still think he would have made a great president. Of course, ego commands me to say that America would be better off if I had been elected in 1972 instead of Nixon.

The press today, with notable exceptions, has let the Bush people get away with a lot that is not in the national interest. I'm not anti-Republican—my mother and dad lived and died Republicans—but what we have under the Bush-Cheney team is quite fraudulent: too many things held in secret, too much sham and not enough substance. And when they do offer substance, it's usually wrongheaded. Witness their war in Iraq, the big tax giveaway, and a mind-boggling national debt, to say nothing of such folly as their opposition to stem cell research in the interest of saving lives.

My faith in the American voter is shaken at times. I still have faith in the common sense of the American people, but they've been misled by our leadership, complicated by too timid a response from the Democrats and the press. I understand why many people are off the track. I think they're inclined to trust the country's leaders, and with bad leadership, you're usually going to get bad results. Voters don't always see beyond the demagoguery and the sham.

With huge issues such as global warming now threatening the world, it is ridiculous to see our leaders playing politics with abortion, marriage by gays, and flag burning. Does anyone believe that some nut burning a piece of cloth or paper with a flag on it is going to threaten our constitutional freedom? And should a bunch of old men and women decide how a desperate young woman handles an unwanted and perhaps dangerous pregnancy? Do genuine conservatives really want the long arm of Washington invading our bedrooms and marital relations?

But I'm hopeful. I think this country has the capacity and the resources for a promising future. So I don't give up on us yet. I've always thought I lived in the greatest country on earth. And we must be great, because we've made such horrendous mistakes and we still survive. It must be our Constitution, our Bill of Rights, and the decency of our people.

I have been married to Eleanor for sixty-five years. That's another reason why we are still young—both of us now eighty-six. We were both twenty-one when we married during my days as a B-24 combat bomber pilot in WW II. I was awarded the Distinguished Flying Cross after completing a full tour of thirty-five bombing missions over Hitler's most heavily defended target. In 2000, I won the Presidential Medal of Freedom, the nation's highest civilian honor. I hold a PhD in History from Northwestern University. I take pride and zest for life from these three honors; from Eleanor and our five children, a dozen grandchildren, and three great-grandchildren; plus my marvelous Newfoundland dog Ursa, an inseparable companion.

LYNNE McTAGGART

Consciousness Over Matter

W hen I give a talk, I usually ask the audience, "How many of you are thinking positive thoughts most of the time?" One or two people raise their hands. Most giggle nervously. Many of us walk around in a constant stream of negativity—judging and criticizing ourselves or others in our thoughts or aloud, berating ourselves for something we did, and running others down for what they didn't do or aren't doing for us. We bathe ourselves and each other in negativity, and receive more from the media through dire news reports, violent movies, and nihilistic music.

Research in many different models and modalities has demonstrated the effects of negative intention. The experiments conducted by Japanese scientist Masaru Emoto graphically illustrate these effects as well as those of positive intention. He found that the molecules (crystalline structure) of water changed according to the water's exposure to negative or positive thoughts. The molecules were thrown into chaotic, even grotesque, disarray simply by the word "hate" directed at the water. With "love" or "gratitude," the molecules formed beautiful and complex structures. Dr. Emoto's research has far-reaching implications since approximately 60 percent of the human body (70 percent of the brain) is water, and water covers about 71 percent of the Earth, with more underground. What kind of internal disarray are we and the world in as a result of all the negative messages we send and receive? Of course, it is not only liquid that receives these messages. All the tissues of our body register this negativity, as do our energy fields, which a wide range of other research has revealed.

One of the hardest things for people to get their minds around seems to be the concept that we're beaming out information every moment, and that our thoughts are actual energies affecting us and everybody around us. If that information, that constant stream of thought, is negative, it's going to have a negative impact. If it's positive, if we're sending out love and good wishes with every moment, then that's going to have a positive impact.

If our consciousness is full of positive intention and positive regard for ourselves, for the water in our bodies, for our own internal ecosystems, it has profound implications for our health and longevity. We all need to ask ourselves whether the messages we are sending promote or undermine our well-being and that of others.

The Power of Intention

When I became aware of the power of intention, I began to watch the flotsam and jetsam that went through my mind. If you do the same, you may be shocked to discover how much of it is negative. Since then I have been trying to surround myself in positive thinking all the time, and be more aware of what I say to and about other people because I know that has an effect on them. If we all did this, we would be healthier on an individual and a global level, and the natural environment would be in better shape.

In addition, research has shown us that people who are positive and engaged live longer than those who are not. "Engaged" means connected to people and activities, and feeling a sense of connection. The sense of being part of a unity rather than being separate and alone is a key factor in health and longevity.

Scientists have been studying animals to understand the elements with which we're all wired. One of these elements is a seeking mechanism. It informs the search for food, but there is also a curiosity, the nosing around that animals do to explore their environment. As with positivism and engagement, people who have a seeking attitude toward life and maintain that curiosity level have increased longevity. The sense that the world still holds something for us is part of positive thinking and the feeling of connection.

Once you understand the power of intention, you understand that life doesn't happen to you—your thoughts create your reality. And who but you is in charge of your thoughts? There is something powerful that you can do for your health and well-being now and to ensure your healthier aging, and it doesn't depend on a medical system, a doctor, or a pill. By taking charge of your own consciousness and turning your thoughts to the positive, you will change your psychological, physical, and spiritual climate to a climate of health.

Once you become aware of the power of intention, you can no longer ignore the fact that you are connected to everyone and everything. With awareness of the effect that thoughts have—remember the water—your thoughts naturally turn in a more positive direction.

Experimenting with Intention

In 2007, I started the Intention Experiment, which is a series of experiments that leading scientists and I conduct via the Internet and at my seminars and conferences to test the power of thought to change the physical world. Studying the effect of mind on matter is the field known as the science of intention. The methodology for the Intention Experiment is distilled from the practices of masters of intention such as master healers, qigong masters, and shamans. Participants in our experiment are asked to follow a simple and practical program derived from these techniques.

My motivation in starting the experiment was to discover how far we could go with intention. What can we do with our thoughts? Can we stop a train? Can we save victims of cancer? Can we reverse pollution? I began working with scientists—physicists, psychologists, and biologists—from different laboratories. We set up experiments in which we ask people to come online at the Intention Experiment website and send an intention to a target at one of the labs. Then we observe any changes in the target. We use blinded experiments so the scientist won't influence the outcome and we have controls for comparison with the targets.

We started small. The first target was a leaf and the intention was to change its light emissions. (All living things emit a tiny current of light, as many studies have demonstrated.) When my first partner in the Intention Experiment, psychologist Gary Schwartz, PhD, director of the Center for Advances in Consciousness and Health at the University of Arizona, suggested this first target, I was dismayed. He said, "Hey, we're doing something that has never been tried before. It will be a breakthrough if we can show an effect—any effect." Then he quoted a line from the movie *Contact* when the scientist played by Jodie Foster wants to go flying off in a wormhole. The other scientist turns to her and says, "Baby steps, Ellie, baby steps." And that's what Gary keeps saying to me, "Baby steps—we've got to walk before we can run."

The test run at one of my conferences produced a huge effect in the leaf's light emissions. We replicated it numerous times with different groups and in different settings, and then moved on to setting the intention to make seeds grow more quickly. I had a lot of speaking engagements around the world last year, which afforded me a chance to try this with a diverse set of audiences. The first time was in Sydney, Australia, where I was presenting to a group of five hundred. We sent our intention to four sets of seeds—three control sets and one target set. The scientists didn't know to which seeds we were sending intention. All the groups I did this with, including a group of some thousands over the Internet, produced an effect on the growth rate of the targeted seeds in comparison to the control seeds. The biggest effect resulted from a group of experienced healers, however. They sent intention, and the targeted seeds not only sprouted earlier than the control seeds, but the plants from the targeted seeds also grew twice as tall.

After these experiments, we turned our attention to water, because, as discussed earlier, effecting changes in water has enormous implications. This time I worked with Konstantin Korotkov, the Russian physicist. We replicated Dr. Emoto's results. Next we're going to try to affect the bacteria in water, so that we can actually change polluted water. This year we're also going to be creating a mini Gaia, like a mini world, in a terrarium, and see if we can lower the temperature of it with our thoughts. If we can, that will have enormous implications for global warming. We also tried our first Peace Intention Experiment, aimed at lowering violence in Sri Lanka, one of the most savagely war-torn areas on the planet, and our data were compelling, showing a large effect. We're planning another attempting to raise the grade-point average in children in one of the poorest parts of America.

What we're doing is bringing controlled, scientific conditions to the study of intention. There is already a large body of science proving that thoughts can affect the physical world. There is also a good deal of research demonstrating precognition, ESP, and other phenomena whose existence skeptics have denied. In my view, the whole point of science is being willing to test the strange and unbelievable. A true scientist is an explorer, delving into the unknown. And much of what we regarded yesterday as unbelievable will be established fact tomorrow.

Tuning In to Other Channels

Beyond the fact that thoughts can actually produces changes on the physical level lies the notion of retroactive intentionality, which is that thoughts in the future can actually change an outcome in the past. There have already been studies that indicate the existence of this phenomenon, which supports the theory that time is not linear. I bring this up, not to argue one way or another, but simply to point out that we need to be explorers in our own lives and to open our minds to receiving information from other sources than those to which we have been trained to listen.

One of these sources may be your future self. In a kind of backward information flow, if you will, your future self may be giving information to your present self. Whether you call the small voice within your future self "intuition" or something else, what's important is not to dismiss what it has to say to you. The analytical left brain tends to close off such information channels. If you want information other than the limited cognitive information we normally feed our brains, you need to consciously open to and tune in to other channels.

When Einstein described how he discovered the theory of relativity, he told of being in an altered state and having it come to him as a gestalt, as a whole. I believe that genius comes from being able to tap into the field, that secret source of the universe, where you can download information.

This source of information is available to all of us. Precognitive information about ourselves and the world is coming to us all the time. We just have to listen to it. That listening becomes more acute as we exercise the facility. The same is true of intentions. The more you practice, the more focused and powerful your intentions become. The only difference between you and an intention master is time and experience.

Debra Muth, BS, MS, WHNP, ND, is co-owner of Spring City Health Centre, an integrative Anti-Aging & Regenerative Medicine clinic in Wisconsin. She is a national speaker and radio and television talk show guest on alternative health topics. She has authored continuing education programs, health newsletters, and magazine articles, and is currently coauthoring several books. She also conducts clinical research with several nutraceutical companies. Dr. Muth was born on November 27, 1966, in Milwaukee, Wisconsin.

DEBRA MUTH

CHAPTER
28

Living Menopause
Audaciously

For many women, menopause is a voyage or even a pilgrimage that takes years to complete. This journey transforms not only a woman's body, but her soul as well.

Menopausal life passage is not just about the body fighting to find hormonal balance. It is also about reclaiming the soul and calling the spirit back. When women reclaim their soul, they transition into a sense of their own identity. Many women change who they are during their lives, making adjustments for their children, husbands, and family, leaving parts of themselves with all the lives they touch. Women who call their spirit back learn to live, move, change, do, feel, think, and interact from a true place deep within themselves. Working from this deep sense of being allows them to be true, once again, to who they are as women.

Hormonal imbalance is a symptom of this life passage. The imbalance is the heart's cry to be absolute once again, and the spirit's desire to return to the place where it can exist in its natural state of strength and courage. The menopausal pilgrimage is about returning to that place, that sacred land at the core of the soul called home. In returning to that home, that inner sanctum, a woman finds the spiritual strength and sense of wholeness she craves, and is once again filled with the zest and self-reliance that she possessed before puberty, adult life, or children and marriage eclipsed them.

There is a widespread misconception that menopause happens to a woman around the age of fifty-one. Actually, though the completion of the menstrual cycle often occurs at that time, many women begin experiencing symptoms as early as age thirty-five. In my medical practice, I see woman undergoing these changes earlier every year, which manifest in a variety of symptoms and stages known as perimenopause (occurring for seven to ten or more years before the cessation of menses). The process of birthing herself, which is what a woman does as she moves through menopause, becomes a lengthy one indeed.

The start of this birthing process begins with a multitude of physical symptoms caused by a reduction of the hormones produced by the ovaries that help regulate a woman's body. Without these hormones, women experience night sweats, sexual disorders, hot flashes, mood swings, and insomnia, to name the most common manifestations. Some women manage these symptoms with little disruption of their daily lives, while others can no longer function in the world as they know it.

When hormonal imbalances begin to assert themselves, women often describe the experience with the following phrases, which I have heard repeatedly in my practice:

"I am no longer myself."

"I am no longer nice."

"I say whatever I think."

"I am irritated with people and depressed."

These questions stem from the emotional changes that occur with hormonal imbalances. Other questions I hear arise from the various demands women have placed on themselves over the years. We run through our busy lives at high speed, trying to squeeze in all the many activities our families or our jobs demand of us. Suddenly, one day in our early forties perhaps, we realize something is different. We find ourselves looking in the mirror and wondering: Who is that person looking back at me? Where did my youth go? How am I going to go on? These questions are a sign that hormonal imbalance is beginning. This is both a physical change and time to reclaim the soul and call the spirit back. If a woman restores her hormonal balance with a natural approach (as follows) and attends to soul work, she can regain her body, mind, and spirit.

Help for the Journey

Hormones dictate the aging process and a loss of hormones translates into the obvious, and not so obvious, signs of aging. What do we believe to be true about aging? From the point of view of many of my patients when they first come to see me, aging means a loss of everything as they know it. It means loss of their sexuality, their physical being, their endurance, their creativity, and even their minds, as they project into the future and the fear of senility. I help them see that they can leave behind the negativity and the sense of loss and become

DEBRA MUTH

Living Menopause Audaciously

For many women, menopause is a voyage or even a pilgrimage that takes years to complete. This journey transforms not only a woman's body, but her soul as well.

Menopausal life passage is not just about the body fighting to find hormonal balance. It is also about reclaiming the soul and calling the spirit back. When women reclaim their soul, they transition into a sense of their own identity. Many women change who they are during their lives, making adjustments for their children, husbands, and family, leaving parts of themselves with all the lives they touch. Women who call their spirit back learn to live, move, change, do, feel, think, and interact from a true place deep within themselves. Working from this deep sense of being allows them to be true, once again, to who they are as women.

Hormonal imbalance is a symptom of this life passage. The imbalance is the heart's cry to be absolute once again, and the spirit's desire to return to the place where it can exist in its natural state of strength and courage. The menopausal pilgrimage is about returning to that place, that sacred land at the core of the soul called home. In returning to that home, that inner sanctum, a woman finds the spiritual strength and sense of wholeness she craves, and is once again filled with the zest and self-reliance that she possessed before puberty, adult life, or children and marriage eclipsed them.

There is a widespread misconception that menopause happens to a woman around the age of fifty-one. Actually, though the completion of the menstrual cycle often occurs at that time, many women begin experiencing symptoms as early as age thirty-five. In my medical practice, I see woman undergoing these changes earlier every year, which manifest in a variety of symptoms and stages known as perimenopause (occurring for seven to ten or more years before the cessation of menses). The process of birthing herself, which is what a woman does as she moves through menopause, becomes a lengthy one indeed.

The start of this birthing process begins with a multitude of physical symptoms caused by a reduction of the hormones produced by the ovaries that help regulate a woman's body. Without these hormones, women experience night sweats, sexual disorders, hot flashes, mood swings, and insomnia, to name the most common manifestations. Some women manage these symptoms with little disruption of their daily lives, while others can no longer function in the world as they know it.

When hormonal imbalances begin to assert themselves, women often describe the experience with the following phrases, which I have heard repeatedly in my practice:

"I am no longer myself."

"I am no longer nice."

"I say whatever I think."

"I am irritated with people and depressed."

These questions stem from the emotional changes that occur with hormonal imbalances. Other questions I hear arise from the various demands women have placed on themselves over the years. We run through our busy lives at high speed, trying to squeeze in all the many activities our families or our jobs demand of us. Suddenly, one day in our early forties perhaps, we realize something is different. We find ourselves looking in the mirror and wondering: Who is that person looking back at me? Where did my youth go? How am I going to go on? These questions are a sign that hormonal imbalance is beginning. This is both a physical change and time to reclaim the soul and call the spirit back. If a woman restores her hormonal balance with a natural approach (as follows) and attends to soul work, she can regain her body, mind, and spirit.

Help for the Journey

Hormones dictate the aging process and a loss of hormones translates into the obvious, and not so obvious, signs of aging. What do we believe to be true about aging? From the point of view of many of my patients when they first come to see me, aging means a loss of everything as they know it. It means loss of their sexuality, their physical being, their endurance, their creativity, and even their minds, as they project into the future and the fear of senility. I help them see that they can leave behind the negativity and the sense of loss and become pioneers in aging—an aging in which youthful vigor, creativity, joy, and fulfillment are part of daily life.

I employ a holistic approach, recognizing that our minds and bodies are not static but continually changing with life. In anti-aging medicine, we intervene before menopause to treat the symptoms and long-term consequences that result from less-than-optimal hormone levels. Practitioners and patients should work together to balance the physical and psychospiritual, using various modalities such as nutritional support, cleansing, herbal medicine, bodywork, and lifestyle coaching to complete the full-spectrum wellness program. Menopause is not a disease. It is a journey that should be traveled with those who support you and help you grow.

With proper attention to hormonal health, women are better able to cope with the challenges of each new stage of life, and the passage to new satisfactions is eased. One of the most common reasons I see women in my practice is to aid in their decision about whether to use hormone replacement therapy. I use bioidentical hormones, which are molecularly identical to those made in the human body. This means they have the same exact chemical structure as hormones produced by our body. A hormone will only act on a part of the body if it "fits." A hormone can be thought of as a key, and its target site (an organ) a specially shaped "lock" on each cell. The hormone will work if the key (hormone) fits into the lock (on the cell). When hormones turn the key, they unlock the feedback system to the entire endocrine system, allowing the organs and cells to communicate with one another and accept the messages from the hormones. Only when the endocrine glands get feedback from the body can they adjust hormone levels and keep them at the right balance. The introduction of bioidentical hormones allows this process to occur, providing women with the proper hormonal balance and the subsequent feeling of being whole, once again. The goal of bioidentical hormone replacement therapy is to alleviate the symptoms caused by the natural decrease in production of hormones by the body. Supplementing with bioidentical hormones can also prevent and reverse osteoporosis, improve lipid profiles, and reduce the risk of heart disease, breast cancer, and Alzheimer's disease, thereby slowing the aging process.

Media reports about the Women's Health Initiative (WHI) trial have fueled anxiety and concern about hormone therapy. Doctors are refusing to start hormone therapy on women experiencing the symptoms of menopause. Even worse, many women are being pulled off of it, despite the fact that they feel great on this treatment and have been using it for years. Headlines in the press have proclaimed hormone therapy to be dead. Many physicians who understand the results of the WHI study, however, have spoken out against the generalization of the results to any woman considering hormone therapy. They rightly assert, as I have, that the WHI results apply only to the two drugs studied: Premarin and Provera. Neither of these synthetic hormones are bioidentical to women's hormones. More important, the majority of the women in this trial were sixty-five years old and had not been treated for the first ten to fifteen years of menopause, a situation not applicable to women seeking treatment for early symptoms of menopause. Alas, such a balanced and intelligent assessment does not make for good headlines.

Then along came Suzanne Somers's book *The Sexy Years*. Suddenly, the term "bioidentical hormones" entered public awareness and these hormones became the new rage. Those of us who practice anti-aging and regenerative medicine are thankful that this book raised the issue again and focused attention on the availability of safe, effective, and, most important, individually tailored hormone replacement therapy.

The conventional method of hormone replacement therapy (HRT) is substandard in comparison to other conventional medical practices for conditions that, over time, lead to an increase in disease. The standard HRT approach is not to test to determine the individual woman's hormone levels, but simply to start a woman on one of the drugs; there is no initial testing and there is no later testing to monitor the results. This is akin to starting a patient on thyroid medication without laboratory testing and then not providing any adjustments based on testing; doctors wouldn't think of doing that.

Balancing hormones is a science and an art, and should involve looking at women as individuals. Women need to be provided with the most updated and best available testing and, if hormone replacement is warranted, the most superiorly prepared bioidentical hormones for bringing balance back to the endocrine system. Tailoring treatment to a woman's specific needs requires reviewing her symptoms, medical history, family history, and personal desires. Each consultation should be unique and include asking women about their feminine being and helping them find their lost spirit.

I do this by talking with my female patients about what it means to have feminine power. Reclaiming our feminine power entails recognizing and honoring the values of female energy, and giving it its due importance and place in our daily lives. Living in our feminine power means living according to our natural way of being, that is, who in fact we are. Living this power means accepting that we have the authority and right to decide what is best for us as individuals.

My patients and I talk about what brings them happiness, joy, and the feeling of being complete. This knowledge is important both spiritually and medically in the passage into menopause.

It is also important for women to discover where they lost their spirit during their life's journey. We talk in depth about what has brought them turmoil and heartache. By working through these issues, women can heal old wounds and grieve losses, and in the process, become whole again. This way of working with women provides them both the physical balance and spiritual balance they need to create the lives they desire.

I became interested in these issues and in alternative medicine as a result of my own medical issues. I was misdiagnosed with fibromyalgia, for which there are no real medical treatment options. I say "misdiagnosed" because no functional medical tests were done to prove this diagnosis. It was a diagnosis of exclusion; that is, doctors eliminated everything else they thought it could be. With no treatment beyond pain pills for the chronic muscle and joint pain throughout my body, I turned to some close friends who opened my eyes to the healing capabilities of spirituality.

As a medical practitioner, I (along with a surprising number of other health-care practitioners) became aware that our Western scientific medicine, despite its wonderful accomplishments, has its limitations. Alternative practitioners assisted me in my recovery. They showed me how nutrition, hormonal rebalancing, detoxification, and a spiritual journey could help me emerge from my debilitating condition. Without them and their knowledge, I am not sure where I would be today, but I do know it would not be doing what I absolutely love. I am not alone in recognizing what alternative healing can do. The general public does as well, as evidenced by the increasing enthusiasm for alternative healing techniques.

The Sacred Descent

In order to grow, women need to address the issues that have held them back spiritually during their lives. Psychoanalyst and developmental psychologist Erik Erikson believed in a psychosocial structure of development in which society plays a major role in shaping one's development over the life course. There are eight stages in Erikson's psychosocial model of development, with the ultimate goal being the achievement of a stable sense of identity. For many women, their sense of identity has been molded and shaped into someone that everyone else believes they should be. Many of us have sculpted ourselves to succeed in a male-dominated world, often losing the feminine side of who we are. We no longer understand the power we hold within us or what is waiting to be tapped into, explored, and released into the world.

To the outside world, a woman who has begun her menopausal journey often appears preoccupied, sad, and inaccessible. Tears flow without reason but are ever-present, whether she cries or not. She cannot be comforted, feels abandoned, becomes forgetful, and chooses not to go out or spend time with friends. She curls up in a ball on the bed, refusing to leave her room. Or she may find comfort in the earth, working in the garden or just walking in nature. She enters a period of isolation, seen by friends and family as depression or a nervous breakdown.

During this journey, women may feel stripped bare or devoured by anger. They may feel a loss of identity, a falling away of the perimeters of a known role. Often there is a feeling of being dried up, raw, and devoid sexually, a gut-wrenching sense of being turned inside out.

Women may move in and out of these feelings and can spend any length of time in this descent, but the truth is that every woman will find her way back. This occurs through a spiritual experience of moving deep into self rather than out of self.

Many women decide that they need to remove themselves from the male-dominated world during this transition. Some women choose to remove themselves physically while others separate themselves in a conscious way on an emotional or mental level.

I think that in *The Heroine's Journey* author Maureen Murdock is really describing the menopausal journey as she explains the descent into the underworld. Women should have great respect for this sacred journey. The process allows each woman to address her feelings and fears about her changing life.

One Woman's Journey

I would like to share a story of one woman's menopausal journey. Katherine, forty-five years old and in her second marriage, was busy with her career as a teacher and near the end of raising her three children. She spent her spare time caring for her parents and in-laws. She thought she was managing her life perfectly. She was always on the go, with minimal time for herself. She had no clue that her life as she knew it was about to come crashing down when her youngest child left for college.

Almost instantly, her life came to a stop. She found herself in the menopausal descent, overwhelmed with fatigue. Having no energy even to dress herself, she was unable to grocery shop, cook, or do laundry. Katherine went into a period of isolation, unable to work or leave her home. When I met her, she had seen eight different doctors, none of whom had been able to help her. They told her she was suffering from depression; one described her situation as a nervous breakdown. She knew it was something very different, but whatever it was seemed to be controlling her entire being.

I was able to give Katherine an explanation for what was happening to her. This menopausal descent is a part of menopause rarely discussed by the general medical community. In her case, this aspect of menopause was triggered by the life-altering event of her last child leaving home. In our lengthy discussion, she admitted she had been experiencing many of the symptoms of hormonal imbalance; she had just attributed them to normal menopause. Wanting to manage it naturally, she never considered hormone replacement therapy, nor did any of the eight doctors from whom she sought care. The unfortunate reality is that our health care system is not exactly user-friendly.

I explained that many of her symptoms were being triggered by hormonal imbalances taking control of her, rather than her having control over them. Menopause, a normal process that every woman goes through, should be manageable without this much difficulty. Most women going through this process are just looking for a reasonable explanation about what is happening to them along with some reassurance that there is an end in sight.

Testing of Katherine's hormone levels showed us which hormones were out of balance and which needed replacement. After starting hormone therapy, Katherine was able to begin to reclaim her life; the imbalance of hormones no longer had control of her. She slowly emerged from her isolation, allowing herself to become acquainted with her feelings, her emotions, and her body. Katherine has been working through this journey for the past two years. She is more herself than when she began this amazing life-altering experience. She has returned to her career, is finding joy in gardening, and learning to live without her children being the center of her life. Did hormone therapy do all of this? Certainly not, but it helped her regain control over emotional ups and downs, which in turn gave her the ability to work through the challenges menopause brought with it.

CHAPTER TWENTY-EIGHT

Succession of Rites

The journey of menopause is not a solitary rite of passage, rather a succession of rites or rituals. The succession of rites marks a woman's way through midlife, validating the struggles of each stage of her voyage, like steppingstones across a rising river. Each woman makes her way through these rites in her own way. Some may find the sacraments painful, while others hardly notice them. Although all women make this voyage, the journey of menopause is a highly individualistic passage; the currents each chooses to sail are hers and hers alone.

Christiane Northrup, MD, is a leading proponent of medicine and healing that recognizes the role of mind, body, and spirit in health. The best-selling author of *Women's Bodies, Women's Wisdom* and *The Wisdom Menopause* says, "I've spent the first half of my life studying and footnoting everything that can go wrong with the female body—and figuring out how to fix it. I'm dedicating the second half of my life to illuminating everything that can go right with the female body, including teaching women how to truly flourish." Dr. Northrup was born on October 4, 1949, in Buffalo, New York. Photo by Barbara Peacock.

CHRISTIANE NORTHRUP

CHAPTER 29

The Wisdom Cycle

For women, issues of aging are often the same issues connected to female health problems throughout their lives. The emotional, psychological, societal, and cultural influences underlying the health problems, if unresolved, influence a woman's experience of aging as well.

As an example of the factors in health beyond the physical, I noticed long ago in my practice as an obstetrician/gynecologist that if a woman comes in with, let's say, eight vaginal yeast infections per year, she does not have a Monistat deficiency. That part of the body, which I call the "lower lips," is trying to tell her something. I often say, "When the upper lips can't speak, the lower lips will." In many cases, a woman with this health condition is involved in an abusive relationship, or a relationship in which she feels she is forced to have sex that she doesn't want to have. Or she might have a job in which she feels forced to do things she doesn't want to do but feels she can't say no. In a culture that, for about five thousand years, has seen the female body as the second-class citizen, with the male body being the "normal" body, you can well imagine that the female body and the organs that identify us as female have a great deal to say.

The first thing a woman needs to come to grips with is that the processes of her body—her menstrual cycle, pregnancy, breastfeeding, and menopause—are imbued with great wisdom that is always trying to lead her back to the truth. And she needs to realize that her female body is not a mistake that is meant to cause suffering because of Eve's sin or other shaming cultural belief. Once a woman accepts all this, she's got a fighting chance to listen to the wisdom of her body.

The Wisdom of PMS and Menopause

Premenstrual syndrome (PMS) provides a prime opportunity for hearing what the body has to teach. PMS first got my attention as a disease state (or, literally, dis-ease state) in the early 1980s. An article in *Family Circle* magazine first brought the issue to the public; this was before the ob/gyn literature began to discuss it. After the article, many women came to me because somebody had named their suffering. I learned all I could about PMS and began a treatment approach. I found that lifestyle changes—exercising more and eliminating coffee and sugar—usually cured it, but the cure only worked for the first three to four months because the woman, invariably, was unable to continue with those lifestyle changes, even though she felt much better. In almost every case of severe PMS, I found that the woman was living in an alcoholic family system of some kind (e.g., living with an active alcoholic or having an alcoholic parent). As we know, alcoholism is associated with blood sugar issues in entire families, but also with emotional issues.

It became clear that PMS did not lend itself to the one-drug, get-rid-of-the-symptoms treatment approach. Healing required addressing the body, mind, and spirit. That's how I learned that what happens just before your period is premenstrual strength—that is what I say that PMS stands for. Everything that you have not wanted to look at comes up and hits you between the eyes. You have a chance then to change your approach to life, to clean up your relationships, your job, and your thoughts, and then you get another cycle to try everything out again. The menstrual cycle is actually a time of deep introspection and renewal, and a woman typically gets in her lifetime about 450 chances to benefit from it.

On the day before menstruation and the first days of bleeding, the veil between the worlds of the conscious and unconscious is much thinner. I like to say that the menstrual cycle is to the monthly cycle as the seasons of the year are to the annual cycle. The PMS time would be the fall of the year, the dark time of year, the time for introspection and deep emotional processing. Anything you have hidden in the dark comes to the surface then. Once you process that, you find that the premenstrual interval is a time of enormous creativity and enormous rebirth.

When I watched women recover from PMS, they were recovering from the notion that their hormones were victimizing them, as though their hormones existed separately from their thoughts and emotions. Once women get this piece, they no longer feel victimized by their bodies. If you don't learn this lesson by the time you reach

menopause, then perimenopause (the years leading up to menopause and the year after the last menstrual period) comes on as PMS
writ large.

Interestingly, dichotic listening tests (in which a different audi-
tory stimuli is given to each ear at the same time) have revealed
that the right hemisphere is more activated premenstrually and
perimenopausally than the left is, and this hemisphere causes us to
be more tuned to the negative in our lives than at other times. Thus,
at these times you can ferret out the negative thought forms that are
going on below your radar the rest of the time, and then you can
transform them. Unless you can begin to hear them, however, you
will not know they are there and you will miss the opportunity for
transformation.

The Life Waiting for You

In 1900, the average life expectancy for a woman was approximately forty-two. The average woman died shortly after seeing her
first grandchildren born. So what happens with women today, for
whom the average life expectancy is eighty-three, with fifty percent
living beyond that age? When we're in perimenopause, at midlife, we
feel as though we are going through a death, I think this is because
for most of written history, that really was the end. For those of us
in the modern world, however, it's a whole new beginning. But the
transition of perimenopause still requires you to die to your old self.
You have to die to some of the dreams you had about a perfect marriage, perfect children, a perfect career—dreams that may never see
the light of day. You realize that you have a finite amount of time left,
and so you need to focus on what you really want to give birth to.
And at midlife, you're giving birth to exactly who you were when
you were eleven, only now you have the ego strength and the skills
to do something about it.

Many women at midlife redecorate their houses with a ven-
geance. The house is a metaphor for the self. They often add color
and feel the need to de-clutter and redo rooms. Many start to ride
horses again if they loved that when they were eleven. Still, they have
to grieve for what will no longer be. Midlife brings the end of many
relationships, jobs, and ways of being in the world. I was very helped
at that stage myself by something that Joseph Campbell said: "We
must be willing to give up the life we had planned in order to have
the life that is waiting for us."

In my case, I faced divorce after twenty-four years of marriage,
and I suddenly went from a household of five to living alone. I came

up in a huge way against some obsolete but cherished beliefs, especially the "happily ever after" one. Whenever you are in that position—when you are between the worlds, as it were—what happens is a tremendous opening to your soul. It's as though the heavens open up and you can reinvent yourself because you can't rely on those old external structures or beliefs that are no longer useful to your growth. It's a time to download more light than ever before.

To find the life waiting for you requires fueling your life from your soul, from source energy. This life can't be fueled by how you look, the kind of car you drive, how handsome your husband is, or how much money you make. It must be authentic. When you fuel your life from source energy, you become more authentic, more yourself, and then more childlike, but with huge skills and wisdom at the same time. There is an added benefit to living an authentic life, along with the joy, release of energy, and fulfillment that comes with living authentically. People who do so actually turn back the clock in their appearance, because the soul has no age.

My mother is eighty-two and she takes a group of women twenty years younger than she into the Adirondacks every summer. They call it Camp Edna. She takes them up mountains, shows them how to pitch their tents and all the other skills of camping, and leads them on hikes. She is one of those of her generation who are reinventing the way aging is done. The baby boomers will carry that reinvention further.

The New Order of Aging

A basic understanding of the new aging is that there is absolutely no reason to have chronic degenerative disease in the second half of life. As a doctor, I can assure you this is true. By chronic degenerative disease, I mean high blood pressure, heart disease, cancer, diabetes, osteoporosis, and arthritis. In most cases, the development of these disorders is a choice.

If you understand that whatever is happening to you is related to your thoughts and emotions, which set the tone for your behavior, then you are in the driver's seat. Yes, we can say that heart disease and high blood pressure are related to lifestyle—lack of exercise, smoking, poor diet. But knowing that, why would somebody do what Dr. Norm Shealy calls "committing slow suicide"? Why aren't people able to change their habits, even when they know that those habits are killing them? Because those adverse health behaviors are driven by an emotion or emotions with which they have trouble dealing and of which they might not even be aware. A friend of mine recently lost thirty-four pounds in a weight-loss program that addresses lifestyle changes and issues for people who are obese. She said it was the hardest work she has ever done in her life because she had to confront her emotional eating. In other words, when you're not pushing down emotions with pastry (or whatever method you use), you have to feel them.

There is no question that there are emotions that we've stuffed since we were little. Here's the problem: These emotions come up and out the same way they went in. In other words, it feels as bad to relive them as it felt to feel them the first time. But to truly release the stifled emotions means feeling what Stephen Levine calls "the pain that ends the pain." Emotions are the digestive system of our energy. If we want to free our energy, we need to get the system moving, and that means getting the emotions moving. Just as the body knows how to heal a cut or a broken bone, it knows how to heal emotional pain. Its methods are movement, breathing, crying, and tears. When you listen to the wisdom of the body, you have the help you need to move through your pain.

A newspaper article I read recently reported that since the vast majority of cases of frozen shoulder occur in women between the ages of forty and sixty, the condition is thought to be hormonal. That's idiotic. A lifetime of suppressed emotions surfacing in body pain is the likely source for the incidence in that age group, as with so many of the degenerative conditions of later life.

I had personal experience with this. When I woke up one morning, my right shoulder felt frozen and hurt enormously when I tried to move it, though I had not injured myself. I knew from my research that the source of frozen shoulder is emotional. Since the emotions were manifesting as a condition in my body, they must be ones I could not consciously feel. I refused to allow myself to develop frozen shoulder. The first thing I did was not panic, and I didn't run to my primary physician either. I went to my acupuncturist to help with the pain in the meantime, and I consulted Louise Hay's book *Heal Your Body A–Z: The Mental Causes for Physical Illness and the Way to Overcome Them*. Under the entry for "shoulder," I learned that one of the issues with conditions of the right shoulder is things feeling burdensome. I used the affirmations to release that sense of burden, such as "I choose to allow all of my experiences to be joyous and loving" and "I release any burdens I am carrying." Each time after saying the affirmations, I consciously stretched the shoulder. Now my range of motion is better than it ever was. But if I had been the average woman who didn't know the role of emotions in the so-called conditions of midlife, I'd probably be disabled by now.

That said, it is still important to observe good lifestyle choices to support the physical health of the body. Releasing stored emotions liberates your body from patterns that can lead to the development of chronic disease, but doing so doesn't mean you can then indulge in poor lifestyle choices without consequence to your health. Given our longer life spans, exercise is no longer optional, for example. If you want to keep your body healthy through the extra decades we humans now live, exercise must be part of your regular routine.

The Real Data

Our prevailing cultural myth is that we get old, sick, worthless, and die. For five thousand years, a woman has been seen as valuable when she could provide sons. So when you're no longer able to have babies, traditionally you've been seen as worthless. If you have that thought and hold that belief, what do you think you're going to see in your life and the world around you? Our thoughts and our beliefs create our reality. So we need to look to the women who are vibrant, wonderful, and happy in their fifties and sixties and decide to make that a reality in our own lives.

The idea of women not being attractive after the age of fifty is changing rapidly, with help from celebrities such as Helen Mirren and Susan Sarandon, both in their sixties and still radiating vitality and sexuality. The commercial world may be trying to keep the old stereotype going because when you create insecurity in consumers (this is particularly true for the huge number of baby-boomer women entering their later years), you have a ready market to sell almost any product you want. But there is no reason for us to buy. There is now data showing that women are having the best sex of their lives in their sixties and seventies. This is the new message that I am getting out now. Women in their sixties are the happiest they've ever been. These are the best years of your life! That's the real data.

The myth that our brains become feeble as we age has also been debunked. We now know about neuroplasticity, which is a character-istic of your brain. Neuroplasticity means that your brain continues to change and make connections between cells as a result of experi-ence, and not only that, but it continues to create new cells. When I was in medical school, the conventional wisdom was that by the age of twenty-five you had all the brain cells you were ever going to have, and thereafter you started to lose them and continued to do so throughout your adult life. This is simply not true. We now know that human beings are capable of growth, change, learning, and flex-ibility for their entire lives—it never ends. As with the body, however, we must exercise the brain. Growth, change, learning, and flexibility require effort.

As the culture catches up with the data of aging, the cultural stereotypes of aging will change. There isn't a question that this will happen because today's younger women in particular are not going to accept being swept under the carpet as insignificant as they get older.

Today we are ushering in the new order of aging.

Dean Radin, PhD, senior scientist at the Institute of Noetic Sciences (IONS)
in Petaluma, California, has been conducting research on consciousness
for more than two decades. He has held positions at Princeton University,
University of Edinburgh, University of Nevada, and three Silicon Valley think
tanks. Among his many writings are more than two hundred journal and
popular articles, and the books *The Conscious Universe* and *Entangled
Minds.* He has appeared on numerous radio and television shows,
including *Oprah* and *Larry King Live.* Dean Radin was born on
Leap Day in 1952, in New York City. Photo by John Zeuli.

Dean Radin

Mind Over Time

Aging is an entropic process. This means that our body, like any physical system, tends over time to go from order to disorder. This natural tendency is closely related to what we see as the unidirectional march of time. If it were possible to slow or reverse the apparent flow of time in the human body, would the aging process slow down or even stop?

Experiments conducted for a half century by numerous investigators worldwide suggest that the mind exerts subtle effects on matter. Theoretical models of these effects indicate that one way they might work is through retrocausal influences, that is, through a reversal of the arrow of time. Such time reversals can be interpreted as "negative entropy," or negentropy.

If there were a way to cultivate negentropy with the mind, it raises the possibility that with appropriate practice we might be able not only to stop aging, but to actually reverse it.

We Are All Entangled

Research in extended forms of consciousness has revealed that our everyday perceptions are highly constrained versions of what we are actually capable of perceiving. For example, most people think of the self as being located inside the head, generated by the brain. But experiments show that your mind is not completely locked inside your head. It is actually distributed through space and probably through time as well. If interpretations of this evidence are correct, then it implies that we have *distributed minds*, that is, our minds extend through time and space. This, in turn, implies that besides our individual selves, there may be the equivalent of a massive, collective mind or self. We are not normally aware of this collective self, except during those unusual experiences we call psychic, or when we get a small glimpse of that large mind in a mystical or near-death experience.

In my book, *Entangled Minds,* I examined this phenomenon of distributed or nonlocal minds in detail. The book's title refers to the strangest characteristic of our most successful theory of matter and energy—quantum entanglement. The mathematics of quantum theory predicts that when two elementary objects interact with each other in certain ways, then when the objects continue on their merry ways, they are no longer separate. For many decades, scientists thought this was just a curious theoretical possibility with no practical import. Then in the 1960s, physicist John Bell figured out a way to test whether entanglement actually exists as the mathematics described.

It took another decade or so before people began to look for, and eventually find, entanglement effects in laboratory experiments. Since then, it has been confirmed many times, and today we know to very high levels of confidence that elementary particles are indeed entangled through space and time. They might appear to be separate, but they're actually not. Once they interact, they remain instantaneously connected, regardless of distance.

If this sort of time-space connectivity is demonstrable in the deep fabric of reality, then what relevance does it have for human beings? When we look out at the world, we normally see things as separate objects. I feel separate from you, and I look at objects in my office and they appear to be separate. So the connectivity that we know exists at the quantum scale doesn't appear to exist at the everyday, macroscopic scale.

But appearances can be deceiving. In fact, it is possible to demonstrate that certain physical properties of objects made out of billions and billions of atoms, such as a cubic centimeter of certain magnetic alloys, can only be adequately explained as aspects of quantum entanglement. Many scientists are now studying quantum effects in larger and larger systems, including biological systems, so it seems increasingly clear that we will eventually find more and more evidence of emergent properties that are ultimately based on entanglement, perhaps including in the human brain.

Separation Is an Illusion

What entanglement *means* is that now we know what the mystics used to talk about, that separation is an illusion and that the world is made up of appearances, was not just a fantasy. It is how the world actually exists at deep levels of reality. This has been confirmed

through two centuries of careful work in experimental and theoretical physics. Given that we know the fabric of reality is a holistic, non-separable tapestry, we might ask: What would human experience be like in that kind of holistic space? The answer is that sometimes you should find yourself thinking what somebody else is thinking, because minds are not quite as separate as they appear to be. And sometimes you might perceive information from a distance, because space isn't as separate as it appears to be. If you imagine what these hypothetical nonlocal experiences would actually feel like, and how they might manifest in the everyday world, it turns out that exactly the same descriptions apply to what is commonly known as psychic and mystical experience.

Of course, to clearly distinguish between conventional and unconventional explanations, we have to turn to laboratory experiments to see whether it is possible in principle for, say, two people to communicate without any ordinary means of communication. Over the past century, many researchers have been investigating this issue. My colleagues and I have been doing this for the past few decades. I will give one example of the kind of thing we do in the laboratory at the Institute of Noetic Sciences.

We take a couple, typically a long-term, emotionally bonded pair, and isolate them in two separate locations, one of which is an electromagnetically shielded room, which we use to rule out the possibility of transmission of electromagnetic signals. We monitor some aspect of their nervous system, typically EEG, skin conductance, or heart rate. We simply ask them to relax for thirty minutes and to think of each other. They both know their partner is sitting in another room at a distance, but that is all they know. Meanwhile, one person, the "sender," sees a live video image of the friend, the "receiver," inside the shielded room, but the image on the screen is not on all the time. It only pops up for ten seconds, at random times, typically about thirty seconds apart. Otherwise the sender is looking at a blank video screen.

The purpose of this type of experiment is that if it is true that we are connected and that separation is an illusion, then if you do the equivalent of poking one of them, then the other one should flinch. That is essentially how the experiment works. The poking doesn't actually involve a physical poke, of course; instead we use the sudden onset of the live video image as the stimulus. The face of the receiver suddenly popping up on the sender's screen creates a startle effect in the sender, and then we look at the physiology of the receiver to see if they responded. To make a very long story short, the answer is that we do see these responses, repeatedly. The receivers in the heavily

shielded room do show physiological reactions that are consistent with the idea that they are somehow experiencing the startle reaction of the distant senders. The way the experiment is constructed ensures that what is being "sent" is not due to electromagnetic or any other conventional signals.

There seems to be something important about the degree of emotional bondedness between the couple, which helps to modulate this phenomenon. My guess is that our emotions modulate how we pay attention to things. You tend to pay a lot of attention to people you love, whether they are present or not. By virtue of paying attention, you exclude a lot of things you might otherwise focus on. In a sense, your attention acts like a laser beam and chops through the illusion of separation, allowing you to perceive what is always there, even when it's not right in front of you. If you hadn't focused your attention, you wouldn't perceive it.

All Is Relationship

One of the central mysteries about consciousness is how does matter become aware of itself in the way that we are aware, in the way that we have personal subjective experiences? No one knows the answer to this yet, or how such a thing could even be possible. There are two main lines of thought about the problem. One is that any sufficiently complex system would give rise to recursive circuits, like a hall of mirrors, and recursion is what we subjectively experience as reflective awareness. This general idea is considered the leading candidate within the neurosciences and Western philosophy in general. I am more inclined to adopt the other line of thinking, which is more compatible with Eastern philosophical ways of understanding the world: Consciousness is a fundamental aspect of reality, it is simply a part of the fabric of reality itself, and thus everything is constructed out of consciousness.

The reason I like this approach is because consciousness is very closely related to information, and there is a branch of physics that proposes that everything is literally constructed out of information. This is in alignment with the idea in quantum mechanics that if you go all the way down to the bottom of matter and energy, all you end up with are relationships between things. Not tinier bits of matter or energy. No objects at all. Just relationships. So what we call an electron or a photon is actually a set of relationships. This means that the fabric of reality is held together by, and constructed out of, pure information. Consciousness, too, seems to be profoundly linked to the idea of information, or to information processing.

Mystics, who are devoted to the experiential expansion of consciousness, are people who have learned, or have spontaneously experienced, such close attention to their own subjective experience that they perceive reality with "naked awareness," that is, they experience the true nature of the world. That state is sometimes described as crystalline, timeless, and beautiful, extending throughout and transcending all time and space. I think the reasons such experiences are often expressed poetically, or in music or art, is because we don't have words to describe pure information without reference to objects.

The Laws of the Universe May Only Be Habits

Recently, I have been studying the role of consciousness in the physical world by investigating how mind and photons interact. For example, one experiment investigates the role of mind in the speed of light. If it turns out that mentally we can alter the speed of light, then the whole structure of what we have assumed to be fixed laws of the universe is brought into question, and physical laws start to look more like habits. If the speed of light is a habit we all agreed upon, perhaps as a result of Einstein's insight, then perhaps this "law" is more malleable than we think.

There is already a great deal of data indicating that through intention the mind can interact with the physical world both inside and outside the body. If you took that same principle and directed intention inside your body in a way that is relevant to slowing the aging process, then it might be possible to develop a way to remain physically as young as you wish. This may be what is happening in some swamis who are in their seventies and eighties and yet maintain such youthful looking appearances. Of course, these unusual cases probably have a great deal to do with long-term meditation practice as well, especially the stress-relieving aspects of meditation.

The release of accumulated daily stress that occurs with regular meditation probably adds years to your life, to say nothing of better health along the way. But if we can go beyond stress relief and begin to directly slow the aging process through focused mind, then so much the better.

Meanwhile, I am anticipating that there will be scientific breakthroughs in the early part of this century that will demonstrate quantum coherence and entanglement phenomena in biological systems. The moment someone can show both theoretically and experimentally that biology supports quantum effects, perhaps as an emergent property of elementary entanglement, then the scientific plausibility and acceptance of psychic and mystical experience will quickly increase. Shortly thereafter, such experiences will no longer be seen as impossible or even as anomalous, but rather as something we would predict *must* occur. At that point, a historical revisioning process will occur in which all of the previous data, data collected for centuries about psychic and mystical experiences that were once dismissed as nonsense, will suddenly be viewed as obvious facts. Former skeptics will then sheepishly admit, "Those people were right all along. But now we understand why."

Gabrielle Roth, philosopher, movement innovator/explorer, theatre director, and recording artist, is the creator of the 5Rhythms movement meditation practice. Her international Moving Center has certified more than three hundred 5Rhythms teachers worldwide. She also teaches experimental and traditional acting. The best-selling author of *Maps to Ecstasy, Sweat Your Prayers* and *Connections,* her work has been featured in *Self, Elle, Mademoiselle, Bazaar, Utne Reader, New Age Journal,* and *Body Mind Spirit,* among other media. Gabrielle Roth was born on February 4, 1941, in San Francisco, California. Photo: Lekha Singh.

GABRIELLE ROTH

CHAPTER 31

The Audacious Self

A ging is inevitable. Doing it audaciously is a choice. And understanding the full impact of this reality and possibility is the difference between ego and essence, being awake or asleep, filled with joy or depression.

Let's face it—being born is an audacious act. Who wouldn't prefer to keep swimming when faced with that dark lonely tunnel of transition? Giving birth is an audacious act, although we don't know it until we are in the middle of it. Surviving childhood is an audacious act, considering how cruel we can be as kids. And navigating the masks, myths, and machinations of a world gone mad requires us, at some point, to step up and into our most audacious self, become a rebel by joining forces with the big heart beating in our cathedral of bones. It requires nothing less than everything to hook up with our most authentic being.

To connect with mine was a public journey, a journey of sweat and service that delivered me, much as a mother delivers her child, into a world that double-dared me in the face of its suffering to get moving and take everybody with me.

From the beginning, dancing was my passion. When I was dancing, I felt uplifted, peaceful, holy, outrageous, sexy, totally myself, and free of all my suffering. Freedom was palpable. It was only natural to want everybody else to have this experience. Rhythm became my refuge and eventually my philosophy, perspective, and practice. This was my offering to others—a revolutionary road rooted in rhythm.

In my youth, my addiction to being a good girl involved a vast amount of self-betrayal and self-loathing, shoved into one skinny little body. When I looked around me, I saw the same repression, self-loathing, betrayal, and suffering everywhere. Sixteen at the time, I had to pay my rent and put myself through college, and the only thing I knew how to do was dance. So I was hired to teach dance to elders and kids and later in rehab centers and psychiatric wards. People couldn't handle steps or routines because they didn't have the physical training for that; my job was to get people moving, wherever I was, however I could do it.

The 5Rhythms (5R) movement practice I developed was born over a decade of dancing, releasing all the joy buried beneath my pain, and catalyzing others to do the same. Thankfully, there's no dogma in the dance. There's nothing the dance can't transform and there's no part of us that has to be left behind. The five rhythms (flowing, staccato, chaos, lyrical, and stillness) are exquisitely accessible. 5R has reached and rocked people in wheelchairs, prisons, theaters, churches, and schools, and crossed borders and boundaries to create a global community of people who sweat their prayers.

An Inner Revolution

Once we identify with the force, the energy of life that is moving in and through us, we start to feel what it means to be a free spirit, to be free of the part of us that is constantly judging, comparing, controlling, analyzing, and manipulating, and holding us back. Nothing less than an inner revolution is required. This revolution is very personal; it involves finding our groove and sinking down into our roots, finding our feet and getting out of our heads, finding our hands and allowing them to be moved by our hearts.

This is audacious and revolutionary because it requires us to stand up to everything and everyone, including the part of us attached to old ways—not our best or higher self, but the personal, driven, and dogmatic self that is in dire need of a Big Dance, a really Big Dance with a lot of sweat. That self is calling out to be turned into a prayer for somebody else and to get over its self-importance. If we hear that call and make that prayer, then we can move very gracefully in and thankfully through the aging process.

The audacious self is the one that shows up and stands in its own truth, taking responsibility for it, and transforming whatever is in the way of being real, being vulnerable, being humble servants of something bigger and more delicate than denial. It listens to the intuitive, instinctive part of us and trusts that this is the voice of divine intelligence. Only through this voice will we receive our mission and find our place on this earth.

The audacious self is always part of us. We simply need to get out of its way and keep moving. By moving, I mean *really* moving, that is, moving with the intention to transform, to let go, to know the self, and to listen to what's real inside of us and move out of apathy into action. What I love about the dance floor is that it reduces our complexity to energy, and energy moves in waves, patterns, and cycles that unite us as humans. We become accessible to each other and we don't need anything except our willingness to move and be moved.

For me, god is the dance, and the body is our spiritual path.

The only thing we have to conquer is our resistance to movement and change. Once we have aligned ourselves with the force that moves us all, things that need to fall away gracefully do. Shifts are simply made; they're not labored over. And they're gradual. In the many years that I've been teaching, I've watched thousands and thousands of people completely reinvent themselves, rejuvenate themselves, and re-*source* themselves. Something drops away when we dance, something heavy and hard, and we begin to witness the joyful, juicy person hidden within us.

The Wilderness of the Heart

The five rhythms are profound teachings and teachers. In the flowing rhythm, we learn how to let the dance in. In the staccato rhythm, we learn how to let the dance out. In the chaos rhythm, we learn how to let the dance go. In the lyrical rhythm, we learn how to let go of letting go. And in the rhythm of stillness, we learn how to let be.

But life isn't simple and for ten thousand reasons, at a very early age, we begin to hold our breath. We unconsciously commit ourselves to a war within, a war between us and the Great Spirit that flows in and out of each and every one of us until we die. Attempting to hold back the spirit of life isn't an act that serves us. It moves us into an alignment with death. Dead things don't move. We pretend to be scared of death; it seems we are afraid of life and all its changes. When we hold our breath, nothing moves below the neck. The whole heart of the body is cut off from oxygen, breath, and feeling and this frozen energy creates numbness.

This is very common and it begins quite early. Something happens and we become afraid of being real, expressing what's going on inside us. Cry and the response is "What's wrong with you?" Get angry and that's not okay either. We get scared and someone calls us a baby or makes fun of us. Emotional repression is totally socially acceptable. We hold our breath because the breath moves our feelings into tears and shouts and trembles. If we're not supposed to feel, best not take a deep breath, best not let life or breath into the body because spirit is a great catalyst and it will move, sometimes stir, and often shake us.

When we start to move our bodies, our feelings begin to move. The feelings that have been repressed, depressed, impressed, and relatively frozen begin to shift and surface. They become integrated into and transformed through the dance organically, without much to-do about it. Keep dancing and we start feeling. Fears begin to move, anger begins to move, sorrow begins to move. Unexpectedly, after a wonderful dance, we suddenly begin to sob or feel inexplicably angry or deeply compassionate for someone, or maybe everyone!

In this way, we begin to move through the physical into our emotional landscape, into the wilderness of the heart, to release all the energy that has been shoved down inside and frozen between our legs, under our arms, in our bellies, caving our chest or raising our shoulders. These feelings move us into their creation stories and these stories bring us face to face with mothers, fathers, friends, teachers, gods, pets, and moments when we turned away from who we are to be who we are not.

The five rhythms connect us to the cycles of life, the patterns, and the vibrations that make up our struggle. And eventually, in our sweet little dance, the true monster emerges and we are confronted by the ego that has been working so hard to keep us secure, predictable, and under control. This boring, robotic part of us that asserted its power over us so long ago and has yet to come up with anything brilliant or anything new, shows up loud and clear to sabotage our dance. Movement is a real threat to the ego's rigid, fixed patterns of being. In the dance, we painfully and directly experience this fixed part of us. Egos resist any change they are not controlling. Egos can dance, but their effort is in being or not being seen. To be truly moved, we have to move beyond that station of the cross into the wild kingdom of being soulful. This is our most audacious act: to take back our bodies, hearts, and minds from this soap-opera character standing in for a true self.

Your Home Rhythm

We are each an embodiment of rhythm. My home rhythm, where I'm most comfortable, and where I was most comfortable when I was nine, fifteen, and forty, is stillness. Libraries were my refuge when I was a child. Solitude, space, and stillness are as important to me as food and water. They are my sustenance. Whereas my husband's home rhythm is staccato and he has always been sustained, fed, and nourished by schedules, rituals, boundaries, things that begin and end, a staccato rhythm, which is the way he moves, speaks, eats, and lives.

Our home rhythm tells us what we need to know to be true to ourselves, and identifying it isn't always easy or obvious. Quite often, we're in relationships in which we've both given up our rhythms to create a kind of third rhythm that doesn't really fit either of us, so that we can stay together or act out a fairy tale of happily ever after. In reality, being able to flow together and being able to accept each other's flow of energy are fundamental to relationships. Accepting our own home rhythm is the first step. If we are denying our own energy, we are not going to be accepting of others' energy.

It's healing to recognize our true internal rhythm, as it reveals so much about us—our tendencies, tempo, and timing—and only when we can sense our own flow will we know when we're off course and off center. These are fundamental things to know. They have a profound effect on how we age because we either age gracefully or with great resistance.

Rhythms of the Life Cycle

The 5Rhythms also reflect the cycle of life we're moving through. Of course, none of these life cycles are fixed. Some people move earlier or later into these various stages. The 5Rhythms are a map to personality, geography, relationship, creativity, and the aging process. They are the medium, metaphor, and medicine of the essential cycles of life.

The birth cycle, the first five years of life, is governed by the rhythm of flow. We are meant in this period to find our flow and to be in touch with nature and dimensions of our essential individuated interpretation of this rhythm. This connection to our own flow is the foundation of all that follows. The tragedy of not embodying this rhythm is that at the end of the aging process, we end up leaving a body we never occupied.

In childhood, after age five, staccato rules. We learn how to focus, express, and define our energy. As flowing is about rooting in the body, staccato is about embodying the heart, its obvious metaphor. As the body is the medium for finding our flow, the heart is the medium for expressing it. If we arrive at elderhood filled with a lifetime of unexpressed feelings, filled with the past, it is daunting to face our inevitable future. The weight of emotional baggage could take an airliner down, much less a soul otherwise ready to take flight.

In puberty and through the twenties, chaos rules. Having embodied both our physical and emotional, feminine and masculine energies, the task now is to find balance. True balance can only be found in surrendering to exploring the extremes and finding ourselves on the line between. No one else can do it like us or for us, and, if we don't do it, it does not get done. If we should end up at our final destination without having done this dance, we will likely be sad beyond belief, for we have missed our crucible and our life can seem like an unfinished symphony.

Before you get depressed at this prospect, however, it is important to know that it is never too late to redeem your enlightenment coupon and seek your response to all that you are and do. This is the process of growing down into growing up and often accompanies maturity.

The maturity cycle, from thirty to sixty years old, is governed by the lyrical rhythm. We bond to make families, offering whatever it is we came here to do, our gift, our work. Everything is maturing. Our style and the rituals of our life become established.

The lyrical pattern is actually the most complex of all the rhythms because it's an integration of everything that came before it. It is rooted in deep, profound self-acceptance and self-love, which is why it is so difficult to attain and impossible to feign. Either we are at peace and at home in our bodies, hearts, and minds, or we're not. If we're not, then our maturity is very painful. In fact, we'll probably spend the entire time trying to stay in puberty. This is how we got to be a culture that is addicted to how it looks, and to looking, talking, and being like teenagers for most of our lives.

After the lyrical cycle, we enter stillness, from the age of sixty onward. I call this the bone cycle. Everything returns to the bones. Bones are what we'll leave behind us, at least for a while. Traces of our steps will be left in bones for our ancestors. When you think of the skeleton, the bones, you think of getting down to the essence of things. That is what the stillness cycle is about—letting go of the trappings and the outerwear, and getting down to the bones.

In the dance, we get used to letting go. It becomes a practice. Most of us fear death, fear being out of control, fear surrender. As we practice letting go, we feel power, grace, and dignity in the birth and death of each dance, each day, each passing moment. We begin to feel the possibility and the freedom in letting go of the past and forgetting the future. It takes on a positive spin as opposed to a negative spin.

If we get to seventy-five and we've never practiced letting go, how we are going to let go of our bodies is beyond me. This is huge and we are small in the face of it. We each need a practice to prepare us for the awesome process of letting go of our memory, our physical agility, our schedule, our work, our status as a sex goddess or the guy with great hair. When we have a practice that sustains us over a vast period of our lives, we gradually integrate changes. With each shift, each turn of the wheel, we are moving with the flow.

My practice has been the 5Rhythms. They have prepared me each step of the way for the next. My dance has changed with each life cycle. In my twenties and thirties, I was into chaotic, deep, over-the-edge, ecstatic dance. My stamina seemed infinite. My dance was juicy, hot, fiery, and risky. That lasted till my midthirties. From then to around fifty, my dance softened and deepened. I still went on a journey, but it wasn't so much about reaching the outer limits or the outer edges of who I was, but more seeking for deeper roots inside myself and for patterns that may have been obscured by the bombast of youth. Reaching into things that were more hidden or required deeper excavation, I felt more like an archeologist.

In my fifties, my dance began to slow down. It became empty, as in the emptiness reached through meditation. Stillness is my home rhythm, and moving stillness my deepest dance. Having attained great heights of ecstasy in my twenties, I welcome the depths of emptiness in my present dance.

Aging on the Dance Floor

We have a 5Rhythms pilot group in London of people between sixty-five and ninety who began the practice as elders. They're amazing. Whenever I lose hope or feel despair, I watch the video of them and see the amount of light, energy, and hopefulness they express. And there are quite a few studies pointing to movement as a deterrent to Alzheimer's and dementia. This is particularly so with freestyle movement, because we're making decisions in the moment and the whole emotional-physical-mental body is engaged in this decision-making process. A recent study by the Albert Einstein School of Medicine found that very few cognitive activities reduced the risk of Alzheimer's and dementia, and of physical activities, including structured dance forms such as ballet or ballroom, only freestyle movement reduced the risk.

This is great news for me! It's scientific backup of something that I intuitively know and have witnessed over the years, which is that people age more realistically on the dance floor than they do off it.

People who move freestyle keep the rebellious teenager within them totally alive. They have a spark, an animated youthfulness that will never die. Obviously, if you're moving your body, it's also not going to get fixed into the shapes of aging that we so often see. I say aging more "realistically" because I don't believe we are destined for fixed shapes. Sure, we're a little stiff and less agile, but hey, audaciousness keeps us fluid. That's my experience so far, in myself and in my observation of other people. (For me personally, the most intense reminder of my age is my vision. In my forties, the things that were close to me became the most difficult to see. What a metaphor!)

A seventy-seven-year-old woman I just worked with in London came to me and said, "Thank you so much for your practice and particularly for the rhythm of staccato because my husband has been quite ill all year and through this rhythm I learned to step up, to ask for what I need, to challenge doctors, to speak up, and I also had a place to put my frustration and my upset, in my dance."

A 5R teacher recently sent me an e-mail about her experience after her eighty-two-year-old father had a bad fall and was in the ICU. At his bedside, she looked into his pale, milky-blue eyes, which were normally hazel, and thought she and her father might be saying good-bye. "We talked for just a few minutes until he tired and I left," she wrote, "and that's when this practice, this incredible web of energetic sanity, took over and dropped me right into Stillness. The hours, the days, the years of moving against, through, with the 5Rhythms took over, held me, carried me, and cradled me. The next week followed the gentle ebb and flow of my life—with my dad in the hospital, with his wife, with the doctors, with all of the phone calls, e-mails, and neighbors—held steady."

We're constantly being tested all the way through life and the 5Rhythms give us tools and practical ways of experiencing, expressing, and expanding our sense of what we can do and who we can be.

Recently, one of the New York newspapers interviewed a number of people who appeared to be in their seventies and eighties. They were interviewed about what they had learned from life. Of these ten people, not one of them said how old they were. They either had a clever way of sidestepping the question or simply refused to answer, as though it was shameful. I found that very sad. Why shouldn't we be proud that we've lived this long and this well and that we have some wisdom to share, that we have reflections that might shine a light for somebody coming behind us, that we are worthy, that in fact we're a library, a wealth of stories and information? The great sadness for me is that we aren't seen this way, that after a certain age one becomes part of the invisible posse. Although I've seen a solitary member of this posse bring Manhattan to its knees just taking three turns of the red light to cross the street.

Communion

The 5Rhythms help move us toward ever-greater communion with each other and the universe because they move us toward ever-greater communion with ourselves, from which everything else flows. For me, enlightenment is organic. If we go through life and receive the teachings of each life cycle, we organically move toward a greater emptiness, toward a unified field as a natural progression. The 5Rhythms embody these teachings and help us navigate the waters.

The dance helps us to ground everything, to get real, to be vulnerable, to awaken to all that we are and all that we are not and to know the difference, to reach down into the audacious self, which is in a constant process of taking risks and letting go.

Zalman Schachter-Shalomi, rabbi, writer, and professor emeritus at Temple and Naropa University, founded the visionary Jewish Renewal and Spiritual Eldering movements. His Spiritual Eldering Institute in Philadelphia and his landmark book *From Age-ing to Sage-ing: A Profound New Vision of Growing Older* brought a whole new concept of elderhood to public awareness. A believer in the universality of spiritual truth, Reb Zalman has traveled the world and studied a range of traditions, learning with Catholic and Buddhist monks, Sufi masters, Native American elders, and transpersonal psychologists. He was born on August 28, 1928, in Zholkiew, Poland.

ZALMAN SCHACHTER-SHALOMI

CHAPTER 32

The Adventure of Age-ing

Aging is inevitable. Doing it audaciously is a choice. And understanding the full impact of this reality and possibility is the difference between ego and essence, being awake or asleep, filled with joy or depression.

I didn't know what was happening to me when I got closer to my sixties. I wanted to continue to be the same workaholic I had always been, but it didn't work anymore. I couldn't keep up in the same way. I became aware of the diminishments that were happening to me. But unless you can admit this and say, yes, I am in this stage of life, it feels like a guilty secret. You can't let it out, you can't share it with other people, and then you have to keep on pretending that you can still do what you used to do.

My inner work had a lot to do with the form of mysticism in Judaism called Kabbalah. Part of the inner work of that is a nightly examination of conscience. You ask yourself: What was this day all about? What did I do, how did I feel, how did I relate to people? When you do this inner work, you begin to raise questions with yourself. You have a dialogue with yourself, and it became clear to me that, with all the spiritual practices I had been doing up to that time, they couldn't quite help me with the new season of life into which I had entered.

Seasons

It was then that I began to look at life from the point of view of seasons. When I sat and meditated to see the panorama of things, it looked to me that the biblical seven years was a very important period. I saw that if you project a lifetime over a year to make it more graphic for yourself and you begin with the feast of nativity, December 25, that's birth, by the end of January, you're seven years old. By the end of February, you are fourteen years old. By the end of March, you are twenty-one. That's the winter of life. Then comes the spring of life. By the end of April, when you are twenty-eight, you have what is called the Saturn return. It takes Saturn about twenty-eight years to go around the sun. And that means a whole new cycle begins in life. And then you go to thirty-five and to forty-two, and by then you are at the end of June. That's the time of "What are you going to do when you grow up?" And you have July, August, September—that's when you make hay when the sun is shining, as it were. It's the time when you do the work in life.

When I looked, I saw that there is a script for all these ages. What do you do from one to seven? You're a toddler, you go to kindergarten. You have a script. What do you do from seven to fourteen, fourteen to twenty-one? You have a script. You have a script for all of life, but by the time you get to retirement age, from then on, no more script. It is very difficult to live without a script, without a defined role. Without a script, you have to play from sixty-five on the same games that you played before. We don't know what's the next thing we're supposed to do.

Now, in aboriginal and native societies that was simple. Because elders had a place and a role, and they sat in council together. Council is very important. In Native American society, women after menopause were the center of awareness, power, and decision-making. That was because they no longer had the role of childbearing, nurturing, and raising the children. So the role, the script, was there. And people were honored for that. When the roles were scripted for people and they knew what they had to do, it was so much easier.

In our society, it isn't so. Along with that, we have been given more years to live. We live with an extended life span and we don't have the extended consciousness that you need to have with an extended life span. Our society is suffering from social mobility and from the lack of models that used to come to us from grandparents. Today requires a new kind of elder. Society has not yet made room for that new kind of elder.

At the same time, in the last fifteen years, a way of thinking about life on this planet has come into its own. People are thinking more and more of Earth as a living being. Scientists have come up with the hypothesis that says Earth (*Gaia*, to use the Greek word for it) is alive. She's a living being and the rivers are her blood and the trees are her lungs. You get the sense of the planet as a being of its own, as having a life of its own. And we are not at the top of the ladder of being, but rather we are like cells, sometimes cancer cells, sometimes white and red corpuscles—it depends what choices we make about life. But we are cells of the global life, of the global body. Earth is try-ing to heal herself.

Meanwhile, time in our society has become a flywheel that is turning so fast today that we don't get an hour for an hour; we get twenty minutes for an hour. We don't live time in the more relaxed way of living with time. It's going so fast that the human body is not about to digest, to work, to repair itself with the speed in which things are driving us today.

So here we have a problem: We have an elder population, more people of age than ever before; the planet is sick and is trying to heal itself; and time is speeded up in such a way that it is unhealthy for human beings and other beings to live at such a speed. This is why elders are needed.

Jung asked the question: Why should people be alive after they have reproduced? Purely from an understanding of evolution, we would say that once you have bred, you can die. Look at the salmon. They swim upstream, they lay their eggs, and then they can die. Alright, we'll give human beings a little more time until they can raise their kids. So they can live to be fifty. But we are now having a life span that's so much longer.

I can't imagine that this is just by happenstance. Something in the way in which Earth needs to heal herself produces more elders at this time. They need to do something to slow the pace of the planet and to infuse society with values. So this is our job, this is our task, and this is what I'm seeing all over the place, whether you call it Spiritual Eldering or Aging with Awareness. There are conferences and books being written. There seems to be a getting ready for the new huge group of people that are now entering the elder years: the baby boomers.

Harvesting

Those who are doing Spiritual Eldering work are beginning to create a shift in the template of what "old" means in society. Instead of thinking of old as worn out, we are bringing back the notion of long-lived. Instead of looking at it as a failure to be old, we look at it as a success. We made it to this time—how remarkable! How much experience we have!

Now, as we look at the cycle of the year, we see that October, November, and December of a lifetime have some very special programs, except we haven't scripted them before. So the work of Spiritual Eldering is for yourself and for people in society to script what it is that we need to do in the October, November, and December of a lifetime.

That's the harvest time. Most people when they get older have a big history of having plowed and sown the seeds, but don't have much history of having harvested their lifetime. No wonder there is such a dissatisfaction with elder years. As it says in Psalm 128, "he is joyous when he brings in the harvest sheaves." That's what our situation is: We haven't learned to harvest.

How do you go about harvesting a lifetime? You need certain tools. The tools are not external tools. The tools are internal tools. These are inner processes, these are things that add to awareness the same way that more memory gets added to the computer. If you have more memory installed and you have it reconfigured so it can handle more memory, then what happens is that it can handle the more difficult program.

Let's look at how memory works for us. Every day I have to go toward the future. As I walk toward the future, who do I see at the other end? The angel of death. Oy, I don't want to look. So I back into the future. But what happens if I back into the future? I see the past. Oy, I remember what I did wrong then, and I remember the disappointment I had there. So I cut myself off from the past. What about the present? I don't want to think about this and I don't want to think about that, and before long, look at what I've done to my consciousness. I don't have much memory of the past, I don't have any free memory of going to the future, and I have very little present memory because of the diminishments that I don't want to be aware are robbing me of awareness. In Vedanta, Indian philosophy, you call this sense *Avideya*, not wanting to know, intentional non-conscious being. There is such a category in the Baltimore Catechism [Christian doctrine]: invincible ignorance.

October

So the work of October is expanding awareness. In the Eastern and Western traditions, awareness was expanded via meditation, contemplation. These tools involve introspection, looking into the recesses of your mind and your motivation and your memory. Most of us don't know how to do that. We are so subject to the flotsam and jetsam that happens in our heads. In the middle of one thought comes another thought; one bumps the other and they don't seem to have any connection. Very few people can do mind steering. It takes a while to learn to steer consciousness and awareness, to hold the course, as it were. Because when you go inside yourself and start checking the past, you come to the places where you don't want to look. Why? Because they make you anxious. That is the file in which you keep the failures—the things you don't like, the things that are not yet reconciled, the things that are upsetting.

Anxiety keeps you away from there. You start to approach and say, "No, let me get a cup of coffee instead." There's always a distraction that's waiting to pull you away from what you don't want to face. But in that file may be that which can make you rich today. You may have felt at the time what you wanted to do and didn't get to, and therefore the thing was a failure. But it was that very failure that moved you in another direction.

I found out when I checked out my failures that the fallout of my failures is where my successes are. The things that I didn't manage to do at that time steered me to other things. I'm grateful for those. That's what people mean when they say "Good grief!"

Reaching into places that may for a moment not feel so comfortable allows you to recover your memory. If you don't recover your past, if you don't recover time for yourself, you won't get to the wisdom. Wisdom comes from having learned from experience.

October is a time when we learn how to use the tools for harvesting life. We learn to do journal work. We learn to talk to one another. There are certain kinds of conversation that I call spiritual intimacy. It sometimes happens when you sit on an airplane next to somebody and you have a conversation in which something comes out of the closet, something you didn't like to talk about to family because of the landmines in the conversation. If you talk about it, there will be an explosion; people will get angry. In a conversation of spiritual intimacy, you can talk about such things and feel seen, heard, and understood. Hearing, seeing, and understanding the other is very, very precious.

Letting go of vindictiveness and doing forgiveness work is another tool for the harvest. To give you an illustration, the prisoner does his time in prison, but the warden does time in prison too. Whenever you hold somebody in the prison of your anger, the prison of your unforgiveness, you tie up vital energy in the grudge. Can you imagine what it would be like if you could let go of all the energy that's tied up in the prisons in which you hold people who have done you wrong in the past?

The work of forgiving self, forgiving others, and letting go of vindictiveness is hard work. Sometimes you cannot do this by yourself, inside of yourself. You need to have tools for that. The tools may be journal work or interpersonal work. Sharing spiritual intimacy and exploring with another gives me a safe place to look at my collusion with my hurt, my participation in being ripped off.

Another part of the work of October is expanding mind to include more of the future, more of the present, and more of the past. When I do a time stretch this way, I get in touch with an aspect of God that's called the Ancient of Days. An aspect of God that fits the younger years might be "a vision of God who helps me in the battle of life." But for the older, there is the Ancient of Days, the witness to everything that ever happened and ever will happen. That's my companion for eldering. This kind of meditative work is what needs to be learned in the October season of our lives.

November

Imagine I've done my work. I've done my eldering. Now a more serene person, I don't have as many long toes that explode if someone steps on them. I am a person who can see contradiction, what kind of compromise is necessary at times, and the paradoxes inherent in life. And then I do what Jimmy Carter did. As an elder citizen of the planet, I do conflict resolution. I build affordable housing for Habitat for Humanity. I fulfill the peacemaking role of elders. Can you imagine if instead of sending young people to Bosnia, we sent several thousand elders who have lived their lives, done their homework, and are able to talk to Bosnians and Serbs, to Muslims and Christians, and ask, with all the meaning of their life experience, "Does it pay to shed blood?"

As Martin Luther King said, "I've been to the mountain." I have a contribution to make that is a deeper and richer contribution by my witness at the painful spots on the planet, and to intervene and say this is my work now. Earth needs a cadre of elders who have become conscious and aware of their task for healing the planet. People who have done their homework in October and who are now prepared to serve in November. To serve in schools in the neighborhood. To serve as mentors. To serve in boardrooms. To serve in so many ways that say, "I have accumulated wisdom out of life experience. I've synthesized it. I've made it something that I can give and share with people."

One of the richest times I had at Temple University were the office hours. At the end of each semester, you have to fill in how many hours you did this, what percentage you did that, and I would put in "20% ear." The dean wanted to know what ear was. "I give ear," I explained. Students would come and talk with me about what had happened in class. When they were able to tell me what they thought and how they thought about it, that's when it entered their consciousness. Mentors are very, very important and that's a job you can do locally while you think globally. That's what elders are needed for.

December

It used to be that life began at home and death was at home. Then we took both to the hospital, and now birth has become pathology and death has become pathology. Intergenerational healing has to be done so that people are not afraid of death, so that death is not pathology.

The work of December is to make natural again the exit from life. Can you imagine if we could get people who are not afraid of dying, who would tell the truth to their children and grandchildren and work with them consciously about death? To be able to say what is it that's unfinished for me and to be able to find ways in which the next generation becomes deputized to take the tradition on just one more step. If December work is done correctly, the work of grieving after a death will be easier. We would remove pathology from the whole process of eldering and, later on, dying and we would make a contribution to the planet. That's the vision of Spiritual Eldering.

As I say in From Age-ing to Sage-ing seminars, "If we don't have extended consciousness to match our life span, we are dying longer instead of living longer." Here are several helpful activities to practice in expanding your consciousness.

1. Learn a new language or a new skill if possible, not only with your mind, but also with your body. If you learn a new language, for instance, learn to write in that language and in that script. If you learn a new skill, practice it for about forty days until you find that your body has integrated it into its habit pattern. That will result in more of the synapses of the brain being connected and accessed, which equals some extension of consciousness.

2. Each time you read something in a book or magazine, or see something on the tube, set the source of your information aside and, relaxing and closing your eyes, imagine what happened before, what is likely to happen afterward, picture the setting and characters in

your mind's eye, so that you almost feel it. The more you are able to do this, the larger your awareness will have expanded.

3. Make an inventory of as many of the experiences you have had that gave you pleasure and made you feel right about yourself as you can remember. Order them from the mildest to the strongest. In your mind, construct a rosary that you can tell at will so that, whenever you wish to change your attitude and mood, you can consult that album of peak experiences. This will refresh your mind and your body, and will have the result that even your T cells (immune-related cells) will increase, as will the vigor with which you face even your diminishments.

4. Study the contemplative teachings of world wisdom traditions. Many a time you have had moments of inspiration and ecstasy, which, alas, disappeared from your memory. Though they are difficult to access, often because you don't have good concepts for them, studying one form of inner teachings as can be found in the Kabbalah, Christian mysticism, Sufism, the Vedanta, and Buddhism will give you a grid with which you can better recall those experiences. Then, using your imagination, paint on the inner canvas of thought and feeling a scene in which you are experiencing that ecstatic moment, that revelation, that theophany. Then, make for yourself a marker, a motto, or a gate through which you can reenter that experience at will.

5. Before you go to sleep, recall some of these ecstatic experiences and fall asleep as you hug them, expecting to have good dreams. If you remember your dreams upon waking, record them in your journal.

6. Mentoring and oral history. If there are some people in your family or friends who would be interested in some of your reminiscences, if they are younger and have a different map of reality from yours, then communicating with them is bound to expand your mind in their direction.

7. Find a piece of music you are fond of and then, with no one else in the room as you play it, dance to it in free form. Visualize yourself, on the inside, as a great ballet

dancer, so even if you cannot fully execute the movements that you imagine, your imagination and what you *can* do will provide you with a way of expanding your consciousness, not only in your head and your heart, but also in your thighs and toes so that they, too, will become awakened.

8. When you enter the December period of your life, it pays to recall, in the most vivid way you can, loved ones who have passed on. This will open entrance for you into the regions you are bound to inhabit after you drop your body.

Norman Shealy, MD, PhD, is one of the world's leading experts in pain and stress management. His patented system (including the TENS unit) for curing chronic pain is used by traditional and nontraditional practitioners in nearly every specialty today. He is founding president of the American Holistic Medical Association and cofounder of the American Board for Scientific Medical Intuition. Among his many books are *Soul Medicine: Awakening Your Inner Blueprint for Abundant Health and Energy* and *Life Beyond 100: Secrets of the Fountain of Youth*. He was born on December 4, 1932, in Columbia, South Carolina.

NORMAN SHEALY

Every Thought Is a Prayer

I am seventy-five years old, but I still feel twenty-six. And in truth, I'm probably healthier than a lot of twenty-six-year-olds. A few years ago, which was the last time I checked, my biological age on the treadmill test for cardiac health was in the mid-twenties. I believe that the attitude I've had throughout my life is largely responsible: I've never practiced being old.

As an intern in medical school, I discovered that there are two groups of people: those who practice being old and those who don't. Many people who practice being old start long before they reach the age when others might begin regarding them as elderly. I call this group the living dead. These are people who are breathing and eating but otherwise not really living. They are rotting away emotionally, mentally, and spiritually.

Depression and Anger

Depression, which is the most common illness in the world, is usually behind this suspended state. I have personally worked with more than thirty thousand people who have been depressed all of their lives. It often starts before the age of three, so most cannot remember ever being truly happy. From my experience in speaking around the country for many years, I have concluded that only about 20 percent of people are really happy, 40 percent are clinically depressed (half of those, or 20 percent of all Americans, are on antidepressant drugs), and 40 percent suffer from what I call subclinical depression—they feel dull and are not happy.

These lifelong depressions typically start with abuse and/or the feeling of being rejected in childhood. My sister is an example of lifelong unhappiness and the consequences it can have. She was two and a half years old when I was born. My mother was very frail after my birth, weighing only seventy-five pounds because of hyperthyroidism. She was weak and preoccupied with the new baby, and my sister felt rejected and never recovered from it. She was unhappy from the age of two and a half. Within six months of my birth, she was grossly overweight, a problem that continued for the rest of her life. She died at age fifty-eight of complications of obesity, high blood pressure, and diabetes, having already lost a leg to the disease. The official cause of death was congestive heart failure.

Research demonstrates the health consequences of unhappiness and unresolved emotions such as anger. One study of nearly thirteen thousand healthy adults tracked them over time to look at the results of depression and anger. Of the people who died of cancer in the next twenty years, 75 percent had a lifelong feeling of hopelessness. Of the people who died of heart disease in the next twenty years, 75 percent had a basically angry personality, feeling they had been abused early in life. Of the people who died of heart disease or cancer, 15 percent had both depression and anger. So 90 percent of all the people who died of cancer or heart disease had anger and/or depression. Further, the people with lifelong depression died, on average, thirty-five years earlier than the people who were happy.

Another fascinating aspect to how we program our state of health comes from the work of Eric Berne, the creator of Transactional Analysis. Through his work, he came to believe that people set the time and cause of their death, usually in early childhood because of some major trauma or stress that occurs. Many years ago, I had a patient with advanced cancer. In my work with her, it emerged that she had set her life's script to die at a certain age because her grandmother had died of cancer at that age. I took her through a twenty-minute, guided imagery exercise on forgiveness. When we were finished, she got up out of her wheelchair and walked out of the room, free of pain. She said to me at some point, "I now realize I cannot afford the luxury of depression." I consider that one of the wisest things a patient has ever said to me. I sent her home with an exercise to do on her own. She was diligent about doing it, and three months later, her cancer was remission and did not return.

A year and a half later, I was in Los Angeles to talk in the hospitals, where she had previously been unsuccessfully treated. We were driving down the highway and she told me that, during the exercise we had done, she had suddenly realized how much she hated her family, and had said to herself, "I'm not going to let the bastards kill me."

This was not what I would call perfect insight, but it was adequate for her.

When she got home, she told her husband that she was going to get well. He responded that she had cancer and was going to die. She concluded her story by saying, "I got well and he committed suicide."

In another case, a woman crippled with rheumatoid arthritis came to me on the seventh day of our working together and said, "I don't have rheumatoid arthritis anymore." I asked how she knew and she said, "If you had rheumatoid arthritis for seven years and it went away, you'd know." Two days later, she told me that she had been married for twenty-eight years and her husband had been unfaithful to her the whole time. She found out about it when their third son was born, and decided she would stay in the marriage until he was eighteen. When her son was eighteen, he was drafted and sent to Vietnam with his two brothers. "I couldn't divorce their father when they were in Vietnam, and I developed rheumatoid arthritis," she said. "When they came home safely, I couldn't divorce their father because who would take care of me? And I kept saying to myself, 'If it weren't for that damn son of a bitch, I wouldn't have this disease.'" In her work with me, she realized that her husband hadn't created her rheumatoid arthritis. "I did," she said, "through my attitude toward him." And she was correct—the rheumatoid arthritis was gone. Her joints and blood work became normal.

All of this illustrates how much your attitudes and emotions determine your state of health. If you practice being old, give way to hopelessness or anger, and do not attend to your mental, emotional, and spiritual health, your body will bear the consequences.

The Pathway of Health

There are actions you can take now to produce an immediate shift in your life away from practicing being old. At the top of my list is to consider this: Every thought is a prayer. As the research and clinical cases I cited demonstrate, you cannot afford the luxury of negative thinking. If you approach life with the knowledge that every thought is a prayer, then everything you do, think, say, and even allow yourself to get into feeling for any length of time becomes critically important. You begin to treat your body as if it is the temple of your soul and you take care of it on all levels.

The critical care of your temple can be summed up as: Think right, eat right, and act right (as in keep your body mobile).

Eating right means you eat real food. Unfortunately, only 20 percent of the food available in this country is real food. The other

80 percent has been worse than prostituted; it's been devastated by the commercial food industry. Real food is fruits, vegetables, nuts, seeds, eggs, and meats, and not the processed versions of any of these. Of all the food sold in grocery stores, 60 percent is processed, in a package, and contains multiple ingredients, which means that most of the time it's junk. In addition, 45 percent of all food consumed in this country comes from McDonald's and other fast-food restaurants, and 99 percent of their food is junk. Eating the American way does not allow for lifelong good health. Real food is what our bodies need.

We also need real water. Your drinking water is just as important as what you eat. Don't drink city water. It has a weapon of mass destruction called chlorine. Chlorine is banned outside of our water supply. It's terrible for your body, so get a water filter that removes chlorine and fluoride. Drink a quart or preferably two quarts of good water a day. You can also drink black or green tea. If you drink coffee, drink Gano coffee, which contains red mushrooms (*Ganoderma lucidum*) prized for more than four thousand years for their energizing quality. There's nothing wrong with having a couple of cups of Gano coffee a day. As for alcohol, if you like wine, have a glass with dinner, but not in the middle of the day.

Acting right means you exercise adequately. You don't have to move elaborately. You can do what I call "free-form" tai chi or qigong, which means to stretch your body and see where your body would like to stretch next. Explore the movements of your own body and when something feels tight or stiff, move it! Stretch it one way and then in the opposite direction. Just play with your body in movement, and learn to enjoy the bliss of living in the temple that it is.

Thinking right means you steer away from negativity and deal with and release your emotions rather than storing them. When it comes to people or events that trigger you, change the things that you can change and that you choose to put your effort into changing. For the things you can't or don't want to invest in changing, detach from them, which means not allowing yourself to dwell on them. It helps in detaching to understand that you don't need to know why something (or someone) is the way it is and you don't need to judge it. You can simply be at peace with it.

Here's how I detach. I take a deep breath, and then I start thinking about something pleasant. For someone who has done this for forty years, as I have, it has become such a habit that it's easy. To train yourself to do this, spend a minimum of twenty minutes a day doing the following exercise.

Concentrate on six phrases: 1) My arms and legs are heavy and warm, 2) My heartbeat is calm and regular, 3) My breathing is free and easy, 4) My abdomen is warm, 5) My forehead is cool, and 6) My mind is quiet and still. Repeat the phrases a number of times. Let a natural rhythm develop in feeling each phrase as you say it and before you go on to the next.

Doing this exercise retrains the brain to follow the pathway of health (keeping the body calm and relaxed), rather than the pathway of stress and reactivity. There is a large body of scientific evidence demonstrating the benefits of this technique, which has been used in the training of Olympic teams throughout Europe for sixty years.

Once you've learned it, you can just take a deep breath, even while you're walking around, and say to yourself quietly, "My arms and legs are heavy and warm." Your response has become conditioned and your mind and body will slip easily into the relaxed state the exercise has trained them to adopt.

The Bliss Molecule

In addition to other benefits, thinking, eating, and acting right all help rebalance the energy system of your body. With the increasing understanding of energy medicine, more people are seeking ways to maintain the health of their energy system. Reiki, massage, acupuncture, and Emotional Freedom Techniques (EFT) are just a few of the many modalities available.

One of the best steps you can take for the health of your energy system and to enhance your well-being is to cultivate bliss in your life. Many people know about endorphins, those feel-good chemicals that are released in the brain during aerobic exercise, for example. Fewer people know about another of our brain chemicals: anandamide, which is affectionately called "the bliss molecule." (*Ananda* is Sanskrit for "bliss.")

When I learned about anandamide (which, by the way, is also found in dark chocolate with a 70 percent or more cocoa content), I began to think about what makes people feel blissful. It can be great music, it can be basking in the sun, it can be swimming, it can be sex. We know that orgasms produce some of the chemicals that make us feel blissful. Saunas to me are blissful. So is massage. I get a massage at least once a week, sometimes twice a week. There are also many aromas that produce the sensation of bliss.

Consider your own life: Are you experiencing bliss? If you're not, you are missing an important component of your well-being. Most of us could use more bliss in our lives. Make a list of all the things that make you feel extraordinarily good and start adding more of them to your daily experience. If you do this, I can guarantee that you won't be in the group that is practicing being old.

Pamela Wartian Smith, MD, MPH, spent her first twenty years of practice as an emergency room physician with the Detroit Medical Center. She is currently director of the Center for Healthy Living and Longevity and founding director of the Fellowship in Metabolic, Anti-Aging, and Functional Medicine. An internationally known speaker on the subject of Metabolic, Anti-Aging, and Functional Medicine, she has been featured on CNN and PBS, among other media outlets. She is the author of four best-selling books, including *HRT: The Answers,* as well as the forthcoming *What You Must Know about Women's Hormones.* Pamela Wartian Smith was born in Detroit, Michigan on July 24, 1954.

PAMELA WARTIAN SMITH

CHAPTER
34

The New Medical Paradigm

This is an exciting time in the field of medicine. We stand on the threshold of a bold new approach to health care that will enable us to extend not only our life spans but our health spans as well. The era of "one size fits all" conventional health care is coming to an end. Individualized care—care that is tailored to each patient's nutritional, hormonal, metabolic, genetic, and spiritual well-being— will extend our vigorous, healthy, and productive years. The science to do this is already here, allowing us to address the root causes of disease instead of using treatment regimens that merely mask symptoms. This new paradigm in medicine is happening now, it works, and I have experienced it firsthand.

My awareness of this new paradigm dawned about fifteen years ago when I was faced with a serious medical issue of my own. A conventionally trained physician, I had been working for twenty years in the emergency department of a large hospital system. After all of the changing shifts and strange working hours, I started experiencing severe insomnia. At first I thought it was temporary due to job worries and keeping a busy schedule at home as well. I tried over-the-counter sleep aids, but none seemed to work well enough to provide a full night's rest. Lack of sleep began to have an impact on my life. At work, I just did not feel as sharp as I should be and I became too tired to make it to all of my kids' school functions. Dragging myself around in a funk was not who I am. I am normally very energetic and upbeat. I became moody and easily agitated. Nothing I tried seemed to help. I began making the rounds, seeking the advice of one physician after another, to no avail. I consulted eleven different doctors from various specialties. The only assistance they offered was sleeping pills and antidepressants. I hated the way these prescriptions made me feel and worried about becoming dependent on them, but almost every doctor I saw thought my insomnia was secondary to depression. I knew I was not depressed. Even as a child, my outlook had been upbeat and optimistic. Could I be wrong? I began to question why neither I nor my fellow physicians could find and fix the cause of my problem.

Around the same time, one of my colleagues in the emergency room invited me to a medical conference being held in another city. It was sponsored by the American Academy of Anti-Aging Medicine (A4M). I had not heard of this academy before or of anti-aging medicine, so it took some convincing before I agreed to go. Skeptical, but intrigued, I took the opportunity to learn something new. My insomnia was not letting me rest anyway, so I thought that by overbooking my calendar I might get some sleep through the sheer exhaustion of listening to a boring lecture or two.

There I was at the A4M conference, expecting to be lulled into a stupor by boredom. But instead, during the second seminar, which was on female hormone replacement therapy, I sat bolt upright upon seeing the second slide of the presentation. It was my "eureka" moment. The slide simply stated that women low in the hormone progesterone suffer from insomnia as one of their symptoms. I had my answer at last. Eleven doctors, twelve counting myself, had not seen the cause of my insomnia, but rather treated the symptom unsuccessfully with various sleep aids, pills, and relaxation techniques. Some of the doctors I saw even went so far as to suggest that my problem was psychosomatic or "all in my head." I had begun to wonder myself if I was becoming detached from reality. But I had not lost touch; I had been misdiagnosed. I was about the right age for entering perimenopause and had undergone a partial hysterectomy after my third child. Even though I still had my ovaries, I learned that the disruption in blood flow to the ovaries as a result of surgery diminishes the ovaries' hormonal output. The seminar opened my eyes.

During that and the other seminars I attended at the anti-aging conference, I learned an entirely new way of looking at the disease process and health care in general, that is, that health is more than just the absence of disease. It involves establishing a reserve of health by working to become hormonally and nutritionally sound above the levels needed just to keep disease at bay. I also learned that the gold standard for determining certain hormone levels was through saliva testing. On returning home, I immediately did my test and eagerly awaited the results. I was relieved when the results showed that I was indeed very low in progesterone. I soon found a compounding pharmacist who was able to prepare the proper dose just for me. Once becoming hormonally sound, I slept like a baby, and have ever since.

No More Widgets

I have continued to attend every A4M conference since then and have found them all fascinating. I have learned a new approach to medicine that is patient-centered and I have come to understand that each one of us represents an integrated web of bodily functions that determines our level of health and is unique in each of us. The concept of the web is common to all living things, but each individual's functional web is different from everyone else's in some way. This web of function includes the food we eat, the way each of our livers metabolize and detoxify our systems, the condition of the gastrointestinal system, our mitochondrial energy production, our hormonal status, and so on—in short, our genetic and chemical makeup coupled with our environment.

What I learned through the study of metabolic, anti-aging, and functional medicine eventually led me to establish the Center for Healthy Living and Longevity in order to treat patients as individuals and not as widgets on an assembly line. I learned firsthand that patient-centered care takes time and much thought and effort. I spend about an hour with new patients on their first visit. In our quest to restore their health, we explore nutritional status, toxic load, intestinal health, hormonal status, prescription and non-prescription drug use, exercise habits, and many other factors. The patient-centered approach to medical care is very much about patient education. The patient partners with the doctor in seeking health. The initial interview process sets up this relationship. Together, we prioritize the patient's various health issues.

We then address those issues, keeping in mind the integrated web of all bodily functions and the bioindividuality of each patient. When hormonal therapy is warranted, we overwhelmingly prefer to use compounded formulations that are chemically identical to what your body makes. These are referred to as bioidentical hormones. The body recognizes the chemical structure and knows exactly how to utilize it; this is not the case with synthetic hormones, which can produce undesirable side effects and increase the risk of cancer.

No two people, not even identical twins, respond to treatment the same way. Research shows that the environment in which we place our bodies governs eighty percent of our response to cellular and organ insult by pathogens, stress, or injury, whereas our genetic makeup dictates only twenty percent. Your environment includes the food you eat, the liquids you drink, your stress levels, sleep patterns, marital status, drug use, type of occupation, toxic exposure, and even social contact. This individuality of patients is why I prefer to have a compounding pharmacist prepare many of the medications I prescribe, formulating them exclusively to meet the specific needs of each person.

Human Beings vs. Human Doings

A benefit to my new practice style is that I have learned to slow down. When I worked in an urgent care facility, I was lucky to get eight or ten minutes with each patient. In our modern culture of instant communication, fast food, and 24/7/365, life comes at us at mach speed. There is little time to ponder our lives, so rather than being proactive in the way we live we become reactionary and automaton-like. We have become "human doings" instead of human beings. The level of stress inherent in the constant motion in which we live is not healthy. It is now well known that stress is the major common denominator in many of our alarmingly prevalent diseases, such as cancer, diabetes, heart disease, and stroke. After I have discussed with my patients the implications of prolonged stress, they begin to prioritize and make time for health, for example, leaving time every morning for wise dietary choices instead of just grabbing a Pop-Tart on the way out the door. Slowing down in order to have a healthful meal with family becomes important. It is unfortunate that many patients do not begin to prioritize in this way until after their triple bypass or stroke.

The anti-aging, metabolic, and functional approach to health is not a quick fix. It often requires a shift in lifestyle on the part of the patient. But the rewards are enormous. I have seen patients increase their levels of health to the point where they no longer need their cholesterol lowering drug or their antidepressant medication. Blood pressure, cholesterol levels, weight, libido, and mood all become normalized. I have never gotten so many tearful hugs from grateful patients as I have since I began to practice medicine in this way. And though I teach my patients a lot, I learn just as much, if not more, from them. It is a joy to be part of their lives and to help guide them toward a truly healthy state.

Why Don't All Doctors Know This?

This type of care, the optimization of health and wellness, seems to be consumer driven. An internet-savvy generation of baby boomers is demanding to know their options. Many of my patients ask me why their primary care doctors don't have the same outlook regarding medical care. In fairness, I have to answer that many doctors just do not have the time to research the latest medical studies and information because of the hectic nature of the mainstream medical treatment model. So many of my patients asking me this question started me thinking: Why not train others to do what I have learned to do?

At first I tried to train other doctors by letting anyone interested shadow me during office hours. They would spend a week learning firsthand the practice of anti-aging medicine. We soon found that a week was insufficient for gaining any degree of proficiency. In addition, medical research and clinical results were pouring into this expanding field, so what doctors learned last week would need to be added to the next. Quality training required that I reach as many doctors as possible with the latest available information.

So, after years of attending the A4M conferences, I approached Dr. Robert Goldman and Dr. Ron Klatz, the founders of A4M, with an idea. With their blessing, I started the Fellowship in Anti-Aging, Metabolic, and Functional Medicine under the aegis of A4M. Initially, there were five learning modules, each lasting three days and held during the A4M conferences. I searched the world over for the best and the brightest to provide the lectures and learning materials. These were many of the same experts I had consulted when building my own practice. With the help of my hard-working staff and members of A4M, the fellowship took flight.

The program proved to be wildly popular among the attendees, as many of these doctors had heard the same questions from their patients as I had. The patient-centered approach was catching on. So many doctors have told me that the fellowship saved their career in medicine. They had become so disgruntled with the way conventional medicine had evolved that they were seriously considering giving up on medicine altogether. Many have told me that their passion for medicine has been reignited. The physicians adopting this new paradigm in medical practice come from many different specialties: orthopedics, ob/gyn, family practice, internal medicine, neurology, radiology, and oncology, among others.

I have been blessed to be the director of the fellowship since its inception and have been thrilled at its appeal and success. There are now eight modules and forty web broadcasts to teach anti-aging, metabolic, and functional medicine. It is a real challenge to keep current with the latest information coming out of clinical trials and published studies. We strive to make sure that whatever the fellowship teaches is scientifically based. Translating clinical trials into the latest and best clinical practices remains a challenge and takes time. It takes about fifteen to twenty years for an approved treatment to become integrated into the medical profession and be widely utilized by physicians. With so many doctors now either interested in or actually participating in the fellowship, however, our knowledge base has expanded exponentially and we expect the process to be accelerated for many of the clearly effective methods we teach.

The Life in Our Years

The completion of the Human Genome Project (the final report was released in 2003) only added credence to the concepts inherent to anti-aging medicine. The project has shown without a doubt that we all metabolize in different ways. One person's genes can even code for more than one version of an enzyme needed for the metabolic process. New lab testing is also helping to further our understanding of exactly how the body works on a cellular and even a molecular level. We can now perform tests for things that were only a dream just a few short years ago, such as genetic testing that may help us to prevent patients from developing debilitating conditions in the future. For example, we can determine ten to fifteen years ahead of time whether a patient is likely to develop diabetes and then shape the individual's gene expression to avoid it. We can do this by making sure the patient places herself in and fosters an environment that will suppress the expression of the gene responsible for the development of the disease. In support of the need to approach medical care differently, we now know that many of the prescription drugs in the conventional medical armamentarium can deplete vital nutrients and enzymes, hindering attempts to regain health.

The preventative potential of anti-aging, metabolic, and functional medicine is enormous and portends vitality for however long we live. This medical paradigm is not necessarily about using science to help us live longer, but it is about living better. What good is it to live to be a hundred years old if you spend the last twenty years drooling unconsciously in a nursing home? To paraphrase Abraham Lincoln, it's not the years in our life, but the life in our years that counts.

Happily, I can say that we have reached a tipping point with the fellowship. There are now enough patients and medical professionals, supported by ample numbers of scientific studies and published papers, for this new paradigm to become mainstream medicine. Additionally, plans are under way for a master's degree program in anti-aging, metabolic, and functional medicine at a major medical school. What an amazing transformation from teaching one doctor at a time in my small office! There are many to whom I am indebted for their part in helping to bring this about. Our noble cause has been transformation of the field of medicine in order to improve the health of all.

The new medical paradigm presented by anti-aging, metabolic, and functional medicine will help change our cultural view of aging from one of inevitable degeneration on the path toward our demise to one that views aging as an opportunity for exercising our new-found options and for recognizing and optimizing the truly malleable nature of our later years. We need to shed the stifling cloak of ageism by learning that aging does not have to be a tragic reduction in life choices and can instead be a comedic expansion of wonderful options for self-expression and the sharing of a lifetime of garnered wisdom. We stand at the threshold.

Gloria Steinem, revered feminist, journalist, and founder of *Ms.* magazine, is author of *Outrageous Acts* and *Everyday Rebellions and Revolution Within,* among other books. A lifelong activist, she speaks around the world on gender, race, and other social justice issues. Among the many oft-repeated Steinem quotations are: "The truth will set you free. But first, it will piss you off," and "Women may be the one group that grows more radical with age." Gloria Steinem was born March 25, 1934, in Toledo, Ohio.

Gloria Steinem

Doing Sixty and Seventy

Age is supposed to create more serenity, calm, and detachment from the world, right? Well, I'm finding just the reverse. The older I get, the more intensely I feel about the world around me; the more connected I feel to nature, though I used to prefer human invention; the more poignancy I find not only in very old people, but also in children; the more likely I am to feel rage when people are rendered invisible, and also to claim my own place; the more I can risk saying "no" even if "yes" means approval; and most of all, the more able I am to use my own voice, to know what I feel, and say what I think. In short, I can finally *express* without also having to *persuade.*

Some of this journey is uniquely mine and I find excitement in its solitary, edge-of-the-world sensation of entering new territory with the wind whistling past my ears. Who would have imagine, that I, once among the most externalized of people, would now think of meditation as a tool of revolution (without self-authority, how can we keep standing up to external authority)? or consider inner space more important to explore than outer space? or dismay even some feminists by saying that our barriers are also internal? or voice thoughts as contrary as: The only lasting arms control is how we raise our children?

On the other hand, I know this stage is a common one. I'm exploring the other half of the circle—something that is especially hard in this either/or culture that tries to make us into one thing for life, and treats change as if it were a rejection of the past.

I'm also finding a new perspective that comes from leaving the central plateau of life, and seeing more clearly the tyrannies of social expectation I've left behind. For women especially—and for men too, if they've been limited by stereotypes—we've traveled past the point when society cares very much about what we do. Most of our social value ended at fifty or so when our youth-related powers of sexuality, childbearing, and hard work came to an end—at least, by the standards of a culture that assigns such roles—and the few powerful positions reserved for the old and wise are rarely ours anyway. Though this neglect and invisibility may shock and grieve us greatly at first, and feel like "a period of free fall," to use Germaine Greer's phrase, it also creates a new freedom to be ourselves—without explanation.

From this new vantage point, I see that my notion of age bringing detachment was probably just one more bias designed to move older groups out of the way. It's even more self-defeating than most biases—and on a much grander scale—for sooner or later, this one will catch up with all of us. We've allowed a youth-centered culture to leave us so estranged from our future selves that, when asked about the years beyond fifty, sixty, or seventy—all part of the human life span if we escape hunger, violence, and other epidemics—many people can see only a blank screen, or one on which they project disease and dependency. This incomplete social map makes the last third of life an unknown country.

We may not yet have maps for this new country, but other movements can give us a compass. Progress seems to have similar stages: first, rising up from invisibility by declaring the existence of a group with shared experiences; then taking the power to name and define the group; then a long process of "coming out" by individuals who identify with it; then inventing new words to describe previously unnamed experiences (for instance, "ageism" itself); then bringing this new view from the margins into the center by means ranging from new laws to building a political power base that's like an internal nation; and finally maintaining a movement as stronghold of hope for what a future and inclusive world could look like—as well as a collective source of self-esteem, shared knowledge, and support.

Think about the pressure to "pass" by lying about one's age, for instance—that familiar temptation to falsify a condition of one's birth or identity and pretend to be part of a more favored group. Fair-skinned blacks invented "passing" as a term, Jews escaping anti-Semitism perfected the art, and the sexual closet continues the punishment. Pretending to be a younger age is probably the most encouraged form of "passing," with the least organized support for "coming out" as one's true generational self. I fell for this undermining temptation in my pre-feminist thirties, after I made myself younger to get a job and write an exposé of what was then presented as the glamorous job of Playboy bunny—and was in reality an underpaid waitressing job in a torturing costume. In the resulting confusion about my age, the man I was living with continued the fiction with all goodwill (he had been married to an actress who taught him that a woman was crazy to tell her real age), as did some of my sister's children, who thought she and I were two years younger. I perpetuated this difference myself for a couple of miserable years. I learned that falsifying this one fact about my life made me feel phony, ridiculous, complicit, and, worst of all, undermined by my own hand. It all had to do with motive, of course, because lying to get the job and write the exposé had been the same kind of unashamed adventure I undertook as a teenager when I made myself much older to get work selling clothes after school or dancing in operettas. Falsifying oneself out of insecurity and a need to conform is very different from defeating society's age bias. It's letting the age bias defeat you.

That was why, when I turned forty, I did so publicly—with enormous relief. When a reporter kindly said I didn't look forty (a well-meaning comment but ageist when you think about it), I said the first thing that came into my head: "This is what forty looks like. We've been lying so long, who would know?" That one remark got so many relieved responses from women that I began to sense the depth and dimension of age oppression, and how strong the double standard of aging remains.

In recent years, I've noticed that even my accidental statement—"This is what forty looks like. We've been lying so long, who would know?"—is quoted without its second sentence. Instead of the plural that said we're all fine as we are—which was the point—only the singular was left, as if there were only one way to look. Small as this may be, it's a symbol of the will to divide and individualize. So is a telephone call I just got from *Redbook*. For an article on aging, the reporter was asking, "How do you stay young?"

There is no such thing as being individually free in the face of a collective bias.

Dear Goddess: I pray for the courage
To walk naked
At any age.
To wear red and purple,
To be unladylike,
Inappropriate,
Scandalous and
Incorrect
*To the very end.**

---

* From "I Hope to Be an Old Woman Who Dresses Very Inappropriately," by Gloria Steinem

I've come to realize the pleasures of being a nothing-to-lose, take-no-shit older woman; of looking at what once seemed to be outer limits but turned out to be just road signs.

When I fear conflict and condemnation for acting a certain way, I think: *What peace or praise would I get if I didn't?*

I recommend the freedom that comes from asking: *Compared to what?* Hierarchical systems prevail by making us feel inadequate and imperfect. Whatever we do, we will internalize the blame. But once we realize there is no such thing as adequacy or perfection, it sets us free to say: *We might as well be who we really are.*

I realize in retrospect that fifty felt like leaving a much-beloved and familiar country—hence both the defiance and the sadness—and sixty felt like arriving at the border of a new one. I'm looking forward to trading moderation for excess, defiance for openness, and planning for the unknown. I already have one new benefit of this longer view:

I've always had two or more tracks running in my head. The pleasurable one was thinking forward to some future scene, imagining what should be, planning on the edge of fantasy. The other played underneath with all too realistic fragments of what I actually dif or should have done in the immediate past. There it was in perfect microcosm, the past and future coming together to squeeze out the present—which is the only time in which we can be fully alive.

The blessing of what I think of as the last third of life (since I plan to reach a hundred) is that these past and future tracks have gradually dimmed until they are rarely heard. More and more, there is only the full, glorious, alive-in-the-moment, don't-give-a-damn-yet-caring-for-everything sense of the right now.

I was about to end this with, *There no second like the next one, I can't wait to see what happens*—which remains true. But this new state of mind would have none of it: *There's no second like this one.*

Nancy Swayzee, NMT, MES, a neuromuscular and exercise therapist, is the creator of Whole-Body Breathworks (exercise program to improve and maintain systemic, organic, and musculoskeletal health) and Breathworks for Body & Soul (movement program facilitating integration of body and spirit). Her video *Fitness Forever,* which arose out of ten years of running hospital fitness classes and provides a medically oriented and approved exercise program, won numerous awards, including the National Council on Aging's Excellence in Health Promotion. She is the author of *Breathworks for Your Back.* She was born on June 30, 1939, in Lincoln, Nebraska.

NANCY SWAYZEE

CHAPTER
36

Like a Little Child

Seeing the world through the eyes of a child is seeing the world for the first time. It is the nature of children to explore their universe without bias. A child's brain is an information gathering, sensory storing system. To an infant, toddler, and child, the world expands as events happen for the first time. Children are naturally audacious.

As an adult, being willing to change your beliefs about yourself is audacious. In my case, I began a new life at fifty. That is when I began to live audaciously. It started with a year of dreams.

As I entered my forties, I began to question where my life was going, as many men and women do. I had been an early starter; my children were grown and my marriage of twenty-six years outgrown. I moved to Colorado to begin a new life. In beautiful Fraser Valley in the heart of the Rocky Mountains, I found myself having other-worldly experiences, unlike anything I had ever had. I had strong déjà vu moments during my daily walks in the forest with my two dogs. After living in an urban setting for my entire life, I felt I had come home.

One night I had three different dreams, each following a short period of wakefulness. In each dream, a falcon appeared, the same bird though in a different setting each time, and each time hovering over me long enough for me to see the markings on the underside of her wings.

The next day, during my mountain walk, a falcon appeared and flew in front of me before rising high into the sky. She appeared two more times during my six-mile hike, pausing the last time to hover not more than twenty feet above me. As I looked up, I recognized the markings of the bird in my dreams.

For several miles, I pondered what this meant. What was she trying to tell me? Suddenly, the message came through clearly: "Pay attention to your dreams."

And so began a year of extraordinary dreams, filled with many strange settings and events. In every dream, I was leading some kind of group. Sometimes I was simply speaking at a podium to a crowd of faces; sometimes I was physically leading them, Pied-Piper style, once on a tricycle.

In my waking hours, I increasingly experienced life with a sense of awe and wonder at the strange events that were occurring. I was journaling my dreams, which were often filled with neon-sign-like messages blazoned across my vision. One was: *Everything is connected and the healing will come from recognizing the connection.*

This message and all the dreams led me eventually to develop Breathworks, my movement program for the integration of body, mind, and spirit. At the time, however, I only understood I was supposed to be teaching something—but what? I believed I had nothing to teach.

Stepping into the Unknown

After a skiing accident that prevented me from running, I began to take an aerobics class. I was forty-seven at the time and the oldest person in the class. To the other, much younger members (most of them hardcore skiers), I was an inspiration of sorts. Jane Fonda's workout was all the rage during the eighties, and as an older woman I was a fun addition to the classes. My classmates convinced me to try teaching aerobics.

To put this extraordinary idea in perspective, I need to tell you that during the crucial first two years of my life, I had been kept in my crib in a dark room for much of the day. As a result, I had been hampered all my life with a type of physical dyslexia and saw myself as awkward, clumsy, and uncoordinated. Despite this, I went forward with teaching. I discovered that I enjoyed it and everyone loved my classes, so I kept on teaching.

A few months after I started teaching, the young woman who owned the aerobics center decided to sell it and move. Everyone began to coax me to buy it and keep it going. I thought, "I can't possibly. I've never done anything like this before!"

Then I had a dream that opened in the Hollywood Bowl, with the seating filled to capacity. On the stage was a table with a typewriter. I came onstage in exercise clothes, climbed on the table, and typed with my abdominals. The audience stood and clapped and cheered their approval.

This was ten years before my first Breathworks book was published. I hadn't even developed the program yet, hadn't formulated the concept of strengthening the core muscles. The dream prompted me, however, to step into the unknown and buy the studio. Little did I know this would become my life's work.

Before all of this, I had lived in response to other people's definition of who I was. I had been a mother, a wife, and even a successful assistant vice president of a bank, but I certainly didn't step out of the box. I was always fearful at any new undertaking, particularly of the physical kind. Yet here I was, taking over a fitness center and beginning to experience the physical body in a completely new way. I was also looking at life in a new way. Through my search for connectedness, I had begun to see things as "whole," the sum of the parts.

Not long after I bought the studio, I was reading a book called *Agartha*, which was channeled material that was popular in the eighties. I came across a line that immediately made me weep. It became the core of the belief system by which I have lived my life ever since. The line read: "True enlightenment is a clear understanding of the perfectness of all things."

At that moment, my whole life made sense. The beauty of the truth of that moment filled me as I suddenly understood that each event in my life had been part of the journey that made me who I was—warts and all. I have repeated that line from *Agartha* over and over during times of challenge and difficulty in my life, and it has changed the way I experience events. It moved me out of thinking of myself as a victim and gave me the courage to believe in the possibility of all things.

The Healing Connection

In 1989, two years after I opened Fit City, I sustained a severe back injury that made traditional abdominal exercises (curl-ups and crunches) impossible for me to do. I began to pore over my physical therapy texts and in a book called *Muscles: Testing and Function with Posture and Pain,* by Florence Kendall, PT, I found the answer. Enter transversus abdominis. Seeing this beautifully compact muscle wrapping around the body (it's referred to as the "corset" muscle), I began to call this deep abdominal muscle "the core."

In 1989, I began to teach Breathworks. Having learned the vital function the transversus plays in respiration, I taught active belly breathing as a means of strengthening the deep muscle. (Further details of this story can be found in my book *Breathworks for Your Back: Strengthening from the Inside Out.*) With every person I worked with, I discovered anew how integrated all our systems are, and that each part of the body is dependent on the health of the whole. The recognition that how we carry our bodies and how we breathe affects the entire physical body and our mental state was like discovering a miracle. It was the neon sign from my dream: *Everything is connected and the healing will come from recognizing the connection.*

Returning to California in 1990, I completed the American College of Sports Medicine course to prepare me to offer Breathworks as a preventive and rehabilitative program for back injury. At the same time, I began teaching my work at Tahoe Forest Hospital, and shortly after developed the Fitness Forever Senior Exercise program and a class for the disabled. I was now fifty-one and smiling every time I remembered how far I'd come.

All of this led me to train as a neuromuscular therapist, which brought the wholeness of the body into even clearer focus for me. Three years later, when my granddaughter was in an accident and suffered a closed head injury, my Breathworks exercises and my knowledge of soft tissue allowed me to play a role in her recovery. Looking for more information that could help her, I came across *Smart Moves: Why Learning Is Not All in Your Head,* by Carla Hannaford, PhD, about the connection between movement and childhood development. The book introduced me to the re-patterning program called Brain Gym. I began to integrate many of the Brain Gym concepts into Breathworks and began to see the powerful connection between repetitive, playful movement and brain function. I witnessed how working with the body assisted the thinking processes and working with the brain improved physical functionality.

During this experience with my granddaughter—up close and personal, frightening and painful—her strength and courage helped me connect with my own lost childhood. She was not the only one needing healing. The healing was traveling both ways. The neon sign about connection and healing was for me this time.

Taking what I had learned from working with my granddaughter, I began working with individuals who had Parkinson's, brain injury, or cerebral palsy, or were recovering from a stroke. This was a powerful experience for me and it allowed the people with these conditions to see themselves differently. They began to see new possibilities, and I began to see the miraculous power of the brain to heal itself.

Wonder-full

For the last several years, I have been teaching my Breathworks brain-based exercises to other older adults, ranging in age from in their fifties to their nineties. In these classes, we play at tap dancing, Celtic dancing, and line dancing—all silly, made-up stuff. We play childlike games with playground balls and tennis balls. It's all very energetic and fun and requires both physical and mental attention: noticing where you are in the sequence of steps, where the ball is, the rhythm of the music. We even dance with the balls, and call this "ball *room* dancing." These men and women all began taking the classes with a set of self-limiting beliefs about themselves. They would say things like, "I can't move that fast" or " I won't remember your name…you know this old brain."

Now they learn new dance routines every few days. They can move their feet to very fast Celtic music or salsa. Their cheeks are rosy, eyes shining, and minds focused. Playing like children, we laugh, at ourselves and at each other. They love what they discover about themselves. They have a wonderful time in the class, as do I in teaching it. We feel totally audacious.

In my lifetime, I have often been ridiculed for my frequent use of the word "wonderful." The ridiculers say, "Can't you find any other word to use?" After pondering, I realized that the definition of the word—full of wonder—is why I choose to use it so often. It best describes what I feel. As the French writer Colette said, "What a wonderful life I've had. I just wish I'd realized it sooner." I am so grateful for the magical life I've had and continue to have.

On this human journey, we must all live with ourselves, which is sometimes frightening and sometimes confusing as we try to figure out who we are. As adults, we tend to define ourselves by our opinions and beliefs. Often these beliefs about ourselves were originally created by someone else. We do not start out believing in our limitations. We enter this life with the audaciousness to believe we can stand up and walk!

I reunited with my inner child when I began my new life. She became a precious part of me that I honor and nurture. Her curiosity and audaciousness has led me to become the person I was meant to be.

CHAPTER THIRTY-SIX

Being present, living in the moment, paying attention—these terms for conscious living are the natural way of a child. They don't mean staying on alert; quite the contrary, these are all ways of achieving a calmness, internal quiet, and joy you may not have experienced before.

By making the choice to live life in the here and now, with acceptance, seeing each event as through the eyes of a child, we can make our experience on earth a series of miracles.

Dick Van Dyke's career as an actor and entertainer spans five decades. Receiving notice (and a Tony Award) for his role in Broadway's *Bye Bye Birdie*, he was chosen over Johnny Carson and Carl Reiner to star in a new TV sitcom in 1961. *The Dick Van Dyke Show* earned him three Emmy awards. Other series followed, including *Diagnosis: Murder*, debuting in 1993. Among his movie credits are *Bye Bye Birdie*, *Mary Poppins*, and *Chitty Chitty Bang Bang*. Dick Van Dyke was born on December 13, 1925, in West Plains, Missouri.

Dick Van Dyke

CHAPTER
37

Learn Everything You Can

At eighty I've come to the conclusion that attitude is everything. It has nothing whatsoever to do with your environment or the situation you're in. It's the attitude you take toward it. By God, I can't think of anything else that works for me more than the way I look at the situation I'm in and at life generally.

The other thing I think is, as a guy gets our age, we start to find out what our character faults and personality defects are, and we go to work on them. I found that, all my life, what ate away at me was procrastination. I was one of those people who put things off. I never got my homework in on time. I never was quite aware what that was doing to me subconsciously. There's eroding inside when you've got something on your mind. I've overcome drinking and smoking and everything else, but I don't think anything has been harder than trying not to procrastinate. When you procrastinate, these problems stay with you. When you act on them, they're gone. Your conscience is clear and you're content and serene. I don't think people realize how much unfinished tasks are eating away at them.

I think if you live this long and are reasonably content, you're comfortable in the world. That's the only phrase that comes to me. I'm quite comfortable in the world and with myself. I find other people's reaction to me somehow reflects that.

When Carl Reiner created what was to become *The Dick Van Dyke Show,* he originally saw it as a starring vehicle for himself. But a writer friend of mine, Aaron Rubin, alerted Carl to me in the musical *Bye Bye Birdie,* and said, "Why don't you check this kid out?" Carl came to see me perform. So did Sheldon Leonard, whose company was developing the TV show. I got the lead in the show—one of the biggest breaks of my life.

I haven't been back to the Broadway stage since *Birdie.* But I've done a number of shows on the road over the years; I did *The Music*

CHAPTER THIRTY-SEVEN

Man and *Same Time, Next Year.* And before *Bye Bye Birdie,* I had been in a show called *The Girls against the Boys.* It was one of the last Broadway reviews. It had quite a cast—Bert Lahr, Nancy Walker, Shelley Berman, and me. It was pretty good. The audience liked it. We ran two weeks and went out of business.

But *Bye Bye Birdie* lives on. It's one of the shows that's been a natural for high schools. I don't know how many high school performances I've seen over the years, but I've seen a lot of them, including productions with my own kids.

I think we have all said, Carl included, that the years of *The Dick Van Dyke Show* were the best years of our lives. We had the most fun and the most creative gratification that we've ever had. It was never like going to work, ever.

We didn't do well the first year. We were on opposite Perry Como, who was very big in television at the time. We got cancelled at the end of the season. Sheldon Leonard saved all of our butts by going to our sponsor, Proctor & Gamble. He went to Cincinnati and talked them into giving us a shot the next year. They left us on over the summer and we picked up an audience, thank God.

I haven't done a regular series for almost five years now. I've been very, very busy. I've gotten into pro-bono work: fundraising and charities. I'm on the board of the Midnight Mission down on Skid Row—chairman of the fundraising committee. We just built a brand-new building down there. I did a lot of begging and pleading for money, but we got it done.

I have a little group—five young guys and myself. We sing mostly children's songs, but jazz versions, everything from *Sesame Street* to all the Disney stuff. We do a lot of benefits. We go to children's hospitals and that kind of thing. It's a lot of joy to me.

I'm also an amateur computer animator. It's a big hobby of mine. I've gotten so good that I've been offered a couple of jobs. I don't know the first thing about the technology of computers. I just make pretty pictures. I learned how to do that. So I do special effects, animation—everything.

I didn't really feel a lot of stress in my younger days. My main stress was having a family and continuing to work. That was my main problem in life—keeping working. Other than that, I just never suffered a lot from stress, even though I didn't know how to act or sing or dance. Every time I'd go out for one of these auditions, I'd lie and say I could sing, and I said I could dance. Somehow, God help me, I managed to do it.

I can remember one big turning point in my life. I had come to CBS in 1955 under a seven-year contract. I was the anchorman on the morning show. Walter Cronkite was my newsman. I was twenty-nine years old. I had no idea what the hell I was doing. I was bad. They took me off. I did some game shows and some children's shows. Finally, at the end of three years, they dropped my contract.

So I'm stuck in New York with my family. I don't know what to do. ABC gave me a game show, which was broadcast out of the old Latin Quarter. But I realized this was not my cup of tea. This was not what I wanted to do. It was an income, but I was unhappy. On my own after work every day, I ran out and auditioned for everything in sight—everything but opera and ballet—musicals, plays, everything. And I got a lot of callbacks. I auditioned for *Bye Bye Birdie*. I got up and did a little soft shoe for Gower Champion and he gave me the job. That was the turning point. I really found what I love to do.

Look at *Mary Poppins*. Can you believe that? I'm not a professional singer or a dancer. I think I get so much joy out of it that I don't stop to think about the fact that I can't do it.

And I managed to carry a tune in *Bye Bye Birdie* with Chita Rivera. She's on Broadway now in her one-woman show, *A Dancer's Life*. They gave me a call the other day. I guess it's traditional between January and February that ticket sales are low and they said Chita's birthday is this month and would I come in and speak on stage and do a number with her? I said, "My God! I would get the biggest kick out of that!"

My career has been a ball. I have been so lucky. Don't think that luck doesn't count. It's incredible how lucky I've been. When I turned eighty, I said I can't believe I've lived this long and feel this good. I'm very big on exercise. Always have been. I've maintained my weight. I'm still dancing, still jumping around.

How to account for my longevity? I smoked for years and years. I had a bout for a number of years with chronic alcoholism. Somehow, my vital organs survived all that. I think genes account for a lot. I've always danced and always moved and always exercised and thank God never had a weight problem, or heart or blood pressure problems.

My main advice to young folks is based on my mistakes. Train! Train and learn everything you can: I had to pick up dancing and singing and everything else along the way, which is certainly stress producing. The more prepared you are, the better off you're going to be.

Alford N. Vassall, Jr., MD, originally trained in engineering physics in Canada (his study included nuclear physics and quantum mechanics) before earning his medical degree from Meharry Medical College in Nashville, Tennessee, with an ob-gyn residency at SUNY-Buffalo. His medical practice has been located in Farmington, New Mexico, for the past twenty-three years. Having developed a quantum physics perspective in his practice of medicine, he regards it as a promising new approach and is dedicated to bringing it to patients and physicians. He was born on September 2, 1950, in Savanna-la-Mar, Jamaica.

ALFORD N. VASSALL, JR.

Living in Your Passion

One of the keys to revitalization in the second half of life is to live in your passion. By that, I mean far more than finding activities you enjoy. Living in your passion is an exchange of energy with the universe that revitalizes your entire system and actually changes how aging affects you.

Before we consider aging in a biologic system such as the human being, let us consider aging in the physics of normal materials. What happens when an object ages? If it is a string or wire, it loses its elasticity, which means that it loses its ability to return the energy stored in the stretch and resume its original form. As for a mechanical system, each time it is used, it gives up some of its substance in order to function. When it has no more substance to give up, the system has aged beyond its ability to function.

This brings us to the concept of yin and yang in traditional Chinese medicine (TCM). According to TCM, yin is dark and yang is light, yin is quiet and yang is motion. Yin can be considered matter and yang energy. It is an important part of the concept that yin arises from yang and yang arises from yin. The yang energy provides the motion for the body. The concept is that a person starts out with a given amount of yin, which is gradually depleted over time until it is all used up, at which point the person dies.

The biologic system, like the mechanical system, wears down and ages when it has to use its substance to function as a system. Eventually, the system becomes depleted, as there is no more substance. The arrest of aging can be seen as the system using the substance efficiently and in such a way that it lasts a long time. Western medical efforts in this area have been devoted to making the system more efficient so it does not waste substance. Thus, health authorities prescribe regular exercise and proper maintenance of body functions, and focus on hormonal agents such as growth hormone to help preserve substance.

Traditional Chinese medicine has a different approach. It seeks to conserve yin (substance). It does this by balancing the yin and yang flows in the body. When the flow is balanced, there is conservation of yin. I have combined the concept of yin and yang with concepts from quantum physics to create a dynamic model that can be used to create a different relationship to and experience of aging. I call this model the "Yin-Yang Energy Induction Model."

Exchanging Energy with the Universe

Let us look at two core principles of quantum physics. The first is that all is connected. The second is that in the absence of an observer there is no reality, which implies a connection between the observer and what is observed.

You may be familiar with the Venn diagram model used in mathematics for set theory. Simply put, the universe is the universal set and each of us is a subset within the universe. What is inside each subset is exactly the same as what is in the universal set: energy.

Energy is characterized by frequency and wavelength. Generally, the shorter the wavelength the greater the amount of energy involved. Within the subset that is the individual, there is a "packet" of different frequencies and wavelengths of energy. Outside the individual subset, there is a matching set of frequencies and wavelengths. This can be compared to a set of guitar strings of a specific length within the subset with equivalent strings outside in the universal set. Thus, playing a particular note within the subset will induce a response from the corresponding note in the universal set. This analogy carries through to the level of thought or emotion since all is involved with energy in some way.

To repeat, frequencies in the subset match frequencies in the universal set and vice versa. Generating frequencies in an individual subset will result in a transfer of energy to the universal set and vice versa. The generation of frequencies in the individual subset arises only from the use of the substance of the individual. But by aligning with the frequencies of the universal set, the individual subset can initiate a transfer of energy. In a real sense, this transfer of energy is a channeling of energy across the interface between the individual and the universe.

Since we are talking about electromagnetic energy, the mechanical equivalent of this is the situation in which there are two tuned induction fields, and the flow of electrical energy in one circuit induces an electrical current in the second by the connecting magnetic fields. Thus the communication and transfer of energy takes place through the magnetic fields. This is the same concept for the transfer of energy between the universe and the individual.

As noted, the frequencies of electromagnetic energy associated with the universal set have corresponding frequencies in the individual subset. This association allows us to create the idea of our two tuned mechanical induction fields. In this situation, the vibration of a specific frequency in one field will harmonically create the vibration of the same frequency in the other. This is the basis of the interconnectivity and communication inherent in the Yin-Yang Energy Induction Model, as well as the ability of the body to use yin-substance to generate yang-energy locally, versus channeling the energy across the induction field.

What does being in your passion have to do with all this? When your inner circuits are tuned and exchanging information, you feel emotionally connected—so well connected, in fact, that you have the sensation of feeling the flow of the universe in that moment. This is when you are in your passion. This elemental feeling is the same as what athletes describe as being in "the zone," that state of perfectly focused energy and oneness that enables the basketball player, for example, to have an uninterrupted run of baskets in a game. This is also the state frequently reached during meditation, when you feel the pure flow of the universe. In this meditative state, you are in tune, matching the field within the subset (you) to the field outside the subset, which is the greater universal set.

Health as Matching the Universe's Energy

When your inner flow matches the universal flow perfectly, it is the state of pure health. There is an implication here for getting to this state of pure health, that is, striving through healthful practices and techniques such as meditation to realign your energy with that of the universe. If you are not in health, then you first must heal in order to connect and transfer energy. The energy of a subset (you) in poor health does not match the energy of the universe.

The body must be maintained properly if you are to align yourself with the universal energy. Food and other items taken into the body affect the body. Nurture your body physically through exercise and diet. Eat carefully, avoiding caffeine, sugar, alcohol, and other products that are naturally unhealthy to your body.

General lack of attention to these areas allows the body to age through failure to maintain its effective repair mechanisms. The body is forced to use as fuel things not meant to be used as such. For example, protein is made from carbohydrates and amino acids. When the body is not getting the proper fuel, it converts one type of protein to another or strips the carbohydrate portion to be used for energy. This happens in starvation, but can also happen in other circumstances such as a chronically poor diet or malabsorption of nutrients due to poor intestinal health. The body also burns some of the yin-substance of the body to produce yang-energy, whether this is to drive enzymatic reactions or for other functions. The result is aging of the body, which can be accelerated, slowed, or continued at the same pace through lifestyle practices.

An example of accelerated use of the yin-substance of the body can be found in methamphetamine abuse. The drug causes a flood of hormones and neurotransmitters (the brain's messenger chemicals), which results in feelings of euphoria and other symptoms associated with well-being. Methamphetamine users accelerate the depletion of their essential yin-substance, and so they age prematurely. It is common to see a twenty-five-year-old methamphetamine user who looks twice his age.

That is an extreme example, but many more typical lifestyle practices, such as choosing to react with stress and failure to maintain adequate nutrition, deplete the yin-substance and accelerate aging. In our society, many people want instant gratification, so they choose not to take care of their bodies and when their bodies begin to fail, they seek a pill or some golden elixir to take away the ravages of aging.

Beyond physical healing and maintenance, the body must be able to support the healed state. This implies the body must be prepared. This is not accomplished simply by exercising and taking care of the body's physical needs, but also calls for synchronization of the body with the mind and spirit. Just as a violin must be tuned in order for it to play beautiful notes in the form of a musical piece, so must the body be tuned physically so that it can manifest its purest form of harmony between the various facets of the mind, body, and spirit. This requires some training beyond simple meditation, such as the meditation of motion as in the dance of Sufism or yoga practice. These movements encourage the flow of energy through the body and maintain the electromagnetic harmony necessary for the nonphysical portion of existence, which connects through energy fields. It is not unusual for people who practice yoga with meditation daily to appear substantially younger than their chronological age. This is because they are involved in energy transfer with the universe.

Unconditional Love Is the Energy of the Universe

This brings us now to the radical concept of universal love. By way of introduction, let us consider a few ideas. First, evidence shows that prematurely born infants fail to thrive without love. It has also been shown that plants grow well in the presence of unconditional love. In fact, love given unconditionally seems to affect positively everything around it. It can even have an effect on your car if you are interested in testing this idea out yourself. You can try this by telling your car each day that it is worthless and does not deserve your care and attention. After delivering this message for a period of time, you will notice that your car will begin to deteriorate. The oil changes won't last as long as they did before. Simple unfortunate things begin to happen to your car. If you do the opposite instead, and tell your car that it is worthy and deserving of your love and attention, you will note that it seems to take you a little farther before needing that oil change and other aspects seem to last longer.

Second, let's consider the emotion of unconditional love. The love a mother has for her child is most often cited as an example of unconditional love. Her love is not conditional on how the child behaves and she holds the belief that her child can be anything he/she chooses to be. She does not withdraw her love for even what appear to be the worst possible negative choices. Unconditional love, then, allows the recipient to experience its highest potential. Taking this to the quantum level, unconditional love allows each quantum state available to each subatomic particle to manifest at its highest potential for the order of the whole. Here, "highest potential" is defined as what serves the whole most effectively.

When this potential is generated, all things organize in their most effective way. That is to say, even the most elementary subatomic particle behaves as if it has native intelligence and consciousness. If you think this is a bit of a stretch, consider the work of Masaru Emoto, as detailed in his book *The Hidden Messages in Water*. He photographed water at the critical temperature of its crystallization. He found that polluted water formed poor, imperfect crystals, and that simply labeling a bottle with the word "love" or a term associated with love in any language was enough to change the behavior of the water during crystal formation. The result was complex, beautiful crystals. This showed that the energy of unconditional love (even with the intent merely recorded on a paper label) was sufficient to change the physical behavior and structure of the water, that is, the water behaved as if it had native intelligence and consciousness.

So what does unconditional love accomplish? We can consider unconditional love a quantum field with coherence (in the same sense that a laser is a coherent being of one wavelength) that allows each subatomic quantum state to achieve its maximum potential. When the body is in health, that is, physically tuned and tuned to the greater whole through meditation combining unconditional love with modes of meditative movement as in yoga or Sufism, then the subset (the individual) is prepared to connect with the set (the universe).

Choosing Connection

There is a choice to be made regarding your own aging. If you are not living (being in passion), then you are dying (losing substance in physicality). You can choose to live in passion, which naturally slows your aging. You do this by attuning your body, mind, and spirit to its natural energetic frequencies and wavelengths, which are those of the universe. When your energies match those of the universe, there is a natural energetic exchange. While this inductive receipt of energy is taking place, you feel in your passion.

The applied quantum physics involved in achieving this energy exchange can be summarized as follows:

- First heal your body and yourself.
- Then revel in the passion you have found.
- Create the state of meditation to enable communication with the greater whole (universe).
- Meditate in the state of unconditional love to all, each thing animate or inanimate, the entire world.
- Incorporate the physical equivalent of meditation in the form of yoga or Sufi dancing.
- As you meditate, give thanks and gratitude to your body for its support and presence.
- In your meditation and at all other times, channel the energy of the greater whole through your body to maintain your body and existence.
- Give thanks and gratitude to the greater whole in each moment as you realize in the moment that you are the greater whole and all that is.

When you are in connection and inductively receiving the energy of the universe, you feel the connectivity emotionally. In this state of heightened connection, you feel limitless in terms of your potential. Each step you take is imbued with this overwhelming sense of the ability to succeed at anything. This connectivity prompts you to greet each day with the questions: What can I do today that will exemplify my passion? How can I spread my passion and my joy? When you share your joy and passion, you confirm your connection and are able to see once more with the wide-open anticipation and excitement of a child.

Andrew Weil, MD, is credited with bringing integrative medicine (a combination
of conventional and alternative medicine) into public awareness. Author of
numerous bestselling books on the subject (including *Spontaneous Healing* and
Eight Weeks to Optimum Health), he is also clinical professor of medicine and
director of the Program in Integrative Medicine at the University of Arizona.
In 1997, *Time* magazine cited him as one of the twenty-five most influential
Americans, and in 2005, one of the hundred most influential people in the
world. Andrew Weil was born June 8, 1942, in Philadelphia, Pennsylvania.

Andrew Weil

CHAPTER 39

Healthy Aging

Aging brings rewards as well as challenges and losses. I want to direct your attention to areas of our experience where "old" and "good" are synonymous. What is it that moves us in the presence of old trees? Why are old wines and whiskeys valued much more than young ones? What is it about aged cheeses that improves them so much? Why does age benefit some violins? Why are some antiques so valuable? I want you to consider the qualities n these things that age develops, then look for corresponding qualities in people.

Yes, aging can bring frailty and suffering, but it can also bring depth and richness of experience, complexity of being, serenity, wisdom, and its own kind of power and grace. I am not going to tell you that this or that diet, this or that exercise routine, or this or that herb will make you younger. I am going to try to convince you, however, that it is as desirable to accept aging as it is to take any other steps to improve your health throughout your life. To age gracefully requires that we stop denying the fact of aging and learn and practice what we have to do to keep our bodies and minds in good working order through *all* the phases of life.

Aging has the potential to bring greater worth to human life. It can:

- Add richness to life.
- Replace the shallowness and greenness of youth with depth and maturity.
- Develop and enhance desirable qualities of personality while lessening undesirable ones.
- Smooth out roughness of character.
- Enhance the mental, emotional, and spiritual aspects of life by the same processes that cause decline of the physical body.

- Confer the advantages and power of survivorship.
- Develop one's voice and authority as a living link to the past.

Remember that what gives value to the things I have described is not what is on the outside but what is within. And remember the importance of patience: you must resist the urge to try fine wine or cheese prematurely. From where I am now, I cannot imagine what I will be at eighty, any more than I can envision a sapling becoming a great, old tree. What are the optimal conditions for human aging to produce greatness? What part of ourselves needs to evaporate in order to concentrate our essence? What do we have to let go?

My main hope for his book is that it will, in whatever measure possible, begin to change the harmful conception most people have of aging: that it diminishes the worth of living. I am under no illusions about the difficulty of this task. Unrelenting images and messages come at us from the media telling us that youth is where it's at, that growing old is a disaster, that the worth of life peaks early. I can only tell you as clearly and strongly as I can that I disagree, and I ask you to look to the examples above and to other areas of your experience to discover and realize the value of aging.

Dr. Weil's Twelve-Point Program for Healthy Aging

1. Eat an anti-inflammatory (wellness) diet (high in fresh food, low in processed and junk food, plenty of fruits and vegetables).

2. Use dietary supplements wisely to support the body's defenses and natural healing power.

3. Use preventive medicine intelligently: know your risks of age-related disease, get appropriate diagnostic and screening tests and immunizations, and treat problems (like elevated blood pressure and cholesterol) in their early stages.

4. Get regular physical activity throughout your life.

5. Get adequate rest and sleep.

6. Learn and practice methods of stress protection.

7. Exercise your mind as well as your body.

8. Maintain social and intellectual connections as you go through life.

9. Be flexible in mind and body: learn to adapt to losses and let go of behaviors no longer appropriate for your age.

10. Think about and try to discover for yourself the benefits of aging.

11. Do not deny the reality of aging or put energy into trying to stop it. Use the experience of aging as a stimulus for spiritual awakening and growth.

12. Keep an ongoing record of the lessons you learn, the wisdom you gain, and the values you hold. At critical points in your life, read this over, add to it, revise it, and share it with people you care about.

Howard Zinn is professor emeritus of political science at Boston University.
His landmark book *A People's History of the United States* has sold more than
1.8 million copies since its 1980 publication. He is currently adapting
the book for a television series, *The People Speak,* focusing on the issues
of class, race, women, and war, and featuring the words of historical figures
Frederick Douglass, Mark Twain, Emma Goldman, Helen Keller, and others
who exemplify the spirit of dissent and rebellion in this country. Howard
Zinn was born on August 24, 1922, in Brooklyn, New York.

Howard Zinn

Outside the Margins of Responsibility

To age audaciously means not to assume that because you reach a certain age you can't do what you did before. This doesn't translate into being unrealistic or failing to acknowledge that you're getting older, but it means not prematurely concluding that your age has to diminish your energy and your activity. It means not letting your chronological age determine what your level of activity, energy, and interests in the world are. It's a matter of not being intimidated by how old you are, and of letting your body and mind, rather than the calendar, dictate what you do.

Being an audacious elder means not only not being intimidated by your knowledge of your own age, but not being intimidated by other people's knowledge of your age. Other people might see you as an older person and might therefore expect less from you, but for you to act toward that expectation is a mistake. If you are audacious, you ignore what might be other people's perception of you as an older person.

I'll put it another way. Not being intimidated by your own age and others' expectations means that what you say to people and what you write or otherwise communicate should not give any clue as to how old you are. That is, someone listening to me talk about what a great society should be like (a recent lecture I gave) should not after listening to me decide that I am an older person.

I think there is more understanding today that older people need not be ruled obsolete. Just as there is now a greater consciousness about women and a greater consciousness about people of different races, I think there's a greater consciousness about older people and their wisdom than there used to be. We still have a youth culture in this country, but I think a vibrant youth culture and more respect for older people can exist side by side.

People get respect according to what they do in their lives. Anybody who does something admirable gets respect—whatever age they are. Personally, at eighty-five, I don't experience ageism except when the respect accorded me turns into patronization. By that, I mean when people are too cautious about my physical abilities, when they insist on holding my arm as I'm walking, when they act as if I'm more infirm than I really am, they make me conscious of my age. That is a form of ageism. Ageism is not just discriminating against somebody because they are a certain age, but it's also being paternalistic. By rights, to be paternalistic toward an eighty-five-year-old person, you should be 105.

The Ultimate Consequence

I've lived my life day to day, week to week, and year to year, always doing the things I wanted to do, which happened to be seen by other people as audacious. So my life is a long and unending stream of slightly audacious acts, a series of small things, all of them involving a little bit of audaciousness.

I say this because after being in the air force in World War II, after risking my life, getting shot at, and after seeing my two closest friends in the air force get killed in the last weeks of the war, I think unconsciously I have been saying to myself ever since that any risk I take is really small, and anything that can happen to me is not terrible. If I had died twenty years ago, or any time after the war, I would have had more life than my two buddies who were killed in their twenties. Unconsciously, I measured whatever risk I was taking against the risk I had once taken, and measured any consequence against the ultimate consequence that my friends endured.

Doing something that might get you into trouble with the government, or even if it won't get you into trouble legally, doing something that might draw down upon you the disapproval of people in your community, takes audacity. It takes audacity to defy those forces and do what you think is right, whatever the consequences legal or extra-legal. But when it came to editing the Pentagon Papers for publication after Daniel Ellsberg gave them to me, I didn't hesitate and, maybe because of my war experiences, I didn't think of it as audacious on my part.

The same is true of writing *A People's History of the United States.* Certainly, I was aware of how radical the book was since I had studied history in orthodox classrooms and read the orthodox textbooks. I was aware that I was doing something outside the margins of the profession and outside the margins of traditional history, but I had no problem with that. Again, I didn't hesitate for a moment.

For one thing, I was writing it coming out of being in the South and involvement in the southern movement, and coming out of the antiwar movement. (I call it the southern movement because I think "civil rights" sounds bland.) Again, I go back to the notion of what it does to a person to go through momentous experiences. In the case of the movements, these were experiences of acting outside the margins. That's what we were doing in the South and that's what we were doing in the antiwar movement. Anytime you participated in a demonstration, anytime you went to jail, you were acting outside the margins of acceptability.

After doing all those things outside of orthodoxy, writing something outside of orthodoxy seemed rather mild, not a very risky thing to do. What would be the greatest risk? That some scholar would deplore what I was doing, which of course a number of scholars did. If you've never lived in any situation other than the academy, then the scorn of another scholar is the worst possible thing that could happen in your life. But in the contexts in which I was living, when Oscar Handlin denounced my book in the pages of the *American Scholar,* I had to laugh.

I grew up reading Upton Sinclair and Jack London, and learning about Clarence Darrow, Emma Goldman, Eugene Debs, and other historic figures who were very audacious and lived exemplary lives in many ways. I was always impressed by people who were intellectuals (not in the high-flown sense but in the sense that they were writers and thinkers) and yet, at the same time, willing to put their bodies on the line and be involved. Upton Sinclair, for instance, was not just a writer. He walked on picket lines. He participated. Of course, Martin Luther King was one of those people, and a lot of the people in the southern movement were like that.

A New Social Movement

I don't think people today are more afraid of possible societal disapproval or consequences from the government for their actions. We are seeing audaciousness around us, though not as much as we saw in the years of the southern and antiwar movements. We are seeing young men refuse to return to Iraq, and we are seeing people all over the country stand on the street in peace vigils and reckon with the reactions of their fellow citizens. The problem is not that there is a greater fear. The problem is simply that so far only a relatively small number of people have been audacious enough to act on the feelings and ideas they have. There are a lot of people in this country who have ideas that run counter to what the establishment wants, but they are not yet acting on them. I don't think the failure to do so comes out of fear of consequences. I think it simply comes out of uncertainty about what effect their actions will have. There is a pessimism that they won't have any effect, which is a common feeling in the early stages of any social movement. When you are obviously not strong enough to bring about a change and therefore the things you do seem ineffectual, only a small number of people are willing to overcome that feeling of ineffectualness and act anyway.

I'm hopeful that we are in the early stages of a new social movement. It seems to me that the realities of what's happening in the country must drive more and more people toward a recognition that something's fundamentally wrong. I'm talking about the obvious failure of the economy in the richest country in the world, the obvious deterioration of the environment when we're supposed to be scientifically advanced and yet are doing nothing to control our environment, and the reality of the war. It just seems to me that all of these must have a corrosive effect on old ways of thinking and we must be heading in the direction of greater consciousness about what is going on. That moving forward has not yet accelerated at a great pace and has not yet resulted in a huge social movement, but the direction we're going gives me hope.

When there's a great movement, most of it consists of people who are not consciously radical or left, but who just recognize what's right and what's wrong. The latter was true of the majority of the black people who participated in the movement. Of the tens of thousands who went to jail, only a small number were consciously radical in what they were doing. We're in the midst of a similar upsurge, not necessarily conscious, and we have yet to see what form it's going to take.

Radical Acts

A radical act today is speaking the truth exactly as you see it without first asking the question "How will this sound?" or "Does this go too far?" or "What will people think?" It is being perfectly honest in expressing yourself, with the total veracity of what you believe in, rather than measuring your words and measuring your actions. If everybody acted fully with regard to the things they believed in, we would immediately have an enormous increase in the amount of radical energy in the world.

Just before he died, Jean-Paul Sartre, who was quite a radical, was asked by a reporter, "Is there anything you regret?" He answered that he regretted not being radical enough. I often feel that way. Generally, people are not radical enough. If they thought, not in terms of the immediate now, but in terms of the future, they'd realize that what is radical today is not going to be radical twenty or thirty years from now. Knowing that would encourage them to act more boldly on what they feel and think.

Finding other audacious people and working together also helps build your willingness to move out ahead. It's hard to do things alone. Working with other people on something you believe in gives you a great feeling that you're doing something right, provides you more energy, and just makes life more interesting. And then, whether you win or lose, whether you achieve something today or tomorrow or next week or beyond, simply the very act of doing something audacious with other people is itself enormously satisfying.

Roslyn, my wife of sixty-four years [Roslyn died in May 2008], had a huge influence on me as a model of how to be in the world in relation to other people, how to do whatever I did, however radical it was, without rancor, without fury, without meanness, trying to hold on to understanding and an attitude of kindness toward other people, no matter how drastic the situation. I think that's a very important influence to have on somebody.

The Advantages of Age

One advantage of getting older is that you have a right, having aged, to say that you've done enough of something and are turning to something else. As for me, I'm not going to write any more books. I'm more interested in theater. My plays are still being put on. My play *Marx in Soho* has been performed in hundreds of venues around the country and various parts of the world, and is still being performed. If I write anything, it'll probably be a new play.

Perhaps the greatest advantage of age is that you are more likely to be audacious. You recognize that there's less that can happen to you that you have to worry about. You can speak more honestly than you've spoken before; do more boldly than you've done before. You have less to lose. You're not going to be around much longer. You might as well make the most of it.

To that end, accept whatever is happening to your body and don't demean yourself because of what's happening to you as you age. Stretch as far as you can within the limits of what aging is doing to you. Don't prematurely lie down and give up.